Betrayed Trust

Thetheleku kaNobanda, chief of the Mphumuza

John Lambert

Betrayed Trust
Africans and the State in Colonial Natal

UNIVERSITY OF NATAL PRESS

ISBN 0 86980 909 1

The financial assistance of the Centre for Science Development towards the publication of this work is hereby acknowledged. Opinions expressed in this publication and conclusions arrived at, are those of the author and are not necessarily to be attributed to the Centre for Science Development.

This book is printed on acid-free paper.

Cartography by Helena Margeot and Toni Bodington, Cartographic Unit, University of Natal, Pietermaritzburg.

Cover design by Yvette Foord.
Cover picture from *The Illustrated London News*, 28 June 1879.

Typeset in the University of Natal Press
Printed by Kohler Carton and Print, P.O. Box 955, Pinetown 3600, South Africa

For Barbara

Contents

Maps and Illustrations

Maps

The maps are based on those appearing in A.J. Christopher, 'Natal: a study in colonial land settlement', Ph.D. thesis, University of Natal, 1969, and on the following in the Natal Archives, Pietermaritzburg:

Natal, Sketch of the District of Natal with its native tribes, March 1853 (C231–2).

Natal, Sketch map of Natal giving the position of the different tribes, 1864 (From CO 179/71 Enclosure no. 4 in Lieutenant Governor Scott's despatch no. 12, 26 February 1864).

Natal, Map of the Colony of Natal, scale four miles to one inch, compiled in Surveyor General's Office, Natal, 1904.

Illustrations

Abbreviations

ABM	American Board Mission
AGR	Department of Agriculture, Natal
AYB	Archives Year Book
BPP	British Parliamentary Papers
CO	Colonial Office, London
CSO	Colonial Secretary's Office, Natal
GH	Government House, Natal
LA	Legislative Assembly, Natal
LC	Legislative Council, Natal
NBB	Natal Blue Books
NGG	Natal Government Gazette
NL & C	Natal Land and Colonisation Company
NPP	Natal Parliamentary Papers
NSYB	Natal Statistical Year Book
NWM	Natal Wesleyan Mission
SANAC	South African Native Affairs Commission
SGO	Surveyor-General's Office, Natal
SNA	Secretary for Native Affairs, Natal
SPG	Society for the Propagation of the Gospel
USNA	Under-Secretary for Native Affairs, Natal
WMMS	Wesleyan Methodist Missionary Society

Glossary

isibhalo	compulsory labour demanded from each chiefdom
ukubutha	to enrol men or women into an age-group
ibutho/amabutho	age-group/s of men or women
isigebengu	adult criminals
ikholwa	a Christian; literally a believer
ukukhonza	to offer allegiance to a chief
umkhosi	annual first-fruits ceremony
amalaita	combinations of young migrant workers
amalala	menials; a contemptuous term used by the Zulu to designate the peoples of Natal's coastal region
ilobola	cattle or other property conveyed in a marriage arrangement from the man's homestead to the woman's
ukulobola	to formalize a marriage through the conveyance of *ilobola*
induna/izinduna	headman/men; chiefly councillors
ukungena	to marry the widow of a deceased brother to perpetuate his lineage
umnumzana/abanumzana	homestead head/s
itishimiyana	an intoxicating drink made from sorghum beer and treacle
amasi	curdled and fermented milk
ukusisa	to place livestock in the care of a dependent who then has certain rights of usufruct
ukutekela	literally to beg, allowing impoverished Africans to obtain food from other homesteads
utshwala	sorghum beer
amatungwa	people originally living north of the Thukela river, encouraged by the Zulu rulers to regard themselves as being of a common descent with the Zulu
umfaans	Anglicized plural derived from *umfana*, young boy
umuzi/imizi	homestead/s

Note on Statistics and Terminology

Much use of official statistics has had to be made in this work. These have to be approached with extreme caution. Colonial officials relied, for the compilation of their statistics, on methods as varied as hut tax returns, police reports and mathematical calculations. Possibly the soundest attitude to statistics was that of the magistrate of Pietermaritzburg who wrote in 1884: 'Having no faith in agricultural statistics, as at present collected in this colony, I omit further mention of them.' The statistics which appear in this work must, therefore, be recognized as providing only an approximate estimation and are given in order to ascertain trends and for comparative purposes. Tables of statistics are provided in my Ph.D. thesis listed in the Select Bibliography.

Because of the difficulties involved in converting acres into hectares, particularly when, for example, referring to the leasing of Crown lands at 1d. per acre, imperial measurements have been retained throughout in this work; one acre being the equivalent of 0,404686 hectares. The currency of the time, the pound sterling, has also been retained as conversion into rands would be meaningless. There are also variations in the spelling of place names. The policy followed is to use the form generally accepted today when referring to geographical names – thus the Thukela River – while using the colonial variation when referring to administrative units such as the Lower Tugela division.

Acknowledgements

My interest in the way in which the settler presence in colonial Natal impinged on the lives of the African inhabitants of the lands between the Thukela and Mzimkhulu rivers began in the late 1970s when Professor Shula Marks of the University of London suggested it as a suitable topic for doctoral research. This book is an expansion of the resulting doctoral dissertation, completed in 1986, that looked at the decline of the homestead economy in Natal in the last decades of the colonial era.

In preparing both my doctoral dissertation and the present book I was indebted to historians of nineteenth-century Natal whose works inspired and directed my own investigations. They include Shula Marks, Norman Etherington, Henry Slater and particularly the late Professor Colin Webb to whose friendship and unstinting support and encouragement from my earliest years as a student at the University of Natal, Pietermaritzburg, I owe so much.

I also owe much to those colleagues and friends whose discussions and comradeship encouraged me to persevere in the often lonely task of research and writing and whose advice and criticisms helped shape this work. I am grateful to Professor Burridge Spies of the University of South Africa for his guidance and helpful criticisms during the preparation of the doctoral dissertation; to Professors John Benyon and John Wright of the University of Natal, Pietermaritzburg, for their penetrating criticisms of the dissertation and suggestions on transforming it into the present work; and to Dr Alex Mouton of Unisa, Dr Sheila Meintjes of the University of the Witwatersrand and Peter Colenbrander for their criticisms and support. Peter, in particular, spent many tedious hours painstakingly improving my literary style. Responsibility for the contents and for the final shape of the book remains mine alone.

A special word of thanks is due to those elderly men and women in Natal who were prepared to welcome me into their homes and share their memories with me, and to Annica van Gylswyk, now of the Scandinavian Institute of African Studies in Uppsala, Sweden, who made my contacts in Natal possible.

I am grateful to the members of staff of the many archives and libraries I visited for the assistance they offered. I should like to mention in particular the staff of the Natal Archives depot in Pietermaritzburg whose friendship and assistance over many years have been much valued. I would also like to thank Toni Bodington of the Cartographic Unit at the University of Natal, Pietermaritzburg, for the skill with which she transformed my drafts into maps. I am also very appreciative of the encouragement and guidance offered by Margery Moberly, publisher, and Jenny Edley, editor, at the University of Natal Press. I also wish to acknowledge the financial assistance provided from the Senior Researchers' Fund of the University of South Africa, and by the Centre for Science Development of the Human Science's Research Council.

Finally, without my wife, Barbara, this book would not have appeared. Her consistent understanding, encouragement and support; her criticism of draft chapters and the long hours she shared with me proof-reading and editing were essential contributions towards this study.

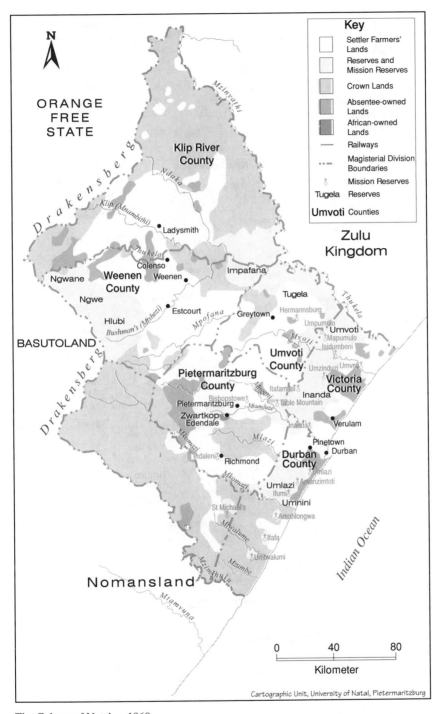

The Colony of Natal, *c*. 1860

The Colony of Natal, *c.* 1880

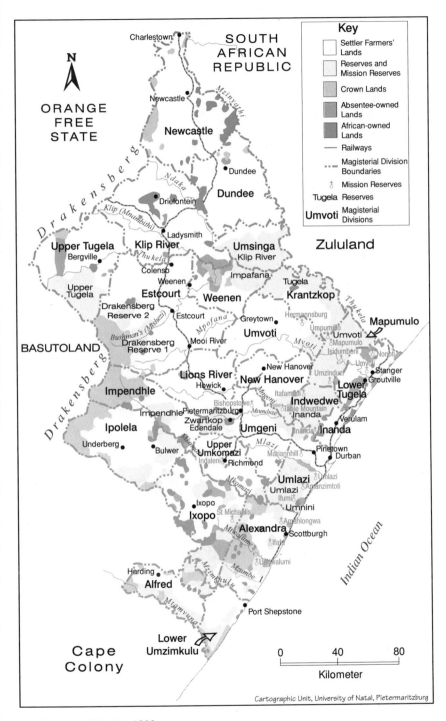

The Colony of Natal, *c.* 1900

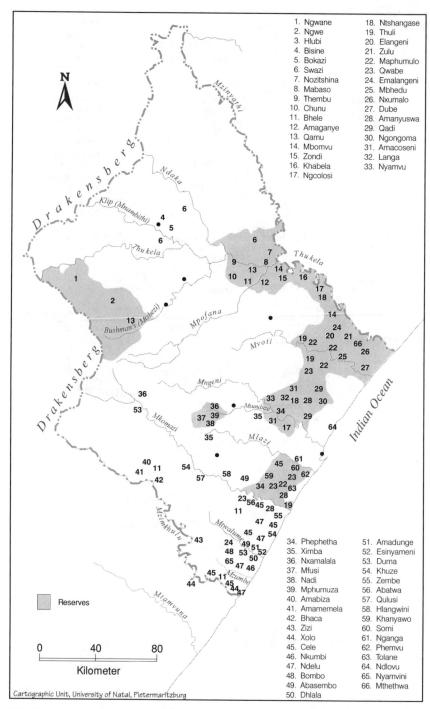

1. Ngwane
2. Ngwe
3. Hlubi
4. Bisine
5. Bokazi
6. Swazi
7. Nozitshina
8. Mabaso
9. Thembu
10. Chunu
11. Bhele
12. Amaganye
13. Qamu
14. Mbomvu
15. Zondi
16. Khabela
17. Ngcolosi

18. Ntshangase
19. Thuli
20. Elangeni
21. Zulu
22. Maphumulo
23. Qwabe
24. Emalangeni
25. Mbhedu
26. Nxumalo
27. Dube
28. Amanyuswa
29. Qadi
30. Ngongoma
31. Amacoseni
32. Langa
33. Nyamvu

34. Phephetha
35. Ximba
36. Nxamalala
37. Mfusi
38. Nadi
39. Mphumuza
40. Amabiza
41. Amamemela
42. Bhaca
43. Zizi
44. Xolo
45. Cele
46. Nkumbi
47. Ndelu
48. Bombo
49. Abasembo
50. Dhlala

51. Amadunge
52. Esinyameni
53. Duma
54. Khuze
55. Zembe
56. Abatwa
57. Qulusi
58. Hlangwini
59. Khanyawo
60. Somi
61. Nganga
62. Phemvu
63. Tolane
64. Ndlovu
65. Nyamvini
66. Mthethwa

Reserves

0   40   80
Kilometer

Cartographic Unit, University of Natal, Pietermaritzburg

Chiefdoms in early colonial Natal

Prologue

On 8 February 1906, twenty-seven armed Africans gathered near the village of Richmond in the heart of the Natal midlands to protest against the imposition of a poll tax of £1 on all adult men in the colony. A small police detachment was sent to intercept the Africans and a handful of protesters were arrested. Making its way to Richmond with its prisoners, the force was attacked at twilight at Trewirgie farm and in the ensuing mêlée the commander of the patrol, Sub-Inspector Sidney Hunt, and one of his troopers, George Armstrong, were stabbed to death.

The incident sent a tremor of panic through Natal's settler society. Faction fights involving Africans were common in the colony, and the deaths resulting from them were scarcely noticed by white Natalians. But this was different. For the first time since January 1879, when Zulu spears had been washed with British blood at the battle of Rorke's Drift, white men had been killed in an armed ambush on colonial soil. In an uprising, moreover, which followed shortly on the heels of the murder of a Camperdown farmer on 17 January after he had insisted that his labourers pay the poll tax.

White supremacy in Natal was based more on the illusion than the substance of power. Realizing how fragile their authority was over the Africans who so vastly outnumbered the settlers, the colonial authorities took immediate steps to punish the offenders. Martial law was proclaimed and the militia was called out. Together with levies from loyal colonial chiefs, the militia flushed out the participants in the skirmish. Those most directly involved in the murder of Hunt and Armstrong were tried by court martial and publicly executed. Others received sentences of twenty years' imprisonment with hard labour, confiscation of property, and lashes.

Although the operation effectively put paid to further trouble in the Upper Umkomazi division around Richmond, it did not have the desired effect of persuading Africans elsewhere to pay the poll tax. Throughout south-western Natal, a region with a long history of unrest and in which the settler presence pressed particularly heavily, there were widespread disturbances accompanied by refusals to pay the tax. African defiance in south-western Natal was met by a sweep of the militia through the region, accompanied by extensive crop and hut burning and confiscation of cattle.

Unrest and defiance of the government were also widespread in the belt of great reserves which bounded the colony along the Thukela River to the north-east. These reserves were arid and comparatively unproductive, yet were the most densely populated African districts in Natal. The domain of important pre-Shakan chiefdoms, now struggling for survival on land allotted in the early colonial period, these reserves proved to be fertile ground for resistance.

In April 1906, resistance turned to rebellion with the uprising of the Zondi chief, Bhambatha kaMancinza, in Krantzkop division on the Natal side of the Thukela River. Bhambatha had been in constant conflict with the colonial authorities since succeeding to the Zondi chiefship in 1890, and in 1905 he had threatened to kill the magistrate of his district should he attempt to collect the poll tax from the Zondi. Faced with resistance elsewhere in the colony, the authorities could not leave this challenge unanswered, and in March 1906 Bhambatha and his followers were ordered to pay the tax in Greytown. On their failure to appear, a force was dispatched to arrest Bhambatha who fled into Zululand where he consulted with Dinuzulu kaCetshwayo, the Usuthu chief and heir to the traditions of the old Zulu kingdom. Bhambatha left his wife and children with Dinuzulu, returned to Natal to arm his people and in April, after a brush with the Natal police, recrossed the Thukela and took refuge in the Nkandhla forest.

Here the Zondi were joined by members of other chiefdoms from both Natal and Zululand. In the skirmishes which followed, the colonial forces, aided by volunteers from the other South African colonies, flushed out the rebels at Bobe Ridge and at Mome Gorge where Bhambatha himself was killed. The military then concentrated on mopping up the last pockets of resistance in the Thukela reserves. By June the rebellion had been crushed, the soldiers leaving burnt-out *imizi* (homesteads) and devastated fields in their wake.

During the hostilities 24 white men had been killed and 37 wounded; among the Africans, between 3 000 and 4 000 had been killed and 7 000 had been taken prisoner. Over 5 000 of the prisoners were tried by court-martial, 4 700 floggings were inflicted and a large number of death sentences were imposed, all of which were commuted to terms of life imprisonment by the Governor, Sir Henry McCallum. Natal's African population slumped into an apathetic acceptance of its inability to challenge the colonial state. During the following several decades, opposition to white rule remained isolated and spasmodic until, in the 1980s, a new period of armed conflict and widespread bloodshed caused havoc in the region.

Although the poll tax was the catalyst which sparked off resistance in 1906, perceptive observers realized that there were more important causes of unrest. The Natal government appointed a Native Affairs Commission to investigate the circumstances behind the uprising. African witnesses to the commission graphically described a situation of official neglect and settler exploitation; of deterioration and disintegration in homestead life and in traditional forms of authority. The overwhelming impression of their evidence is a sense of powerlessness and despair. 'Happy are those who are dead', lamented one witness.

Another's explanation of Bhambatha's decision to rebel would have applied to many other Africans: Bhambatha was prepared to go to 'extremes simply because he was tied hand and foot by the network of troubles in which he found himself . . . He was very much like a beast which, on being stabbed, rushes about in despair.'[1]

The course of the rebellion has been extensively covered in contemporary works by W. Bosman and James Stuart and, in a later work, by Shula Marks.[2] In a wide-ranging study, Marks traces the interrelationship between settlers and Africans, and defines the background to the rebellion. She offers a nuanced picture of a society in crisis; driven to rebellion rather than actively seeking confrontation. A society in which the motives for participation or collaboration were dependent on considerations which varied from conflict within or between chiefdoms, to grievances against the colonial state or settler farmers.

An examination of the homestead economy which underpinned African society is not within the scope of Marks's work. However, an understanding of the changing fortunes of that economy during the colonial period is integral to the comprehension of African society in colonial Natal. Writing shortly before the rebellion, James Stuart, a long-serving colonial official with a keen interest in the African population and an awareness of the injustices under which they suffered, described the condition of most *imizi* as 'to my certain knowledge . . . absolutely horrible and intolerable and nothing amazes me more than the fact that the people have not yet struck out for freedom'.[3]

The Bhambatha rebellion was only one chapter in the saga of the undermining of homestead society in Natal. This undermining was accompanied by the displacement of traditional forms of chiefly authority and the substitution of a system under which the chiefs became puppets of the colonial government, shorn of their traditional status, wealth and power. It was accompanied, too, by the dislocation of African society itself under the impact of a dominant settler culture which drew or forced more and more Africans into the capitalist economy as wage labourers. In the years following the rebellion, the processes of alienation, impoverishment and proletarianization gathered pace. The result by the early 1990s was a region racked with devastating violence and in the grip of an endemic rural poverty obvious to anyone travelling away from the main highways of Natal into KwaZulu. The roots of the violence, superficially explained in terms of a political rivalry between the African National Congress and the Inkatha Freedom Party, lie somewhat deeper – in the colonial struggle for land and resources. The purpose of this work is to trace the origins of this struggle and of the process of rural degradation by focusing on chiefship and homestead society during the colonial era.[4]

Beginning in the 1960s, there has been an upsurge of interest in the society and economy of southern Africa, and in the interrelationship and interaction between the various peoples of the sub-continent. Works such as David Welsh's *The roots of segregation: Native policy in colonial Natal, 1845–1910*, have drawn attention to the impact Natal's segregation policies had on the evolution of apartheid ideology in South Africa. However, fundamental questions about the functioning of African society have been left unanswered.

The wealth of material on Natal's mission-educated Christian community, the *kholwa*, has encouraged research, notably by Norman Etherington and Sheila Meintjes. This has shed light on the way in which an African elite was able to achieve prosperity during the early decades of colonial rule by identifying with settler values. Studies such as these have demolished earlier preconceptions that colonial African society was essentially unprogressive and incapable of change. This view, commonly accepted by settler society, was perpetuated both in the early twentieth century by segregationist writers such as Maurice Evans and, later, by liberals such as the historian C.W. de Kiewiet and the economists D.H. Houghton and S.T. van der Horst. Their works were based on the assumption that African societies are inherently backward in economic terms. This view was proved erroneous in the case of the *kholwa* by Etherington and Meintjes, and refuted in the 1970s for African society generally by Henry Slater and Colin Bundy who focused on the interrelationship between capitalist development and African agricultural practices.

Neither Slater nor Bundy undertook an intensive examination of the homestead economy, and the only major studies of African societies in south-eastern Africa have been for the pre-colonial period, undertaken by David Hedges, John Wright and Carolyn Hamilton. Recent years have seen a proliferation of works, particularly by William Beinart and Timothy Keegan, on the functionings of African societies, on socio-economic interrelationships in southern Africa, and on African resistance to white domination. These have, however, concentrated on areas outside Natal. There has also been an increase in the number of works dealing with the impact of urbanization and industrialization on southern African societies, most notably by Charles van Onselen and Marion Lacey, and under the editorship of Belinda Bozzoli. Works such as theirs have shown how the growth of mining capital and of commercial agriculture destroyed the interaction between settler and African agriculture and hastened the proletarianization of African society. While Maynard Swanson, Keletso Atkins and Paul la Hausse have investigated the impact of urbanization on Natal's Africans, little has yet appeared on the effects of this process on the homestead economy.

Although Africans were recognized as early as 1852 as being the 'only real peasantry of South Africa',[5] Colin Bundy was the first modern historian to popularize the term 'peasant' as a description of African cultivators in southern Africa. The term itself has been widely used by Africanists to refer to agriculturalists 'who control the land they work either as tenants or smallholders, are organized largely in households that meet most of their subsistence needs, and are ruled by other classes, who extract a surplus either directly or through control of state power'.[6] There have been objections to the term, however, as it tends to ignore the differences inherent in rural societies, and to underrate the wide range of agrarian productive relationships which existed in African societies. In colonial

Natal, for example, there were great differences between African cultivators who were labour tenants and those who paid rent; between westernized *kholwa* and the predominantly subsistence cultivators of the reserves. The term remains useful for this study only if it is accepted that there was no single peasantry in Natal, but rather a number of different peasantries. Most were petty commodity producers, but their relationship to the colonial economy differed according to the terms under which they had access to land and resources.

Notes

1. Natal, *Native Affairs Commission, 1906–7, Evidence*, Pietermaritzburg, 1907, Jobongo, p. 712, Mvinjwa, p. 713.
2. For bibliographic details on these and other works mentioned in the Prologue see the Select Bibliography.
3. Stuart Papers [Killie Campbell Africana Library], 2, 'What then is to be done?', p. 3.
4. This work concentrates on the original colony of Natal, the area which formed the colony prior to the annexation of Zululand in 1897 and of the northern districts in 1903.
5. Natal, *Proceedings of the commission appointed to inquire into the past and present state of the Kafirs in the district of Natal . . .*, Pietermaritzburg, 1852, IV, Peppercorne, p. 7.
6. A. Isaacman, 'Peasants and rural social protest in Africa', *African Studies Review*, 33, no. 2, September 1990, p. 2.

CHAPTER ONE

Land and Labour in
the Early Colonial State

In summer, the lands between the Thukela and Mzimkhulu rivers, that sweep down from the Drakensberg Mountains to the Indian Ocean, are a lush green and appear remarkably fertile. This is particularly true of the narrow coastal strip and of the mist belt of the midlands, where the promise of prosperous agriculture is most apparent.

At the beginning of the nineteenth century, the region was home to small bands of San in the foothills of the Drakensberg, and to African communities scattered in loosely linked chiefdoms and grouped together in *imizi*. The former were hunter-gatherers while to the latter agriculture and stock keeping were equally important. During the early decades of the century, however, the region was caught up in a series of upheavals and population movements that encompassed much of the subcontinent. These devastating events, popularly attributed to a convulsive expansion of the previously unimportant Zulu chiefdom from north of the Thukela River, but now increasingly attributed to the repercussions of aggressive slaving raids from Delagoa Bay,[1] caused havoc in the region. Peoples were forced from their homes and whole chiefdoms relocated within the region, attacking and displacing previous inhabitants. In the process, chiefdoms were severely reduced in size or fragmented and, particularly in the south-west, there was widespread poverty and homelessness.

It was into this generally confused situation that the first European settlers made their way in 1824. They were traders and hunters who established themselves at Port Natal where they became exporters of ivory, skins and hides and, possibly, slaves from the south-east African hinterland. Although their trade remained relatively small in scale, they had influential allies among the Cape merchant community; a community which in the 1820s and 1830s frequently urged the British government to annex the port to the Crown. The economic potential of the port did not seem impressive to the Colonial Office in London, however, and successive Secretaries of State for the Colonies refused to extend imperial rule over the region.

The situation changed in the early 1840s, after emigrant Boers from the Cape established the Voortrekker Republic of Natalia in the region. Clashes between the republic and its Zulu and Mpondo neighbours threatened the stability of the whole subcontinent, convincing the Cape Governor, Sir George Napier, of the need for intervention. In 1842 the Colonial Office reluctantly agreed to the annexation of the republic. The Secretary of State for the War and Colonial Departments, Lord Stanley, claimed that Britain was intervening in order to protect the interests of the region's African inhabitants, but at the same time he insisted that the territory be governed at the least possible cost and that it achieve economic self-sufficiency as soon as possible. To save money, the territory was administered as a district of the Cape Colony until 1856, when Natal became a separate colony under representative government with its own executive and legislative councils.

Economic self-sufficiency was not easily attainable. Despite the appearance of great fertility, the lands between the Thukela and Mzimkhulu rivers enjoy few ecological or climatic advantages. The only resource worth tapping in the colonial period, the coalfields in the interior, could not be exploited without the construction of a railway, an expensive undertaking owing to hilly terrain. Other forms of transport within Natal were also hindered by rivers such as the Thukela and its tributaries, with their deep gorges and great valleys. Nor could these valleys support intensive agriculture because of the high summer temperatures and frequent local droughts.

In an attempt to achieve economic self-sufficiency, the new colonial administration encouraged white settlement. During its brief existence, the Volksraad of the Republic of Natalia had made generous land grants to Voortrekker stockfarmers. Although the newly appointed officials, under Lieutenant-Governor Martin West, hoped that the Voortrekkers would remain, relatively few were prepared to accept British rule. By the end of the decade, emigration had reduced their number to 360, mainly settled in northern Natal. In 1850, to encourage these few to remain on their land, they were given title deeds to 1 773 442 acres, an average of 4 926 acres each. Despite this, many more Voortrekkers left the colony after selling their grants to Cape or local merchant firms.

Merchant firms usually bought land for speculative purposes. To profit from their ventures, they sponsored immigration schemes to settle white farmers on the land. The most important scheme was that of Joseph Byrne who, between 1849 and 1852, brought nearly 5 000 British and Irish immigrants to Natal. Byrne's intention was to establish a class of small farmers in the midlands and coastal divisions, and to encourage the cultivation of export crops such as coffee and cotton. The allotments were far too small, however, and the realization that better money could be made in the towns, or by hunting and trading north of the Thukela or in the Transvaal and Orange Free State republics, led many settlers to abandon their land. Of those who tried to farm, few had the capital to do more than scratch a living from the land. By the early 1860s a number had taken out mortgages on their lands and, when depression hit the colony in 1865–70, many had to surrender their title deeds. The depressed price of land encouraged land speculators to continue buying farms as a long-term investment. Individuals and companies steadily increased their land holdings and vast areas of the colony fell into the hands of absentee landowners who, because of their close connections with merchant capital in the Cape and Britain, were able to exercise considerable political influence in the colony. The most important of these land speculators was the London-based Natal Land and Colonisation Company which went public in 1861 controlling 261 619 acres. It steadily increased its holdings which peaked in 1874 at 657 967 acres. By 1870, of a colonial total of 5 025 835 acres in white hands, absentee landlords owned 1 455 314.[2]

For those farmers who managed to retain their lands, the broken nature of much of Natal's terrain, and rapid soil erosion, necessitated considerable expenditure to ensure survival. With limited resources, few farmers could afford to fertilize or irrigate their lands. As a result crops were reaped on an average of only 1 per cent of white-owned land. Because maize and forage required little attention and were readily sold, most white farmers concentrated on them and grew crops such as wheat, barley and oats for home consumption only.[3]

These conditions discouraged intensive agriculture and encouraged stock farming in the interior and in much of the midlands. On the coast, only sugar had promise as an important export crop. Despite minimal and spasmodic financial assistance from the impoverished administration, a plantation economy did develop. During the colonial period, however, although Natal sugar became a principal export, it did not compete successfully with sugar from other producing colonies.[4] The failure to create a viable class of immigrant farmers, or to find a suitable export crop, meant that Natal never became fully integrated into the imperial economy. The Victorian British economy relied on the colonies as suppliers of primary products. Because Natal failed to fit into this pattern, imperial metropolitan interest in the colony was slight; after 1850 no further assistance was given to colonization or to stimulating a viable capitalist farming community.

The colonial government concentrated instead on developing Natal's transit trade with the interior republics. By the late 1850s Durban was becoming a bustling entrepôt. Skins, hides and ivory were declining in importance and the main activity of the port lay in the handling of goods from the interior. Wool, which became the colony's principal export in the 1860s, came mainly from the Transvaal and Orange Free State, and only to a lesser extent from the sheep-farming districts of northern Natal and Umvoti.[5] The colony's dependence on the interior transit trade meant that virtually all its financial resources were diverted into maintaining the main road to the interior, improving Port Natal harbour and, from the 1870s, into constructing a railway to the republics. There was little revenue to spare for improving communications within the colony, thus compounding the difficulties faced by cultivators. Most of the colony's roads were poorly maintained. Even where roads were good, rivers fordable and grazing adequate, an ox wagon could travel little more than fifteen miles a day.[6] Because of this, much fertile land in outlying areas remained Crown land until the 1880s.

The backward state of settler agriculture encouraged both the Natal government and the merchant community to look to the colony's African population as a source of revenue and profit. The return of settled conditions in the region after the defeat of the Zulu king, Dingane kaSenzangakhona, by the Voortrekkers in 1839, had profoundly affected the local African population. By the 1850s, as people returned to ancestral lands or immigrated from north of the Thukela, African numbers had swelled to more than 100 000. Although these people were largely strangers to the market economy, they were better placed than the farmers to support the colony with produce. Prior to white settlement, the homestead economy had been essentially subsistence based, with Africans cultivating crops and herding cattle primarily to meet the needs of their own *imizi*. They had, however, participated in a rudimentary exchange economy, and grain and livestock had been bartered between *imizi*. In addition, in chiefdoms with powerful chiefs, there had been a diversion of both produce and labour from each *umuzi* to the chief.

As early as the 1820s, a number of Africans fleeing the disruptions taking place in the Thukela-Mzimkhulu region had sought protection from the traders around Port Natal. There they had learnt to adapt their homestead economy to meet white needs. In return for land and cattle from the traders, they brought in game, fish and produce to the settlement.[7] By the time Natal was annexed to the Crown in 1843, there were extensive *imizi* around Durban cultivating large tracts of land and supplying produce to the small urban market. By 1850, the settler, James Methley, was writing of 'potatoes of several kinds, Indian and Kaffir corn, beans, fruits and a variety of other vegetables' being sold by Africans who 'having no European competition to contend with, are beginning to find that the trade of a market gardener is one of the most lucrative'.[8]

As the settler community slowly grew from the late 1840s, and urban and village settlements expanded, Natal officials became more aware of how dependent the colony was on the homestead economy for food and revenue. In 1846 a Location Commission was appointed to enquire into the best way of governing the African population. Its report, which was presented in 1847, reflected this growing realization. The report recommended that the Africans be segregated in reserves where villages could be established, and superintendents be appointed to assist with agricultural and industrial training. The commissioners believed that the reserves could nurture an African peasantry capable of breaking away from traditional agricultural practices.[9]

The Natal administration accepted the commission's recommendations but, fearing an exodus of the remaining Voortrekker families, was only prepared to allocate reserves in areas which were not wanted by white farmers. So great was white opposition to the plan, however, that the system was abandoned before any reserves could be allocated south of the Mkomanzi River. Because of this, only seven reserves were demarcated with only one, the Klip River reserve, in the Voortrekker stronghold of northern Natal and none in the south-western districts. It was only in the late 1860s that reserves were proclaimed in the south-west. In contrast to the large tracts set aside in the 1840s, these were small areas surrounded by Crown and private lands. The final acreage set aside for reserves was just over two million, an area incapable of housing more than half the African population.

In addition, the British government refused to agree to the expenditure which the commission's recommendations required. As a result, neither the aim of the Diplomatic Agent to the Native Tribes (later Secretary for Native Affairs), Theophilus Shepstone, to compel all the Africans to move onto the reserves, nor the commissioners' hope of 'uplifting' reserve inhabitants could be realized. Equally important, with few exceptions, such as Zwartkop near Pietermaritzburg, Umnini on the south coast, and Drakensberg 1 and 2 in Weenen county, the reserves were in the coastal hinterland, the Thukela valley, or the Drakensberg foothills. Because of their mountainous or broken nature, all these areas had been rejected by the Voortrekkers and early settlers as unsuitable for white occupation. As the terrain made them inaccessible by wagon, and as roads were virtually non-existent before the 1890s, they remained effectively isolated from the colonial market.

In southern and south-western Natal, most of the land reserved for Africans was in the coastal hinterland bordering on the steep and rocky Mzimkhulu and Mkomanzi valleys. These lands had a low annual rainfall, averaging between 600 and 700 millimetres, and were subject to frequent summer droughts making them unsuitable for agriculture. From the time of their establishment, these small and scattered reserves suffered from serious overcrowding since much of the ground was too broken and vulnerable to erosion to be occupied. Part of the Umlazi reserve was later described as being only fit for baboons.[10] Because the terrain was unsuitable for irrigation, there was no incentive to improve cultivation methods.

Eastern Natal included the Inanda, Umvoti, Tugela, Impafana and Klip River reserves; a great block of 1 085 388 acres stretching from east of Pietermaritzburg to the Thukela River as far north as Msinga. These reserves, like their southern counterparts, were situated in the coastal hinterland and riverine areas. They were dissected by great valleys formed by the Thukela and Klip rivers. Most of the terrain in the five reserves was exceedingly steep and broken. The reserves had a low annual rainfall of less than 800 millimetres, between three and five dry summer months each year, and frequent droughts. Describing the Inanda reserve shortly after its proclamation, the American missionary Daniel Lindley said that a 'more broken, worthless region could hardly be found'. In 1852, the Impafana reserve was described by its magistrate, G.R. Peppercorne, as 'worthless as the sands of Arabia', while Shepstone acknowledged that it would not be able to support its population.[11] Although the reserve lands were subject to excessive erosion and incapable of high grain yields, parts of the Inanda and Umvoti reserves had a higher average annual rainfall of 850 to 1 300 millimetres and included veld suitable for year-round grazing. In the valleys there were large areas of sweetveld for winter grazing. The higher-lying grounds had a short sourveld grass cover which provided grazing in spring and early summer. To obtain maximum benefit from these two veld types, cattle have to be moved between them seasonally. As early as the 1850s, human population pressure made this difficult. Population and grazing pressure caused a rapid degeneration of the grasslands, the disappearance of the woodland and the undermining of both agricultural and pastoral lands.[12]

The problems facing the inhabitants of the reserves in the sourveld grasslands of the highland and upland areas adjoining the Drakensberg were less severe than those problems prevailing in the coastal hinterland and riverine valleys. In the Upper Tugela reserve, however, extremely cold winters made cultivation difficult, while the sourveld of the region was only suitable for summer grazing. In this reserve, and in those in Impendhle and Ipolela, the inhabitants faced the problem of heavy summer rains which tended to erode topsoil. Continual ploughing and grazing rapidly exhausted the veld and destroyed the topsoil.

With the exception of parts of the Inanda and Umvoti reserves, only the Zwartkop, Umnini and Drakensberg 1 and 2 reserves were suitable for extensive agriculture or large-scale stock keeping. The Drakensberg 1 and 2 reserves contained pasture suitable for all kinds of stock, while the Umnini also had fertile lands suitable for sugar, subtropical fruits and vegetables, and a nearby market in Durban. Zwartkop was the best-placed reserve in the colony. It was situated in the mist belt a few miles from Pietermaritzburg and was well watered by the upper Mzinduzi.

Although few reserves could support their populations, the situation was alleviated by the close proximity of other categories of land in the colony. Until the 1880s, with few accurate surveys or fences, and with so much land in the hands of absentee landowners or of the Crown, Africans could move relatively freely onto under-utilized land to establish new gardens and to graze their cattle.[13] This was particularly so in south-western Natal and the western midlands where the reserves were small and interspersed among vast stretches of Crown land.

Like the reserves, most Crown land had been rejected by the settlers, either because of the nature of the soil or climate, or because of unacceptable distance from markets. An attempt in the 1850s to prevent Africans from squatting on Crown land came to nothing and, until the 1880s, the government made little attempt either to sell the lands or to remove African squatters from them. Because of this, Africans seldom distinguished between reserve and Crown land. Some chiefdoms were in fact placed on Crown land in the 1840s by the government, either because land was not available for them elsewhere or for a specific purpose. To cite examples, Ndimndwana and his Nyamvu chiefdom were settled on Crown land in Alexandra county for the former reason; while part of the Duma chiefdom was placed on Crown land in Ipolela as a barrier against San raiders from the Drakensberg.[14]

Because of the colonial administration's reluctance to alienate land set aside for white settlement, the objective of totally segregating Africans on reserve land was never feasible. Although, at High Commissioner, Sir Harry Smith's insistence, Africans in northern Natal were removed to reserves in the foothills of the

Drakensberg, Shepstone took no steps to evict those on private lands in the midlands and on the coast. As a result, there were almost as many Africans on white-owned lands as in the reserves. Because the Executive Council was afraid that Africans on these lands would be subject to only limited control, it sanctioned an anti-squatting law in 1855.[15] The law remained a dead letter, both because it could not be enforced, and because of the political influence of the colony's absentee landowners who drew rents from the squatters. Moreover, the presence of *imizi* on white-owned lands could be advantageous to farmers. Two forms of land tenure became widespread on the colony's farms: labour tenancy, commonly found on white-occupied farms and particularly prevalent on the Afrikaner farms of northern Natal; and rent tenancy, usually on the lands owned by absentee landowners and speculators.

During the early decades of colonial rule, few farmers could afford to employ labourers. Even among the more established farmers and planters in the coastal and midlands districts, few had the financial resources to use wage labour and even then they only occasionally drew labour from the surrounding reserves. In northern Natal, where few reserves had been established, most farmers were dependent on labour from Africans living on their farms. Africans who refused to become labour tenants were faced with expulsion and, with few reserves and with most Crown land leased by stockfarmers for grazing, most had little choice but to submit.

As they seldom practised winter feeding, stockfarmers had to rent or own farms in both the sweet- and sourveld zones. It was fairly common for these farmers to allow labour tenants to maintain *imizi* on winter-grazing sweetveld farms, where they themselves cultivated little or no land, and to grow crops and graze their cattle on farms in both zones. In return, the tenants agreed to supply labourers from their *imizi*, usually for six months of the year at a nominal wage, or for an annual cow or ewe for each labourer supplied. Although, legally, the agreement could bind only the tenant, he seldom worked himself but supplied labourers from his *umuzi*, each of whom received payment in cash or kind. The farmers also insisted that everyone in the *umuzi*, male and female, had to be available for weeding and harvesting, work for which they received no pay. On a few farms, mainly in northern Natal, tenants became share-croppers, or had to offer their maize surplus to the farmer at a fixed price, normally below market value. On many farms no rent was asked, and where it was required it was purely nominal.[16]

Labour tenancy did offer some advantages to the Africans, the most important being that it enabled them to escape from chiefly authority and obligations, allowed them to accumulate cattle herds, and gave them access to some of the best agricultural land in the colony. And, as most farmers cultivated little land, their tenants' agricultural needs were easily met. None the less, conditions for labour tenants were usually worse than for other Africans in the colony, and encouraged resentment and social friction. Because the farmer contracted with the *umnumzana* (homestead head) for labour, and not with his dependants, the latter often tried to evade obligations which they saw as enforced labour. A major cause of tension was that most farmers demanded labour at the busiest times of the year such as harvest-time, when the *abanumzana* needed labour for their own lands. The resulting conflict of interests caused farmers to complain that their labourers were apathetic and inefficient, while the tenants complained that they could not work their own land. There was considerable truth in the tenants' complaints; while they were theoretically free to work on their own land for six months of the year, in practice these were off-season months for maize cultivation. Tenants were often unable to plant more than the bare minimum needed for subsistence, and were obliged to send their sons out to work to supplement the *umuzi*'s income.[17]

Labour tenancy was also a very insecure form of tenure, and when a tenant was evicted he lost his gardens and grazing. A farmer's power to evict tenants if they failed to fulfil their labour commitments created a climate of uncertainty which discouraged attempts to improve cultivation. Surplus cash tended to be invested in cattle which created further problems for, as the herds grew, so did the possibility of friction between tenants and farmers. Although the *umnumzana* contracted with the farmer to supply labour, there was seldom a written contract. In an attempt to regularize labour tenancy, the Legislative Council passed Act 15 of 1871, section 20 of which stated that verbal contracts could only be binding for a short period. Despite this, both farmers and tenants resisted written contracts: farmers because they would have had to stipulate the periods during which labourers had to work; and tenants because they suspected documents which they could not read, and because they knew that it was difficult for them to be sued for breach of verbal contract.

Labour tenancy was the norm in the stock-farming districts of northern Natal, and was as much the product of the African need for land as the farmers' need for labour. On white-farmed land elsewhere, in the midlands and in the coastal divisions, where Africans had easier access to other types of land, few tenants were prepared to accept pure labour tenancy. Conditions of tenancy varied from farm to farm but, in return for gardens and grazing, tenants usually worked for a set period each year and paid an annual rent, equivalent in early years to the hut tax of 7s., which Africans had to pay each year, and rising by the 1870s to £1 or £2. Most tenants also received a wage, usually of 10s. a month. In addition, some landowners required their tenants to provide them with one or more sacks of maize a year, or to offer them first refusal of their surplus crop.[18] That these Africans enjoyed far greater freedom of choice than those in northern Natal is evident from the numerous demands from farmers in the midlands and coastal divisions for a tightening of labour conditions.

But during these early decades few farmers were in a position to lean too heavily on their tenants. Not only could Africans find alternative land if conditions became onerous, but many of the farmers were dependent on them for their own survival. Co-operation between farmers and tenants was to the advantage of both parties. Farmers often relied on their tenants for produce and vegetables, while Africans were remunerated for herding and kraaling the farmers' cattle and hired out their oxen when the latter's fields had to be ploughed.[19]

For Africans who were not prepared to accept labour tenancy, but were reluctant to move to reserve or Crown lands, a more attractive choice was rent tenancy on absentee-owned farms. Both the individuals and the companies who had purchased these lands believed that their other investments in commerce would in the long run increase the price of land and justify their speculation. In the short term they hoped to make their lands pay through commercial farming, particularly in cotton. Certainly until the depression of the late 1860s, few regarded rentals from African squatters as an important source of revenue. They did not have the ability to force payments from *abanumzana* who believed they had a prior right to the land, while the government did not have the resources to enforce payment.[20] Rents were accordingly low; on the Natal Land and Colonisation Company lands in the 1860s they were the same as the hut tax, 7s. per annum.[21] The depression, accompanied by drought between 1865 and 1868, made commercial farming of these lands unfeasible while the surrendering of mortgaged lands increased the amount of land in absentee ownership. By the 1870s the prospect of using rents as a source of revenue had become far more attractive, and the landowners were encouraging more Africans to squat on their lands. On Land and Colonisation Company lands, 1874 was a crucial year in the evolution of rent tenancy. Rents rocketed in that year to a minimum of 20s. per hut and were as high as £3 in the fertile mist belt of Pietermaritzburg county.[22] Although squatting on rent-free Crown lands was theoretically preferable to rent tenancy, pastures and arable lands were usually better on private farms and many Africans chose to pay rent for these advantages. Until the early 1880s, the price of maize rose steadily and rents could be met through grain sales.[23]

Rent tenancy had the great advantage that while land prices remained low and there was little profit to be made from improving farms, few landowners either objected to the stock numbers owned by an *umuzi* or restricted access to arable land. Because tenants were seldom expected to supply labour, they were free to use their time for their own production.[24] In addition, by accepting rent tenancy, they could not only escape specific labour obligations on farms, but could themselves choose when, where and to whom they would supply labour. At the same time, because many of these lands were situated close to villages or to white-occupied farms, rent tenants were assured of a regular market for their produce.

There were naturally also disadvantages to rent tenancy, and the files of the Land and Colonisation Company are full of complaints by tenants. The absentee owners in general, and the company in particular, had strong connections with official and urban interests in both Natal and London. The colonial Attorney-General, Michael Gallwey, for example, was one of nine shareholders of the company resident in the colony. In any conflict between landowners and their tenants, the former could depend on official support.[25] As a result, as their position improved in the 1870s, owners were prepared to sue tenants for non-payment of rent or to evict them. Rent tenants thus had very little security of tenure. Moreover, when the land was sold or let and a farmer took occupation, tenants could either be evicted or forced to provide labour as well as rent. Until the 1870s, however, the reluctance of speculators to sell land at a low price ensured that few tenants faced eviction.

The final category of land available to African producers was that possessed by Christian missionary societies. Missions such as the American Board Mission had been established in Natal since the 1830s. Around each mission a nucleus of Christian families, known as the *kholwa*, had grown. The colonial government realized the 'civilizing' potential of these missions and, from 1855, granted twenty reserves to the missionary societies, varying from 5 500 to 12 922 acres in extent and totalling 153 273 acres. Most reserves were in the midlands and coastal district with only two in the interior. Each consisted of a glebe, which was the personal property of the mission and housed the mission buildings, surrounded by rent-free lands set aside for Africans. Each one was held in trust by a board, usually comprising the Secretary for Native Affairs and the chairman, secretary and treasurer of the mission. The trustees exercised a very limited authority over the inhabitants of the reserves.[26]

During the course of the nineteenth century, lands were also granted to, or purchased by, missionaries to be used as mission stations (as distinct from reserves). Unlike the latter, these were not held in trust for their inhabitants and the missionaries exercised the ordinary rights of landowners on them. By the end of the century, 95 such stations existed with a combined size of 140 998 acres, virtually equal to that of the mission reserves.[27]

The missions contained a potential challenge to the homestead economy. Holding a strong Victorian belief in the link between industry and Christianity, missionaries encouraged the growth of a peasantry capable of supplying the colony's needs. On virtually all their reserves and stations they attempted to break down the homestead mode of production and encourage individual tenure and the cultivation of cash crops. In this they were only partly successful. No more than a handful of the inhabitants of mission reserves were converts and the rest retained their homestead lifestyle. It was only a small group of *kholwa*, often comprising families who moved onto the reserve from outside the area, who accepted individual plots of land and European practices such as manuring their gardens and planting crops in rows.[28]

The encouragement of individual tenure was closely linked to the question of allowing African land purchases. The Locations Commission had recommended the introduction of individual tenure in the reserves to encourage peasant agriculture. But the colonial administration feared that this would lead to a loss of land if owners sold their holdings to whites. As a result the Executive Council had decided that land grants should only be allowed on the mission reserves and, as a further safeguard, the mission reserves' deeds of grant stipulated that such grants should only be allowed to *kholwa*.[29]

The American Board missionaries, in particular, wanted to promote small-scale agricultural settlements. They began granting small allotments to *kholwa* and, by the 1860s, they had granted 2 534 acres at Umvoti, 712 at Amanzimtoti and 199 at Ifumi. Most of these were village or agricultural allotments of less than 30 acres.[30] On these lands a new set of production practices and economic relationships developed. An elite group of *kholwa* families emerged, distinguished by their production of crops specifically intended for sale on the colonial markets. These families prospered and became more and more enmeshed in the capitalist economy. The Umvoti mission village of Groutville was on the important trade route to Durban from the Zulu kingdom. Possessing lands ideal for sugar cultivation, it became the most advanced and prosperous of the settlements.[31]

The financial collapse of the mid-1860s forced a number of *kholwa* small-holders to borrow money, or mortgage their lands, in order to pay for improvements. The Americans, afraid that the *kholwa* would lose their lands when loan and mortgage repayments were demanded, began to reconsider the advisability of the grants. They were also concerned that some of the owners had reverted to polygamy. To try to ensure that the land remained in *kholwa* hands, the Americans abandoned freehold title in favour of leases.[32]

The Americans were not the only missionaries to experiment with individual ownership. In 1851, the Reverend J. Allison of the Wesleyan mission bought the 6 123-acre farm Welverdiend on the outskirts of Pietermaritzburg, and adjoining the Zwartkop reserve. Renamed Edendale, it was divided into village and garden allotments, and sold to members of the mission. Each purchaser had absolute freehold rights over his own allotment, and no restrictions were made on alienation. Communal grazing rights were administered by three trustees – the resident missionary, a representative elected by the owners, and another nominated by the first two trustees.[33]

Edendale was ideally situated to serve the Pietermarizburg market. It was paid for within four years and 1 000 acres were under cultivation by 1860. The inhabitants were also affected by the financial crisis of the 1860s and a number of plots were either mortgaged or sold. Disenchanted with individual tenure, some of the owners decided to buy land elsewhere under communal tenure. In 1867, under the leadership of Johannes Kumalo, they bought the farm Driefontein to the north of Ladysmith. In Kumalo's words, the land was acquired 'when we were in great trouble . . . we formed a company, and we obtained the land in order to hide our heads in it . . . We were in a state of poverty.'[34]

With the economic recovery of the 1870s both Edendale and Driefontein flourished. Visitors to Edendale were impressed by its rich and abundant crops, vegetable gardens and irrigation. The owners of Driefontein prospered and during the following years acquired five neighbouring farms which gave them two blocks of land amounting to nearly 37 399 acres.[35]

*   *   *   *   *

The opportunities enjoyed by *kholwa* and homestead Africans to sell produce were largely created by the white farmers' inability to service the market. None the less, the settlers were antagonized by their success. Not only did the farmers believe that Africans undermined their own attempts to supply local markets, but African self-sufficiency and access to other categories of land made it difficult for the farmers to find labour. The settlers' demands that the government should abandon the reserve system, end its support of the missions and of absentee landownership and, particularly, secure a labour supply for their own needs, were a constant refrain in the colonial period. As early as the 1850s, the demand that 'the lazy Caffres ought to be made to work' was being voiced.[36]

Until the 1870s the ready market for their produce meant that few Natal Africans were dependent on wages and those who entered the labour market usually did so for short periods and earned relatively high wages. Because of this, many African wage labourers in Natal had come from north of the Thukela, either as migrant labourers or as freed slaves or refugees who were obliged to register as labourers for a three-year period.[37] A large proportion of the colony's African men did, however, seek occasional work. In 1846 the *Natal Witness* commented that from 'first to last in this town [Pietermaritzburg] the Caffres may be seen at work, making bricks, tending tradesmen, cultivating gardens, and serving as domestics'.[38] In 1852 Magistrate Peppercorne pointed out that Africans appeared to do all the unskilled work in the colony, an observation which Lieutenant-Governor John Scott echoed in 1863: 'They are policemen, government messengers and post carriers; in domestic service they are cooks, nurses, grooms and general house servants; they are farm labourers and waggoners, and in short perform nearly the whole of the unskilled labour of the colony.'[39] Scott estimated that at least 20 000 colonial Africans were in service annually.

Yet, as Scott further pointed out, the Africans 'exercise almost as freely as the white colonists the right to dispose of their labour and time in accordance with their own requirements or natural wants'.[40] This observation reveals the extent to which colonial Africans were using the opportunities offered by white settlement to earn money for a variety of purposes. In 1852 the American missionary, Lewis Grout, isolated two principle motives for Africans to become labourers: to buy cattle for use as *lobola*, and to earn money to pay the hut tax. Peppercorne pointed out that Africans would rather earn money to pay taxes than part with their cattle.[41] He could have added that to many inhabitants of the Thukela reserves, migrant labour was essential for raising money for food as well as taxes, while to chiefdoms such as the Hlubi of the Drakensberg reserve, the money earned after 1869 in the Griqualand West diamond fields was useful for buying guns.[42]

The main concern of coastal and midland farmers whose hold on their labour tenants was tenuous was not, therefore, that Africans be made to work *per se*, but that they be made to work as agricultural labourers. The truth was, however, that few farmers were able to match the wages paid by urban businessmen, sugar estates, transport riders and diamond mines. Not only could these employers offer higher wages, but they could also afford to pay chiefs to supply labourers to them.[43] As few farmers were in a position to compete with these wages, they demanded government assistance, including the extension to their farms of the forced-labour *isibhalo* system. Under this system chiefs had to provide labourers to the state each year.

Unfortunately for the farmers, the colonial government's main requirement was to raise revenue and its interest in the Africans as a labour force was restricted to the work which they were obliged to provide to the state. Although magistrates were instructed in the early 1850s to try to persuade chiefs to encourage their men to work for the settlers, the Executive Council was only prepared to use persuasion, and reprimanded magistrates who exceeded their instructions by ordering labour from the chiefdoms.[44] By the late 1850s, officials were also inclined to guard jealously the administration's own prerogative in the use of *isibhalo* labour. In 1859, Scott warned magistrates against providing labour for farmers, a warning which was repeated by his successors in 1869 and in 1878.[45] Yet, to placate the farmers, the government recognized the labour rights which they exercised over their own tenants while it also adopted a policy which was to contribute towards settler supremacy. Instead of labour, settlers were offered financial benefits; there was no land tax and agricultural implements specifically for their use were imported duty free. This was only made possible, however, by raising revenue both directly and indirectly from Africans.

From the inception of British rule, the administration viewed Africans as a source of revenue and a system was evolved which placed the main tax burden on them. At High Commissioner Sir Harry Smith's insistence, the annual 7s. hut tax was introduced in 1849. In its first year the tax raised £8 831 and enabled Natal to repay debts it had incurred to the Cape Treasury.[46] The hut tax would have more than paid for schools, superintendents, and teachers in the reserves, but was diverted instead into the general colonial revenue each year. It was increased in 1875 to 14s. and remained the main source of direct taxation in the colony until 1910. In addition, Africans were required to pay a dog tax of 5s. from 1877 and marriage fees (including a marriage registration fee of £5 between 1869 and 1875). Indirect taxation was also so structured as to place the maximum burden on Africans. While few imports specifically for white use were taxed, heavy duties were placed on goods imported for mainly African consumption. Whereas, from 1860, the average colonial duty was 6 per cent, that on cotton sheets and blankets was 15 per cent, picks and hoes were taxed at 1s. each and beads at 9d. per pound.

It is difficult to ascertain exactly how dependent the colonial exchequer was on African revenue as the available statistics are exceptionally scanty. By the 1860s the hut tax covered the expenses of the entire civil establishment. By 1882 it contributed £66 571, while annual fees and fines, paid primarily by Africans, brought in £15 509, the dog tax a further £10 000, and the duty on imports for African use an estimated £17 051. These figures suggest that in that year Africans contributed at least £122 080, in direct and indirect taxation, of a total colonial revenue of £657 738; an average of £1 6s 0d for each of the colony's 93 803 huts.[47] Although the amount of revenue they contributed was less than that raised through customs duties on goods destined for the Transvaal and Orange Free State, Africans were the most important internal source of revenue throughout the colonial period.

The main purpose of taxation was to provide revenue for an impecunious colony, but both the imperial and colonial governments linked tax to the question of labour.[48] It has been submitted that Natal officials used taxation as a weapon to force Africans onto the labour market. This accusation was particularly levelled at them for introducing the £5 marriage-licence fee in 1869; for introducing the tax on hoes and picks; and for doubling the hut tax to 14s. per hut in 1875. These assertions cannot be either proved or refuted. It has to be borne in mind, however, that the doubling of the hut tax was designed to replace the marriage-licence fee which was not bringing in the expected revenue, and that the tax on hoes and picks was introduced when the government needed extra revenue for railway construction. The relevant documents which link the issues of taxation and labour suggest that officials often used the mobilization of labour as a mere pretext for levying taxes on Africans. Clearly, in the early colonial decades Natal was dependent on Africans for produce and revenue. While this situation continued, the government was not prepared either to bow to settler demands for labour, or directly to threaten the viability of the homestead economy.

Notes

1. For the controversy raging in southern African historiography over the existence of the 'Mfecane' and the role of slaving in the upheavals which took place in the early nineteenth century in the subcontinent, see the report on the colloquium on the 'Mfecane' in *South African Historical Journal*, 25, November 1991, pp. 154–76.

2. H. Slater, 'Land, labour and capital in Natal: the Natal Land and Colonisation Company, 1860–1948', *Journal of African History*, 16, no. 2, 1975, pp. 266–70; A. J. Christopher, 'Natal: a study in colonial land settlement', Ph.D. thesis, University of Natal, 1969, pp. 218, 223–46. There is no foundation to the claim by C. W. de Kiewiet, accepted by many later historians, that speculators owned up to 5 million acres, see *A history of South Africa: social and economic*, Oxford, 1941, pp. 71–2.

3. *Natal Mercury*, 27 June 1871; J. Robinson, ed., *Notes on Natal: an old colonist's book for new settlers*, Durban, 1872, p. 170.

4. P. Richardson, 'The Natal sugar industry, 1849–1905: an interpretative essay', in B. Guest and J. M. Sellers, eds, *Enterprise and exploitation in a Victorian colony: aspects of the economic and social history of colonial Natal*, Pietermaritzburg, 1985, pp. 186–91.

5. *Natal Mercury*, 3 January 1856; *Natal Almanac*, 1865, p. 89, 1868, p. 159.

6. Robinson, *Notes on Natal*, p. xix.

7. C. Ballard, 'Traders, trekkers and colonists', in A. Duminy and B. Guest, eds, *Natal and Zululand from earliest times to 1910: a new history*, Pietermaritzburg, 1989, p. 119.

8. J. E. Methley, *The new colony at Port Natal with information for emigrants*, London, 1850, p. 24; see also J. Bird, *The annals of Natal, 1495–1845*, vol. 2, Cape Town, n.d., p. 311; *Natal Mercury*, 19 September 1856; *Natal Witness*, 4 October 1864.

9. D. Welsh, *The roots of segregation: native policy in colonial Natal, 1845–1910*, Cape Town, 1971, pp.12–13, 177.
10. Secretary for Native Affairs (SNA), [Natal Archives], 1/1/115, 525/89, Clarence to SNA, 14 May 1889.
11. Welsh, *Roots of segregation*, p.178; Natal, *Proceedings of the commission . . . 1852*, II, Shepstone, p.37, III, Peppercorne, p.66.
12. Natal, *Proceedings of the commission . . . 1852*, VI, Mesham, p.11; J. Tyler, *Forty years among the Zulu*, Boston, 1891, pp.38, 73–82; M.S. Evans, *The problem of production in Natal*, Durban, 1905, p.7.
13. *Legislative Council (LC) Hansard*, I, 12 February 1880, Griffin, p.629.
14. SNA, 1/1/69, 865/84, Magistrate, Alexandra to SNA, 2 December 1884; 1/1/85, 448/82, SNA to Governor, 20 March 1884.
15. Colonial Office (CO) 179 [Public Record Office], 38, no.13, Acting Lieutenant-Governor to Secretary of State, 14 April 1855, pp.53f.
16. Natal Parliamentary Papers (NPP) [Natal Archives], 107, no.5, Report of commission . . . to enquire into the existing relations between masters and native servants, 31 July 1871; *Natal Almanac*, 1873, p.93.
17. SNA, 1/6/6, 257/76, Magistrate, Umsinga to SNA, 23 March 1876; R.H. Smith, *Labour resources of Natal*, Natal Regional Survey, Report no.1, Cape Town, 1950, p.47.
18. SNA, 1/3/17, 393/67, Magistrate, Inanda to SNA, 18 September 1867, p.340; Umgeni Magistracy, [Natal Archives], Add 3/3/2/1, Return of natives residing on farms in Umgeni division in 1876.
19. SNA, 1/1/4, 26/51, Henry to Diplomatic Agent, 1 July 1851; Sutton Collection [Natal Archives], 1, Diary, 1 June 1874, 8 June 1874; R.E. Gordon, *Dear Louisa: history of a pioneer family in Natal 1850–1888*, Durban, 1970, *passim*.
20. SNA, 1/1/2, 97/49, Francis to Diplomatic Agent, July 1849; 1/1/3, 35/50, Wilson to Diplomatic Agent, 8 April 1850; 48/50, Wilson to Diplomatic Agent, 7 May 1850.
21. Natal Land and Colonisation Company (NL&C) [Natal Archives], 2, no.52, Secretary, London to General Manager, Durban, 4 February 1864; 50, no.75, Ralfe to General Manager, Durban, 27 June 1864.
22. NL&C, Townsend to General Manager, Durban, 123, no.185, 22 March 1875; 124, no.291, 6 July 1875.
23. See *Natal Mercury*, 23 November 1875; SNA, 1/6/6, 253/76, Magistrate, Upper Umkomanzi to SNA, 28 June 1876.
24. NL&C, 92, no.176, Fannin to General Manager, Durban, 8 September 1869.
25. NL&C, 82, no.42, Fannin to General Manager, Durban, 28 August 1867.
26. Natal, *Report on the Native mission reserves*, Pietermaritzburg, 1886, p.1; American Board Mission (ABM) [Natal Archives], A/3/39, Kilbon to Secretary, Boston, 14 March 1882.
27. Natal, *Report . . . Native population*, 1898, pp.A40–8; 1905, p.189.
28. See N. Etherington, *Preachers, peasants and politics in southeast Africa, 1835–1880: African Christian communities in Natal, Pondoland and Zululand*, London, 1978, pp.117f.
29. *LC Sessional Papers*, 22, 1890, Reprint of the report of the Select Committee no.7, 1862, pp.519, 536–9, 553–60.
30. ABM, A/3/39, Goodenough to Secretary, Boston, 7 July 1891; *Natal Government Gazette (NGG)*, supplement, March 1881.
31. See ABM, A/3/41, Report of Umvoti station, June 1897 which refers to the earlier period.
32. Natal, *Report on the Native mission reserves*, p.2; see also ABM, A/3/49, Goodenough to SNA, 25 June 1894; Natal, *Report of the Lands Commission, February 1902*, Pietermaritzburg, 1902, pp.27–8.
33. Natal University, Department of Economics, *Experiment at Edendale: a study of a non-European settlement with special reference to food expenditure and nutrition*, Natal Regional Survey, Additional report no.1, Pietermaritzburg, 1951, pp.1–7.
34. *South African Native Affairs Commission (SANAC)*, 3, Cape Town, 1905, Kumalo, pp.485, 488; see also Colenso Collection, [Natal Archives], 2, Colenso to Colley, 21 December 1880; see also Etherington, *Preachers*, p.123; Shepstone Papers, [Killie Campbell Africana Library], 11, Edendale to H. Shepstone, 7 July 1893.
35. Lady Barker, *Life in South Africa*, New York, 1969, p.82; R. Plant, *The Zulu in three tenses: being a forecast of the Zulu's future in the light of his past and his present*, Pietermaritzburg, 1905, p.92.

36. E. W. Feilden, *My African home: or, Bush life in Natal when a young colony [1852–7]*, London, 1887, p. 110.
37. Natal, *Report of the commission appointed to inquire into the past and present state of the Kafirs in the district of Natal, and to report upon their future government* . . . n.p., 1852–3, p. 44; SNA, 1/1/6, 39/56, GN 1856; *Natal Mercury*, 20 November 1869, 23 September 1873; *Natal Witness*, 19 August 1870.
38. See J. Clark, *Natal settler-agent: the career of John Moreland, agent for the Byrne emigration scheme of 1849–51*, Cape Town, 1972, p. 22.
39. Natal, *Proceedings of the commission* . . . *1852*, IV, p. 6; CO 179, 68, no. 105, Lieutenant-Governor to Secretary of State, 25 September 1863, p. 78, separate, 20 November 1863, p. 447; See also *Natal Mercury*, 23 December 1852.
40. *South African Archival Records*, Natal no. 5, Cape Town, 1964, Lieutenant-Governor to Secretary of State, 30 December 1858, p. 262.
41. Natal, *Proceedings of the commission* . . . *1852*, IV, Peppercorne, p. 5; V, Grout, p. 76.
42. J. Wright and A. Manson, *The Hlubi chiefdom in Zululand-Natal: a history*, Ladysmith, 1983, p. 52.
43. SNA, 1/3/8, 96/59, Magistrate, Lower Umkomanzi to SNA, 4 July 1859, pp. 132f; 1/3/23, Magistrate, Pietermaritzburg to SNA, 6 March 1873, pp. 29f.
44. Welsh, *Roots of segregation*, p. 123; CO 179, 35, no. 35, Lieutenant-Governor to Secretary of State, 29 May 1854, pp. 181–3.
45. *LC Selected Documents*, 12, 1859, Circular to magistrates, 9 May 1859, p. 1; 35, 1870–71, Correspondence on Bill 18, 1869; Colonial Secretary's Office (CSO) [Natal Archives], 2552, c15/78, Manning to Lieutenant-Governor, 27 February 1878.
46. CO 179, 10, 163, Governor, Cape to Secretary of State, 30 October 1850, pp. 107–10.
47. *Natal Mercury*, 31 July 1869, *NBB*, 1882, pp. R5, W29–57; Natal, *Report of the Natal Native Commission, 1881–2*, Pietermaritzburg, 1882, p. 50.
48. CO 179, 5, no. 92, Governor, Cape to Secretary of State, 24 May 1849, pp. 137ff.

CHAPTER TWO

Chiefship in Early Colonial Natal

One of the most daunting tasks facing the new colonial administration in Natal in the 1840s was to provide a system of government which would accommodate both the Voortrekker and the African inhabitants of the region despite the great disparity in their social structures. The intention behind the establishment of the reserves was to segregate all Africans on their own lands. Although colonial authorities did not aim to perpetuate African forms of administration, the refusal of the British government to allocate imperial funds meant that the location commissioners had to abandon their intention of providing an administrative infrastructure in each reserve. With few resources at its disposal, the government had little alternative but to continue recognizing the authority of the chiefs.

As early as 1847, the Colonial Office instructed Lieutenant-Governor Martin West to interfere as little as possible with the internal affairs of the chiefdoms, and to avoid undermining the chiefs in the eyes of their people.[1] Thus was introduced into Natal an administrative system that was to be followed throughout British colonial Africa into the twentieth century. By recognizing the chiefdom or, in colonial terms, the 'tribe', as the basic unit of social and political organization, the colonial administration was able to reduce imperial expenditure by governing Africans indirectly through their chiefs. In 1849, an Order in Council established a separate administrative system for the Africans of Natal by recognizing the laws, customs and usages that had governed relationships in the region before the settlers' arrival. Although this effectively acknowledged the authority of chiefs, they were deprived of the power of life and death over their people and were intended, in practice, to exercise their authority as agents of the colonial government. The Lieutenant-Governor was constituted Supreme or Paramount Chief with the power to appoint and remove chiefs and to amend and alter 'native' law. From 1850, magistrates were appointed specifically as Administrators of Native Law to try ordinary criminal cases, while the chiefs retained jurisdiction only in civil and minor criminal cases. Cases involving crimes between Africans and settlers were tried before the colonial judiciary.[2] The status of chiefs as government servants was underscored in 1863 when they began to receive nominal salaries.

Perpetuating chiefly authority was easier in theory than in practice. The events of the early nineteenth century had caused havoc not only within the chiefdoms of the Thukela-Mzimkhulu area, but also with the institution of chiefship. In the eighteenth century, chiefdoms had been fluid communities with an ill-defined jurisdiction in which *imizi* had been bound together by ties of neighbourhood, kinship (real or fictive), clientship and marriage. They were given cohesion through 'acts of allegiance made by people to chiefs, and through the partial redistribution of accumulated tribute from the chief to favoured or politically important adherents'.[3]

Although kinship was only one of the ties holding people together, it was important ideologically in the maintenance of social and political cohesion, and conferred legitimacy on the chief. Chiefdoms defined themselves in genealogical terms as a grouping together of lineages or descent groups. People who were prepared to adapt, or manipulate, their traditions of origin so as to claim kinship links with a chiefly lineage, and hence membership of the chiefdom, could be accommodated. In this way *abanumzana* were able to transfer allegiance from one chief to another. This perpetuated the fluid and unstable nature of the chiefdoms and militated against the long-term consolidation of chiefly power.

Related chiefdoms could be grouped together in paramountcies but, where they existed, the paramount chiefs exercised little more than a formal authority over their subordinate chiefs. By the end of the eighteenth century, however, far-reaching changes had taken place that enabled several chiefdoms to expand their domains and to establish centralized control over both their own people and subordinate chiefdoms. The most obvious expression of these changes was the emergence of the *amabutho*, or young male groups, which were bands of men required to provide labour or military services for their chiefs.

By the 1820s, the Zulu chiefs, Shaka and his successor Dingane, were either directly or indirectly subjugating the chiefdoms of the region and taking over the labour services of their *amabutho*. Without the resources to impose direct control over the region, Shaka and Dingane used chiefdoms such as the Cele, Thuli, Bhaca and Hlangwini, which had survived the upheavals, to exercise authority on their behalf and collect cattle tribute from the remnants of the other chiefdoms. But, to stress their inferior status *vis-à-vis* the Zulu, the chiefdoms of the southern region were ideologically distinguished from those of the Zulu heartland north of the Thukela. The latter were incorporated closely into the Zulu kingdom and were encouraged to regard themselves as being *amantungwa*, of a common descent with the Zulu; while the former were distinguished as inferior *amalala* (menials), firmly excluded from centres of power and prevented from organizing *amabutho* for military service.[4]

The upheavals within the Thukela-Mzimkhulu region, and the concomitant ideological and political changes, had far-reaching effects which lasted well into the colonial period. Thus, when the British established their authority in Natal they were confronted by a widespread breakdown of chiefly authority amidst which the remaining chiefs were competing energetically to re-establish their dynasties.

In establishing an administrative framework, Shepstone had to take into account the fact that some Africans belonged to chiefdoms which had been powerful in pre-Shakan times. Their chiefs took advantage of the 'breaking of the rope', that is the civil war between Dingane and Mpande kaSenzangakhona, to reassert their independence and to establish power bases for themselves south of the Thukela. The Thembu and Chunu, for example, were *amantungwa* chiefdoms which had consolidated their position north of the Thukela earlier in the century, but had been driven south of the Mkomanzi River where their chiefdoms had been broken up and scattered during the 1820s. Rather than *khonza* (offer allegiance to) *amalala* chiefdoms such as the Cele, the remnants of the two chiefdoms had retraced their steps to their original lands, prepared to *khonza* Shaka and accept a subordinate place in his kingdom. During the breaking of the rope they threw off their allegiance to the Zulu, crossed into Natal and settled around the junction of the Thukela and Mzinyathi rivers. Similarly, the Mthethwa and Qwabe chiefdoms, which had been driven out of Zululand during the upheavals, used the opportunity to reconsolidate in the Thukela valley coastal hinterland, while the Ngwane chiefdom returned to its lands in the upper Thukela region.[5]

Although chiefdoms such as these recognized British authority over Natal after 1843, and were given reserves by the colonial administration, it was difficult for the fledgling colony to impose its authority on them. There were other Africans, however, particularly in south-western Natal where the devastation of the 1820s had been particularly severe, whose chiefdoms had ceased to exist as political entities and whose community and kinship ties were shattered. To add to the confusion, there was a constant stream of refugees into the colony from the Zulu kingdom. While many came as small groups, others were well-organized and powerful chiefdoms, such as the Hlubi under Langalibalele kaMtimkulu.

Faced with this situation, and with limited resources at his command, Shepstone acknowledged the authority of the fifty-six existing chiefs. He did little to interfere with their control over their people, except to try to restrict them to specific lands and to forbid them from using their powers of life and death over their followers. Those Africans without community ties, or without chiefs, were either placed directly under an existing chief (a policy which had drawbacks in that discrimination against the newcomers was always possible),[6] or were organized into nine new chiefdoms under chiefs appointed by Shepstone. In order to bolster the position of chiefs, Shepstone recognized their role as allocators of land to their people. Within his reserve the chief had the sole right to allocate land which was held under communal tenure by his people. This right did much to strengthen the position of chiefs in the early colonial years.

Although there were a number of minor disputes between chiefs jostling to improve their position, most were restrained 'from hostilities with each other by fear alone', as Lieutenant-Governor West pointed out to the Governor of the Cape in 1846.[7] Indeed, fear of reprisals could have played a part in the relative peace which prevailed in Natal during these early years. Although Shepstone was obliged to condone many acts which would not be tolerated in later years, a chief who endangered the general peace of the colony, challenged British authority, or threatened the interests of the settlers was summarily dealt with. Cattle stealing was a direct threat to the settlers' interests and when the first serious case occurred, in Pietermaritzburg county in 1854, the guilty chief, Mdushana kaSonyangwe of the Bhaca, was fined 500 head in addition to the 100 that had allegedly been stolen. Justifying the heavy sentence, Shepstone asserted: 'I am quite convinced that if the Government does not take decisive action in this the first instance of such a serious crime, there will soon be no chance of any white man keeping his cattle.'[8] Yet both Shepstone and successive lieutenant-governors all recognized that the colonial administration, lacking means of enforcement, could not simply impose decisions on Africans. Shepstone learned a salutary lesson as early as 1847 when he deposed Fodo kaNombewu, the hereditary chief of the Hlangwini, who had threatened to attack his neighbours, and replaced him with his (Fodo's) uncle. Within a few years, the refusal of the chiefdom to obey their new chief obliged Shepstone to reinstate Fodo.[9]

It is perhaps no coincidence that in both these cases, Shepstone took action against chiefdoms which had enjoyed authority under the Zulu state. In enforcing his will, he tended to exploit the tensions and rivalries which were a legacy of the Shakan period, pitting the chiefdoms against each other and making use of their military forces. But in order to do so he had to allow the chiefs to continue the *amabutho* system of age-group regiments; a policy potentially dangerous for the colony. It did, however, enable him to summon levies from chiefdoms to deal with unrest. So, for example, when the Hlongwa in south-western Natal proved refractory in 1849, he ordered their paramount chieftainess, Mhlase, to take action against them. Similarly, in the same year, when Langalibalele and Phuthini kaMatshoba refused to obey his orders to remove their chiefdoms from land in Klip River assigned to the trekkers, he used a force of African police drawn from the Sithole, Thembu, Chunu and Ngwane chiefdoms against them.[10]

Colonial dependence on chiefly co-operation in subduing recalcitrant chiefdoms ensured that the administration carefully protected the interests of 'loyal' chiefs. For lesser chiefs, particularly in south-western Natal where most chiefdoms were small, this meant protection from overweening neighbours. Colonial support was also crucial for those chiefs appointed by Shepstone to rule over the newly created chiefdoms and, indeed, with this support a number of them rose to positions which rivalled those of the hereditary chiefs. This was particularly true of Shepstone's *induna*, Ngoza kaLudaba, who was appointed chief of the 'government tribe', the Qamu chiefdom. The new chiefdom consisted of so many fugitives and remnants of chiefdoms that by the time Ngoza died in 1869 it was the largest chiefdom in the colony.[11]

But in the early years of colonial rule, it was the hereditary chiefs who benefited most from the colonial presence, particularly those whose chiefdoms had been prominent in pre-Shakan times. While Zulu client chiefdoms such as the Cele, Thuli, Bhaca and Hlangwini sank into relative insignificance, chiefs such as

Langalibalele of the Hlubi, Phakade kaMacingwane of the Chunu, Nodada kaNgoza of the Thembu, and Zikhali kaMatiwane of the Ngwane, harnessed the changed conditions in Natal to aggrandize themselves. The destruction of Zulu power south of the Thukela freed them to exercise greater authority over their people, while the weakness of the colonial state gave them considerable latitude for action. Phakade and Nodada were particularly noteworthy in this respect. Once they had thrown off their allegiance to the Zulu state and established themselves south of the Thukela they consolidated their position through a policy of incorporation.

Living in the remote north-eastern area of the colony, with only sparse white settlement, both chiefs could ignore the boundaries of their lands. They extended their influence over surrounding Crown lands, more richly blessed with arable and grazing land than was the arid Impafana reserve that had been allocated to them. Both recognized the importance of appearing loyal and of supplying levies when necessary. In return they were left with a large measure of undisturbed control of their chiefdoms, enjoying a special relationship with Shepstone which at times enabled them to ignore the presence of their nearby magistrates with impunity.[12] Given the pre-Shakan prestige of their chiefdoms, their status as *amantungwa*, and the lands at their disposal, they rapidly attracted newcomers willing to *khonza* them. These included not only neighbouring people but also those from further afield, amongst whom were refugees from the Zulu kingdom. By the 1870s the once-small remnants of the two chiefdoms had overtaken the Qamu chiefdom and become the largest chiefdoms in the colony.[13]

In the Natal midlands, the Mphumuza chief, Thetheleku kaNobanda, also provides an excellent example of how a chief could use the colonial presence to strengthen his position. The Mphumuza were a junior branch of the Nadi chiefdom and, during the 1830s, both branches had been assigned land at Dingane's command by the Hlangwini chief, Fodo, in what was to become the Zwartkop reserve. Thetheleku's father, Nobanda kaNgwane, had been killed while fighting with the Port Natal traders against Dingane in 1838.[14] Possibly because of this, Thetheleku enjoyed a special relationship with the colonial administration from the earliest days of British rule, and was able to build up a more influential position for his chiefdom than its status warranted. Shepstone regarded him as an authority on African law. He was made an assessor at Langalibalele's trial in 1874, and on that chief's return from exile in 1887 he was made his custodian. His influence was widely recognized by Africans throughout south-eastern Africa. He was able to ignore the authority of the paramount Nadi chief and further strengthened his position by forming marriage alliances with heads of great chiefdoms such as the Chunu and the Mbo. He was in time to marry twenty-three wives.[15]

Although hereditary chiefs attracted followers primarily because of the resources at their command, their prestige and legitimacy as hereditary leaders cannot be underestimated. Throughout the colonial period they generally enjoyed far greater loyalty from their followers than did appointed chiefs who only held their position through official favour. They regularly consulted their leading *abanumzana* and reputedly showed greater concern for the welfare and interests of their people.[16] A comparison between Phakade and Ngoza is illuminating; despite Ngoza's prestige as Shepstone's trusted induna, his status, as an appointed chief, was considerably less than that enjoyed by Phakade. On his death in 1869 Ngoza's chiefdom disintegrated whereas Phakade's continued to grow under his successor, Silwana.

Hereditary chiefs were also better placed to continue to exact services from their people. In 1852, the American missionary, Aldin Grout pointed out that the 'bone and muscle of chieftainship consists in the right of the chief to demand, gratuitously, the service of his people to provide both for his subsistence and his aggrandisement'.[17] Here again, Phakade offers a good example. He lived in quasi-royal state in his main *umuzi*, as befitted his Chunu chiefdom. He also made extensive use of the *sisa* system which enabled men with large herds to build up a patron-client relationship with poorer men by allowing them the use of some cattle. In this way Phakade was able to secure the allegiance of poorer men in his chiefdom, and to attract people from other chiefdoms.[18]

The services which the chiefs claimed from their adherents were varied. Influential *abanumzana* had to assist their chief in his judicial functions, while other male members of the chiefdom were expected to pay periodic visits to the chief's *umuzi* to pay homage and to offer labour services. These included the building and maintenance of the chief's *umuzi* and the clearing of land for his gardens, and such visits were always of short duration. In addition, a chief was entitled to a head of cattle from each man willing to *khonza* him, while some could ask for an annual payment of one head from each *umuzi*.[19] But the services and tribute which the chiefs claimed were not solely for their own benefit. The cattle, for example, were intended as a bank to be used for *sisa*'ing purposes, while the labour was to insure that sufficient grain was stored in grain pits against future shortages. Moreover, even powerful chiefs lacked the coercive powers necessary to rule without some degree of popular consent, while a chief who did try to impose his will risked having people transfer their allegiance elsewhere. This practice became fairly widespread in the colonial period; for example, in two related Mbo chiefdoms in Alexandra, Kaduphi attracted men from Mabuna because of his reputation as a better and more just leader. Similarly, George Fynn's habit of ill-using and flogging his men provoked an exodus from his Nkumbi chiefdom.[20]

An outward sign of a chief's authority was the extent to which he was able to organize male age groups within his chiefdom into *amabutho*. Here, too, it was predominantly the hereditary chiefs, and particularly those of the great chiefdoms of the interior, who had sufficient authority to maintain *amabutho*. Both Langalibalele and Phakade steadily *butha*'d new age regiments until the former had eleven *amabutho* and the latter thirteen.[21] The *amabutho* appear to have been used primarily for supplying men for labour services. To prevent the chiefs from using them for military aggrandizement, Shepstone only allowed them to be assembled with the permission of the Supreme Chief. Except when assembled to assist the state against rebellious chiefs, the *amabutho* were only convened for celebrations such as the *umkhosi* ceremony.

The *umkhosi* or First Fruits ceremony symbolized the chief's control over homestead production. No men were allowed to drink beer until they had been enrolled in a regiment, and no one could eat the new mealies until the chief had presided over the ceremony. At the ceremony the chief was ritually strengthened, the ancestral spirits were propitiated, and the allegiance of his people was renewed. The ceremony emphasized the authority of the chief within his chiefdom but, as it could only be held with the Supreme Chief's permission, it also symbolized the chief's subordination to the administration. Although no request to hold the ceremony was ever refused in the early colonial decades, the paucity of such requests in the SNA files suggests that few chiefs were in a position to call regiments together. Most requests came from a handful of the great chiefs. For a chief such as Nodada of the Thembu the ceremony had special significance. He claimed a paramountcy over a number of lesser Thembu chiefs in the colony and used their presence at his *umkhosi* to underline their subordination to him.[22]

The 1850s were a time of fluidity in Natal, during which neither settlers nor administration were secure enough to assert authority over the African population as a whole. Consequently, most chiefdoms were able to function without much white interference. Many chiefs also used the British presence in Natal to further as well as to safeguard their interests. At a time of growing African involvement in the colonial economy, chiefs such as Thetheleku enriched themselves by supplying the market. Others directed the young men of their chiefdoms to supply labour to the settlers. Instances of chiefs receiving payment from planters or other employers for each labourer supplied were common.[23] In addition, chiefs like Langalibalele drew tribute from returning migrant labourers. This became a particularly useful source of revenue after the opening of the diamond fields.[24]

The great chiefs who were thus able to control their subjects were emboldened to resist what they regarded as intolerable demands by the state. An attempted cattle census in each chiefdom in 1850 was summarily rejected by the chiefs and had to be abandoned. In the same year Shepstone summoned a number of chiefs to send levies to help imperial troops fight against the Sotho. In response the chiefs met in the Zwartkop reserve and resolved to ignore the summons.[25] But colonial initiatives like these bred suspicion amongst the chiefs and caused spreading discontent. In addition, forced removals of chiefdoms such as the Hlubi and Ngwe from Klip River in 1849, and the resultant loss of cattle and grain,[26] sent a ripple of alarm through the chiefdoms.

African resentment at the colonial presence was further fuelled during these years by the introduction of several measures which had important long-term consequences. A particularly far-reaching measure resulted from the colonial concept of the chiefdoms as 'tribes'. This concept was accompanied by a tighter territorial definition of chiefship arising from the attempt to confine chiefdoms to clearly defined geographical areas with all Africans in an area under one chief. Chiefs were allocated specific reserve lands on which to settle their people. But with limited reserve lands available, it was not possible to give chiefdoms sufficient land, or in some cases to allot any land at all. Shepstone therefore had to turn a blind eye to the encroachment of chiefdoms on Crown lands and, as mentioned, was even obliged to locate some on Crown lands himself. Because of this practical breakdown of the territorial concept, boundaries of chiefdoms were ill defined and members of different chiefdoms intermingled.[27] This often meant that a chief might claim jurisdiction over *imizi* and resources of other chiefdoms. Even in the late 1840s, this situation resulted in clashes between chiefdoms, while in later decades, as land resources became more limited, it led to numerous faction fights.

A second innovation was the hut tax which chiefs had to ensure was paid by their subjects. Convincing the *abanumzana* to remit the tax each year was an onerous and unpopular duty and led to considerable disaffection. This was particularly so in the early 1850s. When the tax was introduced in 1848 most chiefs believed it was a single payment for permission to live on reserve lands;[28] when they realized that it was to be an annual tax there was considerable resentment and numerous refusals to pay.

Probably the most unpopular innovation was the introduction, in 1848, of the system of *isibhalo* or forced labour. The chiefs' control of labour resources enabled the government to demand that they provide the state with one labourer for every eleven huts in their chiefdoms each year. The men served for six months, beginning at 7s. 6d. per month with rations and rising by 1875 to 15s. The system was justified on the grounds that it was based on the *amabutho* system and on the right of the Lieutenant-Governor, as Supreme Chief, to call up men. However, it was widely resented, particularly as no chief had been consulted before it was introduced.[29] *Isibhalo* labourers were used on public works, usually on the colony's roads, but also as postal runners, on the harbour in the 1860s and, by the end of the century, as game and quarantine guards. The system was also widely used during the Anglo-Zulu War when, in addition to the troops levied from each chiefdom, men were also called out to work as bearers, drivers and team leaders.[30]

Although the Supreme Chief had the right to call upon all Africans for *isibhalo* service, and indeed did so during the Anglo-Zulu War, the right was usually exercised only in respect of Africans on reserve and Crown lands. Africans on private lands were excluded so as not to interfere with the rights of farmers to their labour. The *isibhalo* system gave rise to great disaffection. Even in the 1850s, many chiefs found it impossible to fill their quotas, especially as the wage rate was comparatively low. As a result chiefs often had to exert pressure on *abanumzana*, and frequently called out labour tenants despite the protests of the settlers.[31] Some chiefs also used the system to harass men who had fallen foul of them, while exempting favourites or men willing to pay bribes.[32] The system did much to poison the relationship between chiefs and subjects. Although some chiefs exploited it as an additional political control, most found themselves squeezed between the pressures exerted on them by the government and those exerted by their people.

Because of exactions such as these, more powerful chiefs refused or delayed compliance with colonial demands during the early 1850s. In 1854 Phakade delayed paying hut tax while Langalibalele regularly refused either to supply labourers for *isibhalo* service, or to collect hut tax.[33] It is possible that these chiefs were testing to see how far they could assert their independence before Shepstone reacted.

The Sidoyi and Matshana affairs of 1857 proved a turning point in the attitude of these chiefs to the colonial administration. In southern Natal, Sidoyi kaBaleni, chief of a related branch of the Hlangwini chiefdom which had fallen foul of Shepstone in 1847, attacked a neighbouring chiefdom and refused to account for his action to the local magistrate. A few months later in northern Natal, Chief Matshana kaMondise of the Sithole also ignored his magistrate's orders to surrender men accused of murdering a supposed witch. Shepstone's reaction to this flouting of colonial authority was ruthless; both chiefdoms were broken up and the chiefs' property was confiscated. These were the first instances of chiefdoms destroyed for disobedience, and the other chiefs would have realized that Shepstone was acting arbitrarily. There was no precedent in African law for breaking up a chiefdom as punishment for the actions of its chief. The chiefs knew that Shepstone, by 'eating up' the chiefdoms and allocating Matshana's reserve to his personal *induna*, Ngoza, was acting as autocratically as had Shaka.[34]

Incidents such as these epitomized chiefly hostility to Shepstone's control. However, the ease with which these chiefs were crushed persuaded other chiefs of the futility of opposing the colonial administration. At the same time, attempts by the Legislative Council to exploit these incidents to gain control over African policy confirmed Shepstone in his belief that peace could only be maintained if his control over the chiefdoms was interfered with as little as possible.

After 1857, and before 1906, the only major African challenge to British authority in Natal came from Langalibalele, whose relations with his white neighbours and the administration were consistently marked by friction. He had manipulated the colonial presence to make his people powerful and prosperous. By the early 1870s, the Hlubi chiefdom had expanded from 7 000 people in the 1840s to 10 000, and these people were to be found scattered throughout the western area of Weenen county. With the cattle wealth that he had accumulated and his reputation as a rainmaker, Langalibalele had become one of the most influential chiefs in Natal. He travelled with a large retinue of well-mounted men and by the 1870s he had forty wives including as his chief wife, the daughter of King Sobhuza of the Swazi.[35]

Yet the presence of his chiefdom in an area with a relatively settled white farming community ensured that, unlike Phakade or Zikhali, he was constantly falling foul of the administration. As a hereditary chief of proud lineage, his reluctance to accept conditions which would undermine his popular prestige was notorious. Both he and his neighbouring chief, Phutini of the Ngwe, were prepared to hold ceremonies without permission, even at the risk of alienating the colonial administration. Their most serious offence was to hold dances at which the men of their *amabutho* were doctored by tasting the gall of an ox whose hind leg had been skinned and cut off while the animal was still alive. The endurance of the ox during this ordeal was thought to presage the prowess of the chief and his warriors in coming battles.[36]

Ceremonies such as these, and the growing wealth and influence of the Hlubi chiefdom, alarmed both the settlers of Weenen county and the administration, and the latter grew more determined in seeking a pretext for cutting Langalibalele down to size. In 1873, he failed to comply with a demand from his magistrate to register guns which his followers were bringing back from the diamond fields. When ordered to appear before Shepstone, he panicked and, with a number of his people, fled to Basutoland. In the skirmish that followed between the Hlubi and colonial volunteers, three volunteers and some two hundred Hlubi were killed.

After sixteen years of peace since the Sidoyi and Matshana incidents, both Benjamin Pine, in Natal for a second term as Lieutenant-Governor, and Shepstone were unnerved by the clash and reacted with a ferocity out of all proportion to the occasion. There was widespread shooting and homestead burning among the Hlubi and related Ngwe peoples. Once all signs of opposition had been crushed, harsh punishments were meted out to these chiefdoms, and their land and cattle were parcelled out amongst the settlers. Langalibalele was banished for life while seven of his sons, two *izinduna* and two hundred followers were imprisoned.[37]

These excesses provoked criticism in Britain and led to the replacement of Pine by Sir Garnet Wolseley who was made Special Administrator, ostensibly to bring order to the colony's African policy. The only changes that were made were the passing of a Native Administration Act in 1875, and what was intended as a preliminary Code of Native Law in 1878. These were the first legislative attempts to define the official role of the chiefs and to subordinate them to a codified legal authority. The most important of these restrictions were judicial. The chiefs were deprived of their power to try minor criminal cases, which now came under the ordinary criminal jurisdiction of the colony. Although chiefs retained the right to try property, marriage, inheritance and other civil cases, appeals were allowed to magistrates in their capacity as Administrators of Native Law, while a Native High Court was established to hear appeals against the magistrates' decisions. The increased powers of the magistrates were to circumscribe the position of the chiefs considerably, particularly after Shepstone's resignation late in 1876.

The chiefs recognized the extent to which their authority depended on their retention of judicial powers. Therefore, wherever possible they continued to try criminal cases and to impose fines upon their people. Practically speaking, although this was now illegal, until at least the 1890s few magistrates were able to cope with the burden of work so that chiefs were often left to judge criminal cases.[38] Despite the restrictions placed upon them, those chiefs who could continue to distribute and redistribute reserve and Crown lands, were able to retain much of their authority. They could still call on their principal followers for assistance in administering their chiefdoms and on their subjects for labour service. But as the settlers consolidated their position on the land during the 1870s, the authority of the chiefs was undermined amongst their followers on white-owned land. The chiefs obviously had no power to distribute land on private farms. Moreover, the subjects of various chiefdoms tended to be hopelessly intermingled on these lands and it was virtually impossible to ascertain what powers of jurisdiction the various chiefs could exercise. Chiefs testifying before the Native Affairs Commission in 1881 protested bitterly at their inability to enforce their traditional obligations on these lands and many echoed Thetheleku's complaint: The farmers 'lessen my power. They are a source of trouble to my people.'[39]

On farms with resident owners, tenants were now being prevented from obeying chiefly summonses or, often more importantly, could be assisted in disobeying them. This weakened the chiefs' ability to call men out both for *isibhalo* labour and for services on their own land. They were also unable to protect their followers from the exactions of the farmers which many labour tenants used as an excuse, or pretext, for refusing to render traditional tribute or services.[40]

By the late 1870s the African population had increased threefold since the introduction of British rule, and numbered just under 300 000. Few chiefs could still provide sufficient land for their followers' *imizi*, with the result that many chiefdoms were beginning to fragment. This was particularly the case in the interior where, with only six reserves, the chiefdoms were scattered over private and Crown lands in 'apparently hopeless confusion'.[41] Throughout the colony, fragmentation also occurred when either a chief and some of his followers moved to a less crowded district, leaving the remnant under an *induna*, or else an *induna* was appointed to move with a section of the chiefdom. In an attempt to maintain some cohesion for the chiefdoms, the government gave these *izinduna* limited powers under the overall authority of their chiefs. Although most *izinduna* remained loyal to the chiefs who had appointed them, a number began to assume the status of chiefs in their own right and were eventually recognized as such by the government. The recognition of the chiefly powers of these *izinduna*, and the growing number of chiefdoms resulting from fragmentation, meant that by 1882, 173 chiefs were recognized by the colonial administration of whom 99 were hereditary chiefs, 46 were appointed and 28 were *izinduna* with the authority to administer splintered fragments of chiefdoms.[42]

Even where the *izinduna* remained loyal to their chiefs, the very fact of administrative fragmentation weakened the ties binding the communities together. In the 1870s the resources of the Umnini reserve were no longer sufficient for its inhabitants, and the Thuli chief, Mnini kaManti, began a long struggle to find land for some of his followers in Alfred county. Similarly Thetheleku's Mphumuza chiefdom outgrew its part of the Zwartkop reserve and, in their search for new lands, the Mphumuza people expanded throughout Pietermaritzburg and Weenen counties. These two chiefdoms had been allocated reserves which their chiefs were able to use as a base for maintaining authority. Other chiefs were less fortunate; Thulasizwe of the Swazi had no reserve, and Thinta of the Mtungwa had a reserve consisting merely of two small farms.[43] In these extreme cases, political and territorial fragmentation left the chiefs with few people over whom they could exercise authority.

The declining ability of some chiefs to provide land and other resources for their followers also led growing numbers of people to look elsewhere for pastures and gardens. Consequently, many decided to *khonza* chiefs like Thetheleku who remained influential enough to find land for them.[44] The extent to which these shifts of allegiance undermined bonds of kinship is problematic. It is uncertain whether kinship redefinition accompanied political transference. Vilakazi refers to men of the Qadi chiefdom who changed their allegiance to obtain land elsewhere, but who retained their kinship links with their original chiefdom.[45] Yet the transference of allegiance would have done little to strengthen kinship ties within African society. This would have been particularly true in the artificially created chiefdoms under appointed chiefs. These usually survived only for as long as the original appointed chiefs were alive, but tended to splinter after their deaths. Even the favour bestowed upon it by the government was insufficient to prevent Ngoza's Qamu chiefdom from splintering into nine separate chiefdoms by the end of the century.

With the reserves unable to contain a growing population, those chiefs whose lands bordered on mission reserves were naturally determined to assert their authority over their subjects who lived across the borders. Their powers were restricted, however, in that the missionaries controlled the distribution of their own reserve land and were able to apportion it between subjects of the different chiefdoms.[46] Despite this, the missions' deeds of trust had not deprived these chiefs of their powers of jurisdiction. As land shortages grew within the colony, and as chiefs sought new lands for sections of their chiefdoms, so it became more difficult for the missionaries to control the allocation of land. Conflict arose when chiefs claimed jurisdiction over the reserves' inhabitants, called them out for *isibhalo* service and placed *izinduna* on the lands. The mission-reserve inhabitants, unwilling to acknowledge chiefly demands, tried to play off the missionaries against the chiefs and *izinduna*, a situation which later in the century was to lead to the breakdown of control within mission reserves.[47]

The problem was exacerbated by the religious conversion of members of a chiefdom on a reserve. Few chiefs were prepared to accept either this further erosion of the loyalty of members of their chiefdoms, or the withdrawal of their people from their traditional obligations. A number of missionaries recognized that some men converted simply to escape subordination to their chiefs. The result was not only the hostility of many chiefs to the missionaries and to the *kholwa*, but also chiefly contempt for the inhabitants of mission lands.[48] Consequently, some chiefs tried to prevent missionaries from working on the mission reserves, or brought in people from outside to interfere with their work. For all his good relations with the colonial administration, Thetheleku had a hearty contempt for Christianized Africans. As early as 1862, clashes between his followers and their neighbours in the *kholwa* settlement of Edendale were common and laid the basis for a long-standing bitterness between the two groups.[49]

But conflict between *kholwa* and chiefs was not always the norm. Many chiefs recognized the advantages their chiefdoms could reap by having access to mission resources, and co-operated with neighbouring missions and their *kholwa* inhabitants. The relations which existed between the Qadi chief, Mqawe kaDabeka, and the *kholwa* of the Inanda mission reserve are a case in point. Despite remaining heathen and polygamist, Mqawe generally enjoyed excellent relations with the American Board and with the *kholwa*, most of whom belonged to his chiefdom, and amongst whom were members of his family, the Dubes, who were prominent in the American Board congregation.[50] Etherington suggests that Mqawe's attitude was the result of the scarcity of arable land in the Inanda reserve, and his realization that co-operation with the Americans was the best way of ensuring that his chiefdom retained access to mission lands. Because of his attitude, the *kholwa* and heathen members of his chiefdom shared the mission reserve with little friction.[51]

By the end of the 1870s, the colonial administration was gaining the upper hand over the chiefs and had reduced their potential threat to settler security. Yet, to the extent that it remained unable to devise a viable administrative system for the African population, chiefs continued to retain some political control over their subjects. Despite their declining power, they remained indispensable as collectors of taxes and providers of labour. In the months leading up to the outbreak of the Anglo-Zulu War they provided manpower for the very defence of the colony.[52] Chiefs like Thetheleku, Mqawe, Phakade and Zikhali's successor, Ncwadi, responded to the call for troops with alacrity. Memories of their subordination to the Zulu kingdom in the 1820s and 1830s contributed to their willingness to stop what they would have seen as a revival of Zulu power. Thus they supplied not only followers, but even men of their own families. At Rorke's Drift in January 1879, Phakadi lost three sons, including his heir Gabangaye, and two grandsons.

The Anglo-Zulu War was to prove to be the high-water mark of colonial/chiefly collaboration. Yet in destroying the Zulu military machine, the war removed a crucial element in the official need to retain the power of the great chiefdoms as a bulwark against invasion from north of the Thukela. In the years ahead, the remaining powers of the chiefs were to be whittled away until by the end of the century they retained little authority over their subjects.

Notes

1. CO 179, 2, no. 1657, Secretary of State to Governor, Cape, 10 December 1847, pp. 407–10.
2. *South African Archival Records*, Natal no. 5, Lieutenant-Governor to Secretary of State, 30 December 1858, pp. 263–4.
3. J.B. Wright and C. Hamilton, 'Traditions and transformations: the Phongolo-Mzimkhulu region in the late eighteenth and early nineteenth centuries', in Duminy and Guest, eds, *Natal and Zululand*, p. 58.
4. Ibid., pp. 59–72; see also C. Hamilton and J.B. Wright, 'The making of the amalala: ethnicity, ideology and relations of subordination in a precolonial context', *South African Historical Journal*, 22, 1990, pp. 3–23.
5. J.B. Wright, 'The dynamics of power and conflict in the Thukela-Mzimkhulu region in the late 18th and early 19th centuries: a critical reconstruction', Ph.D. thesis, University of the Witwatersrand, 1989, *passim*.
6. CO 179, 15, no. 117, Report by Shepstone, 14 August 1848, p. 207.
7. CO 179, 1, no. 10, Lieutenant-Governor to Governor, Cape, 11 April 1846, p. 167.
8. Sir Theophilus Shepstone Papers [Natal Archives], 70, Shepstone to Cato, 2 December 1854, p. 56.
9. Natal, *Proceedings of the commission . . . 1852*, II, Shepstone, p. 24.
10. *South African Archival Records*, Natal, no. 3, Report by Shepstone, 20 May 1849, pp. 98–101, 14 October 1849, pp. 197–201.
11. SNA, 1/4/12, c96/03, Under-Secretary for Native Affairs [USNA] report on chiefdoms, 15 June 1903.
12. SNA, 1/1/3, 78/50, Stadler to Diplomatic Agent, 9 October 1850; 1/3/8, 211/59, Magistrate, Weenen to SNA, 31 January 1859, p. 307.
13. Natal, *Proceedings of the commission . . . 1852*, II, Boshof, p. 34; Natal, *Report of the Natal Native Commission, 1881–2*, p. 33.
14. C. de B. Webb and J.B. Wright, eds, *The James Stuart archive of recorded oral evidence relating to the history of the Zulu and neighbouring peoples*, 4, Pietermaritzburg, 1986, Mqiakana, pp. 1f.
15. *LC Sessional Papers*, 10, 1873, Umkuba, p. 85; Wright and Manson, *Hlubi chiefdom*, p. 81; W.R. Guest, *Langalibalele: the crisis in Natal, 1873–1875*, Durban, 1976, p. 100; SNA, 1/4/12, c96/03, USNA report on chiefdoms, 15 June 1903; Webb and Wright, eds, *James Stuart archive*, 2, Macebo, 2 November 1898, p. 43.
16. *NBB Departmental reports*, 1885, p. B39; *SANAC*, 3, J.W. Shepstone, p. 41; D.H. Reader, *Zulu tribe in transition: the Makhanya of southern Natal*, Manchester, 1966, pp. 264–5.
17. Natal, *Proceedings of the commission . . . 1852*, V, Grout, p. 31.
18. SNA, 1/3/3, Magistrate, Weenen to SNA, 38/54, 25 March 1854; 52/56, 21 March 1856.
19. Natal, *Proceedings of the commission . . . 1852*, II, Shepstone, p. 30; VI, Shepstone, p. 73; Natal, *Report of the commission . . . 1852–3*, p. 34; J. Shooter, *The kafirs of Natal and the Zulu country*, London, 1857, p. 104; SNA, 1/3/9, 56/59, Magistrate, Lower Umzimkulu to SNA, 12 March 1859, p. 85.
20. SNA, 1/1/16, 73/66, Shuter to SNA, 11 October 1866; 1/1/36, 54/80, Magistrate, Umgeni to SNA, 26 January 1880; 1/1/45, 176/81, Magistrate, Alexandra to SNA, 29 March 1881.
21. Webb and Wright, eds, *James Stuart archive*, 2, Mabonsa, p. 17, Magidigidi, p. 86.
22. Ibid., 1, Ingaba, p. 291; see also Shooter, *Kafirs of Natal*, pp. 25–6.
23. *Natal Mercury*, 31 May 1860, 14 August 1863; *Natal Witness*, 25 October 1872.
24. R. Turrell, *Capital and labour on the Kimberley diamond fields, 1871–1890*, Cambridge, 1987, pp. 19–23.
25. Natal, *Report of the commission . . . 1852–3*, pp. 25–6.
26. Natal, *Proceedings of the commission . . . 1852*, III, Howell, p. 14.
27. Natal, *Report . . . Native population*, 1879, pp. 1, 27; Natal, *Evidence . . . Natal Native Commission, 1881*, Trotter, p. 83.
28. CO 179, 34, no. 43, Lieutenant-Governor, Natal to Secretary of State, 18 July 1854, p. 44.
29. I. Machin, 'The isibhalo labour system in colonial Natal', History workshop, Natal in the colonial period, University of Natal, Pietermaritzburg, 24–25 October 1990, pp. 3, 6.
30. L.J. Heydenrych, 'Die geskiedenis van Port Natal-hawe, 1845–1897', D.Litt. et Phil. thesis, Unisa, 1990, p. 123; GH, 1273, 122/07, Governor to Secretary of State, 2 August 1907, pp. 113f; SNA, 1/1/31, 62/78, Report by Magistrate, Umgeni, 20 December 1878.

31. SNA, 1/1/14, 14/64, Hayes to SNA, 11 February 1864; 79/64, Memorial of Umcana, 8 July 1864; see also Natal, *Evidence . . . Natal Native Commission, 1881*, Teteleku, pp. 178–9.

32. SNA, 1/3/8, 57/59 Magistrate, Inanda to SNA, 21 September 1859, p. 76; Natal, *Evidence . . . Natal Native Commission, 1881*, Walker, p. 72, J. W. Shepstone, pp. 104–5; Machin, 'Isibhalo labour system', p. 7.

33. *South African Archival Records*, Natal no. 3, 28 January 1851, pp. 264–7, Natal, no. 4, 10 September 1853, pp. 136–9; *Natal Mercury*, 21 June 1854; SNA, 1/1/6, 33/56, SNA to Magistrate, Weenen, 24 December 1856; Wright and Manson, *Hlubi chiefdom*, pp. 41–2; N. Etherington, 'The "Shepstone system" in the colony of Natal and beyond the borders', in Duminy and Guest, eds, *Natal and Zululand*, p. 179.

34. SNA, 1/1/8, 72/58, Minutes, 1858.

35. Wright and Manson, *Hlubi chiefdom*, p. 50; *Natal Witness*, 18 December 1866.

36. SNA, 1/3/6, 96/57, Deposition of Moodie, 13 March 1857, p. 303; 1/3/14, 14/64, Magistrate, Weenen to SNA, 22 January 1864, pp. 58f.

37. B. Guest, 'Colonists, confederation and constitutional change', in Duminy and Guest, eds, *Natal and Zululand*, pp. 151–5.

38. Natal, *Report . . . Native population*, 1879, p. 5; SNA, 1/1/45, 176/81, Magistrate, Alexandra to SNA, 29 March 1881.

39. Natal, *Evidence . . . Natal Native Commission, 1881*, Teteleku, p. 183, see also Umneli, p. 315, Faku, p. 337, Silwane, p. 354.

40. Ibid., Teteleku, p. 179.

41. SNA, 1/6/6, 202/76, Magistrate, Klip River to SNA, 22 July 1876.

42. Natal, *Evidence . . . Natal Native Commission, 1881*, J. W. Shepstone, p. 97; J. W. Shepstone Papers, [Natal Archives], 4, p. 27; Natal, *Report of the Natal Native Commission, 1881–2*, p. 33.

43. Natal, *Evidence . . . Natal Native Commission, 1881*, Umnini, p. 196, Tinta, p. 293, Tulasizwe, p. 302. Natal, *Report of the Natal Native Commission, 1881–2*, p. 41.

44. Ibid., Teteleku, p. 182.

45. A. Vilakazi, *Zulu transformations: a study of the dynamics of social change*, Pietermaritzburg, 1962, p. 10.

46. L. E. Switzer, 'The problems of an African mission in a white-dominated, multi-racial society: the American Zulu Mission in South Africa, 1885–1910', Ph.D. thesis, University of Natal, 1971, pp. 83–4.

47. See Natal, *Evidence . . . Lands Commission (1900–01–02)*, Kuzwayo, p. 294, Unzuzu, p. 296.

48. Society for the Propagation of the Gospel (SPG) [Rhodes House Library, Oxford], CLR 137, Callaway to Secretary, 4 June 1869, p. 379; Wesleyan Methodist Missionary Society (WMMS) [University of London, School of Oriental and African Studies], 17, no. 622, Cameron to General Secretaries, 3 September 1866; See also B. Hutchinson, 'Some social consequences of nineteenth century missionary activity among the South African Bantu', *Africa*, 27, no. 2, 1957, p. 162.

49. SNA, 1/3/8, 57/59, Magistrate, Inanda to SNA, 21 September 1859, p. 71; 1/3/12, 5/62, Supreme Chief v. Saliwana, 19 December 1862, pp. 21f.

50. Natal, *Report on the Native mission reserves*, p. 5.

51. Etherington, *Preachers*, p. 70.

52. Natal, *Evidence . . . Natal Native Commission, 1881*, T. Shepstone, p. 278.

CHAPTER THREE

The Changing Homestead

It was not only the position of the chiefs that was affected by the establishment of the British presence in Natal; throughout the colony the pre-capitalist structure of African society was modified. As with chiefship, that structure had already come under considerable strain as a result of developments prior to the annexation of Natal.

Until the late eighteenth century, African society had been organized in clusters of *imizi* which were loosely linked together within a chiefdom by ties of neighbourhood, kinship, clientship and marriage. Although an *umnumzana* received his land from his chief, in practical terms his authority carried more weight in his own *umuzi* than did that of the chief. His authority was passed on to the chosen son of his chief wife, and the continuation of his lineage ensured the material, social and spiritual well-being of the *umuzi* members. Were he to die without sons, his widow could be united in a *ukungena* union with his brother to bear heirs on his behalf and ensure the continuation of the lineage.

As a result of the expansion of Zulu power south of the Thukela, the authority of the *abanumzana* was subordinated, either directly to that of the Zulu king, or to those chiefs through whom he ruled in the region. To give effect to this subordination, the unmarried men of the *imizi* were organized into *amabutho* and were required to provide the Zulu state with labour service. Yet, although Shaka subjected the *imizi* to Zulu authority, the process of centralization also strengthened the control that an *umnumzana* exercised over his *umuzi*. This was particularly true of the women. Their already inferior social status was further depressed in that new labour demands were made on them to compensate for the removal of male labour from the *umuzi*. The position of the *umnumzana* was also strengthened by the control over marriage that was imposed by Shaka. This control, which delayed the marrying age of men and women, enabled *abanumzana* to marry more wives and, therefore, to increase the size of their *imizi*. It also lengthened the period during which their daughters were under their authority. The destruction of Zulu power south of the Thukela in the 1830s and the arrival of white settlers did little immediately to alter this situation.[1]

Each *umuzi* consisted of a central cattle kraal surrounded by the huts or households belonging to the wives, dependent relatives and widowed mother of the head. The eldest son seldom left his father's *umuzi*, and the younger sons generally stayed until they married a second wife. Because of this, an *umuzi* usually included the households of their wives. The *umnumzana* managed rather than controlled the *umuzi* property, and his rights over that property were restricted by the rights of its members. For example, while he controlled distribution of the resources within the *umuzi*, he was obliged to set aside gardens for his wives and his sons' wives, and to allocate cattle for the use of each household. In return, he was entitled to produce and labour services from the inhabitants of each household within the *umuzi*, and could use these to augment his authority and wealth. He also had considerable legal authority over his dependants and was responsible to his chief for their good behaviour.

The *umuzi* was not a static entity but grew as the *umnumzana* or his sons married, and contracted as the sons left to establish their own *imizi*. Within each *umuzi* there was a sexual division of labour. Men were responsible for the husbandry of livestock, building and maintenance of the huts and cattle kraals, digging grain pits and for clearing the land for gardens. Women and girls were responsible for agricultural production, domestic labour, thatching huts, and portering. In the manufacturing field, there was also a sexual division between men who produced wooden and iron articles and baskets, and women who made pots and mats.

Life within the *umuzi* was thus defined by a rigid differentiation between the roles of men and women, which began before puberty and which stressed the dominant status of the male. Both the survival and the reproduction of the *umuzi* were secured by the control of the *umnumzana* over the labour of the young men, and over both the labour and fertility of the women within it. Control over women's fertility was secured through the *lobola* or bridewealth system, without which no socially recognized marriage could take place. Through the giving of *lobola* by the *umuzi* of the husband to that of the bride's father (or brother), a woman passed from the authority of the male members of her *umuzi* to that of her husband.

African law prohibited marriage within a lineage and *lobola* was seen as a political and economic means of stabilizing relationships between lineages. It was a recognition not only of the wife's position in her husband's *umuzi*, but also of his ties with her lineage. Because of this, the stability of a marriage concerned both lineages. *Lobola* was not a sale, but a sign of the woman's transfer from her father's *umuzi*. While in some of the smaller chiefdoms in south-western Natal all the cattle had to handed over before the marriage, in most chiefdoms marriage could take place after the delivery of only one head, on the understanding that the husband would deliver the balance when he could afford to do so.[2] Acceptance of cattle by the bride's father was, however, conditional. If the bride did not remain faithful to her husband, or if she proved infertile, the husband could demand a return of his *lobola*.

But the giving and acceptance of *lobola* did not only affect men. The transaction also guaranteed that, despite her subordinate status, a woman had a considerable measure of security. Provision was made for her throughout her life, either in the *umuzi* of her father or brother, or in that of her husband or her son. The rights enjoyed by women differed from chiefdom to chiefdom, but in most the 'great wife' held authority over the distribution of milk and beef within the *umuzi*. The position of a lesser wife was also protected; although she could neither inherit nor bequeath cattle, it was the practice in most chiefdoms that once gardens and cattle had been allocated to her household, they remained her property and could not be alienated without her consent or that of her sons.[3]

Mechanisms for providing the impoverished with the wherewithal for survival were an important feature of African society, and failure to meet such social obligations was regarded as a serious offence. As Diana Wylie has pointed out in a study of patriarchy in Botswana, 'patriarchal society rationalized a society where the rich distributed rather than accumulated their wealth'.[4] The *ukutekela* custom gave members of an *umuzi*, whose crops had failed, the right to obtain food from other, more fortunate *imizi*. Failure to provide food in such a case was considered to be a serious infraction. In a society which did not amass capital, this was an important factor in reducing the likelihood of severe distress. The custom known as *ukusisa* also played an important role in providing men with resources that they otherwise would have lacked. It involved not only cattle but also horses, sheep, goats, pigs and even fowls, and was particularly important in drought years. Since a man's stature was enhanced by the number of his dependants, chiefs and *izinduna* with large herds could *sisa* cattle to strengthen and expand the patron-client relationship with their people. In this way impoverished Africans were able to use stock which the owners themselves did not need. At the same time, the donors remained entitled to any increase. This could prove advantageous: in Impendhle in 1882 Mahakanci *sisa*'d a mare to Valulisana, and by 1892 its increase was six horses.[5]

To the inhabitant of an *umuzi*, cattle were the 'joy of his heart and the pride of his life'. They comprised his wealth, indicated his social status and were his sacrificial link with the spirits of his ancestors.[6] Not only could they be used to acquire dependants but, as *lobola*, they provided the vital bridewealth a man needed in order to marry and fulfil his role in a polygamous society.

Although, in pre-colonial days, *lobola* items included hoes, brass beads, silver or copper necklaces, and goats as well as cattle, the increased availability of the latter from the 1840s led to them becoming the accepted medium. In 1850 the immigrant, Thomas Duff, mentioned that *lobola* normally consisted of ten head. A wealthy man could also give cattle to a dependant to use as *lobola*; in return he had a claim on the bridewealth of the eldest daughter of the union.[7]

As the primary form of transferable wealth, cattle were seldom slaughtered for food. Beef was eaten infrequently, normally at religious ceremonies or at social feasts such as those connected with marriage. Cattle were, however, an important source of milk. This was seldom drunk fresh, but was curdled and fermented in a gourd or sack and the finished product, *amasi*, was drunk by adults, children and, particularly, by new-born babies and by boys at puberty. For the first eight days of a male child's life and the first six of a female's no feeding was allowed at the mother's breast and cow's milk was substituted; at puberty a boy was presented with his own cow which he had to milk directly into his own mouth to ensure strength and virility.[8]

The African diet was balanced and ensured a healthy existence. In addition to milk, protein was provided by groundnuts and beans and, on the coast, by fish. Carbohydrates were supplied by sorghum, maize, pumpkins and sweet potatoes. These also provided bulk and were supplemented by wild fruit and veld vegetation, game and game birds. Other than milk, the most important of these foods were maize and sorghum. These complemented each other as maize is resistant to drought while sorghum grows more quickly and is not as susceptible to bird damage. Maize was usually eaten as porridge and in some areas in the form of green mealies, while sorghum was normally brewed to make a nourishing beer, *utshwala*. This was regarded essentially as a man's drink; it had a low alcohol content of 2 per cent by weight, but it could be very intoxicating if allowed extended fermentation. It was used as a form of both tribute and patronage and provided a popular form of social intercourse. As a form of social control, neither young people nor women were permitted to take part in public beer drinks.[9]

The African diet, and the sufficiency of food, varied according to the seasons. Except in the late 1860s, the region generally experienced only short and localized droughts until 1878, and it is likely that from spring until the beginning of winter the food supply was adequate in all but the most arid areas. In spring the veld provided an abundance of natural vegetation, herbs, berries and wild melons and roots. In areas like the Thukela valley, the shortage of grain frequently meant that these were a major source of food.[10]

The harvesting of green mealies and vegetables usually coincided with the *umkhosi* festival in January, while the time of greatest plenty arrived with the harvesting of the ripe maize in March/April and of sorghum in April/May. From October to May there was generally sufficient food to provide two meals a day, but the period from winter until early spring saw a dearth of food – the hungry season. Although most *imizi* had grain pits for storing surplus grain their inhabitants were reluctant to use this supply in case of a shortfall the following season. As a result, these months, which also coincided with the period of hardest work in preparing the gardens, were a time of nutritional deficiency. In times of severe drought, such as in the late 1860s and in the summers of 1877/8 and 1881/2, the subsequent hungry seasons were times of considerable distress.[11]

In the early decades of colonial rule, Africans in Natal generally responded successfully to the opportunities opened up by changing conditions. During the Shakan period, the *imizi* of Natal had been drained of both labour and produce to provide for the maintenance of the Zulu state and many had been stripped of cattle. The imposition of white rule was, therefore, at one level little more than a change of paramountcy. The homestead economy now had to be adapted to meet the needs of a new ruling elite, one which was urban based and part of an imperialist, capitalist community.

The destruction of Zulu power south of the Thukela provided an opportunity which was seized by the *abanumzana* to consolidate their position. Once the need to supply the Zulu king with cattle fell away, the *abanumzana* were able to build up their herds. The possibilities were also enhanced for acquiring cattle either from white farmers and traders, or from refugees from north of the Thukela. There was a brisk import trade in cattle from Zululand during the early colonial years, while in the 1860s and 1870s purchases were also made from Pondoland and from as far afield as Tsongaland.[12]

Easier access to cattle enabled the *abanumzana* to marry more frequently. There was a marked surplus of women over men in the colony and, by the late 1840s, it was estimated by Grout that the average *umuzi* in Umvoti reserve had eight huts and that, on average, each head had four wives. A few years later, the Wesleyan missionary, William Holden, visited *imizi* on the south coast and noted that of 201 married men, 95 had three or more wives.[13]

In the early colonial decades, relative freedom of movement between reserve, Crown and private lands as well as across the Thukela also meant that many *imizi* could move their herds to exploit summer and winter grazing. The need to move cattle was particularly pressing on the coast, in the arid coastal hinterland, and in the Thukela valley reserves where bioclimatic conditions ruled out year-round grazing. However, in the Thukela valley reserves, the combination of aridity and overpopulation meant that many *imizi* would have been unable to move their herds between summer and winter grazing. As early as 1852, Magistrate Peppercorne pointed out that *imizi* with only two or three huts in the Impafana reserve seldom possessed cattle, and estimated that the average hut in the reserve had only two. Men in areas such as the Impafana reserve did, however, have the option of accumulating cattle and *sisa*'ing them to *imizi* elsewhere which had sufficient pasture. In this way their cattle could be scattered over a number of *imizi*.[14]

By using the *sisa* system, men could continue accumulating cattle even when grazing was limited. This could, however, contribute to overstocking. By 1869, the first year that cattle statistics were gathered in the colony, Africans owned an estimated 334 563 head, with each hut in the colony having an average of five head. Overstocking was particularly marked in the reserves, where a delicate balance existed between cattle numbers and the condition of the veld. In most reserves growing impoverishment of the grasslands resulted in steady deterioration of herds making them more susceptible to drought and disease.[15]

With the introduction of the plough, oxen acquired agricultural importance and their agricultural value was enhanced. They were also seen as a trading commodity and Africans were occasionally prepared to sell stock when prices were high. As early as the 1850s, the Hlubi were selling surplus stock, while during the Anglo-Zulu War 13 per cent of African-owned cattle in Umlazi were sold to the military.[16]

With official and commercial encouragement, homestead agriculture expanded rapidly. This is reflected in the official estimation of the amount of crops reaped. Despite the extreme caution with which official agricultural statistics in the colonial period must be treated, the estimated figures for 1867 (the first year in which figures were presented) and 1882 attest to the increase. In the former year the total acreage reaped by Africans was believed to be 90 057 and in the latter 279 298.[17]

In both years, well over half of the acreage was under maize. Until the 1880s, the price of maize showed a steady increase and many *imizi* were able to meet the financial demands made on them by the administration and the settlers by expanding their maize production for the market.

The settler demand for maize meant that there was little incentive for most Africans to change their pre-colonial lifestyle. Despite Shepstone's hopes that the *imizi* would produce export crops,[18] they continued, as before, to be based on primary production and subsistence cultivation. In the pre-colonial period there had been little continuity of settlement except in the riverine areas. Traditionally, shifting cultivation had been followed whereby land was cultivated for as many years as it remained fertile. It was then allowed to revert to bush while trees would be burned in a new area and vegetation cut back for new gardens. For as long as this system continued, and for as long as it was possible for people to move between sweet- and sourveld grasslands with their cattle, the Africans were able to live off the environment and maintain productivity in a time-honoured fashion. Through centuries of experience of the vagaries of the region's climate and the infertility of its soils, they had evolved a subsistence agricultural economy suited to the region's environmental conditions.[19]

Yet it was a system which depended on unrestricted access to land, the very condition which the colonial presence was destroying. It was also a system in which homestead gardens sometimes underproduced and in which there were often shortages in the last months before harvesting. And, although part of the harvest was stored in grain pits against future crop shortfalls, a year of total crop failure could mean famine. Restrictions imposed by the white presence meant that it was harder to ensure good crops by traditional methods while, particularly in the Thukela valley, many *imizi* frequently could not cultivate at all and had to subsist by bartering stock for grain or by sending men out as migrant labourers.[20]

Some adaptation was accordingly imperative if the *imizi* were to continue to provide for all their members. But to a conservative rural society which feared that change would anger dead ancestors, innovation could be introduced only gradually. Reluctance to change was strengthened by the considerable influence of witchcraft, which discouraged men from flouting custom by modernizing. Even homestead Africans who supplied produce to markets did so by increasing the amount of land under cultivation, rather than intensifying their agricultural methods.

The differing proximity of markets, whether urban or amongst white farmers, led to an economic differentiation amongst Africans and tended to determine which of them remained subsistent cultivators. Le Roy Ladurie has suggested that the frontier of an economy is determined by portability rather than by the limits of arable land.[21] This is true of Natal: Africans in divisions such as Umgeni, Umlazi and Inanda with access to Durban or Pietermaritzburg were far better placed to benefit from market opportunities. The steady opening of stores catering for the needs of Africans, around Pietermaritzburg and on the north coast, shows the extent to which African residents there were being drawn into the cash economy; by 1879, there were 40 in Umgeni and 46 in Lower Tugela. In these stores cash sales of produce and cash purchases, rather than bartering, had become the norm with Africans.[22]

But market accessibility was only one factor in the growing differentiation between rich and poor. *Abanumzana* who enjoyed a close relationship with their chiefs were favoured in the allocation of new gardens and could thus grow and sell more produce than could less-favoured members of the chiefdom. To consolidate their position further, these heads were able to use the money they received to invest in more cattle. Cattle used for *lobola* could increase the number and labour power of households within their *imizi*, thus further improving their ability to supply the market.

The differentiation between rich and poor is also reflected in the distribution of plough ownership. Although ploughs were expensive to buy, the government provided them to Africans who were prepared to diversify their crop production, while those who were close enough to a market were able to accumulate the purchase price. In remote areas, such as the Thukela valley reserves ploughs were owned by few *imizi*, while in divisions such as Umgeni and Upper Umkomazi they became common.[23]

The settler presence in Natal had, therefore, created a situation in which African society was becoming restratified. The ability to accumulate wealth and prestige no longer necessarily depended, as it had done in the pre-colonial period, on the relationship between an individual and his chief, or even on the genealogical status of the chief. The Mphumuza were a junior branch of the Nadi chiefdom, yet Thetheleku was able to use the position of his chiefdom near Pietermaritzburg to build up an important and influential position and to become the dominant chief in the Zwartkop reserve. The meshing of homestead production into the market economy meant, however, that wealthy men who had previously used their surplus resources to provide for their dependants were now increasingly diverting those resources for sale in the market. This threatened people who had previously depended on wealthy individuals in times of shortage, and undermined the patron-client relationship integral to the functioning of African society.

The new differentiation in African society was most evident in relation to marriage. The wealth generated through sales by men in *imizi* close to a market ensured that they could obtain wives by offering more cattle than could poorer men. In Natal generally, the amount of *lobola* passing hands between *imizi* steadily increased. In 1857 Shooter wrote that it was much higher than in Zululand because of the ease with which Natal Africans could procure cattle. This development also made polygamy easier for *abanumzana* who controlled the distribution of wealth, but put marriage beyond the means of many young men. In 1863, the Methodist missionary, J. Jackson mentioned that it was not unusual for a young girl to be married to an older man for twenty to thirty head of cattle, while in 1866, his colleague, T. Kirby, referred to men having to pay £100 for a wife.[24] The marked surplus of women over men which had characterized the early colonial years was changing and Shepstone was alarmed at the growing number of unmarried young men and at the proliferation of lengthy and costly *lobola* court cases. He accordingly consulted with the chiefs to find an acceptable limit to the number of cattle which could be asked by a father. As a result the number of cattle was regulated in 1869 – a commoner could not receive more than ten head for his daughter; the brothers and sons of hereditary chiefs could ask for fifteen head; an appointed chief for twenty; whilst no limit was placed on the number a hereditary chief could ask.[25]

The marriage regulations were promulgated at a time of economic crisis in the colony, and the financially straitened administration used the opportunity to impose a fee of £5 on all marriages. Because of this, the regulations were considered both by contemporary and later critics to be a way of forcing young men onto the labour market, rather than an attempt to alleviate a growing marriage crisis. Shepstone had proposed a sliding scale starting at £2 for the first wife, with the intention of helping younger men, but the Colonial Office insisted on a fixed rate. The colonial administration, in need of revenue, finally opted for £5.[26] Whatever the motive for the regulations, they did improve the marriage prospects of young men. The limitation on the number of *lobola* cattle helped end the monopoly of marriage by older, wealthier men and, particularly after the replacement of the marriage fee by a 14s. hut tax in 1875, it enabled young men to marry independently of the wishes of *abanumzana*. Despite the overall control an *umnumzana* exercised over the resources of each household within the *umuzi*, it appears that a woman could, through selling her surplus crops and fowls, eggs, etc., build up her household's cattle herds for use as *lobola* for her sons.[27] The limitation on the amount of *lobola* now made it much easier for her to raise the required amount. In areas away from markets it was also possible for young men to raise money by working as migrant labourers in towns and on farms. By the 1870s new and lucrative opportunities for wage labour were also available on the diamond fields and on the colony's railway and harbour works. The presence of white farmers and absentee landowners also provided an alternative source of land to young men wanting to marry and establish their own *imizi*.

As the number of young men marrying increased, so the size of the *imizi* and of the cattle holdings in each shrunk. With less cattle in each *umuzi*, the potential for a man to have more than one wife was reduced and polygamy was weakened. By the 1880s few men, other than chiefs, had more than two wives and many had only one. As no magistracy records include hut tax receipts, it is impossible to ascertain the average number of huts in an *umuzi*. But a survey was conducted of Durban county in 1882 which shows that, of the 1 130 *imizi* in the county, only 43 had ten or more huts, 239 had two huts and 299 had only one. The figures give an average of 3,4 huts to an *umuzi*, with 47,7 per cent having two or less. This decline is also reflected in marriage statistics. In 1871, 4,9 per cent of marriages were of fifth wives and upwards; by 1880 this had dropped to 3,3 per cent. Over the same period the number of first marriages increased from 56,8 to 60,7 per cent of the total number.[28]

In general, African dependence on sales for money was greatest in those *imizi* on the rent-tenancy farms, and on reserves close to Pietermaritzburg and Durban where land, transport and marketing conditions encouraged the growing of surplus crops. These Africans were the most important suppliers to the urban markets of maize, forage and firewood and, particularly as the time for the collection of hut tax and rents drew near, they bypassed markets and hawked grain, vegetables, fowls, milk and firewood directly to the inhabitants of the towns and villages.[29]

In some *imizi*, and particularly those of chiefdoms which were prepared to capitalize on the settler presence, the inhabitants adapted and diversified their agricultural practices. Although this happened mainly on mission and rent-tenancy lands, there were *imizi* in the Zwartkop and Umnini reserves and in parts of the Inanda, Umlazi and Drakensberg 1 and 2 reserves where market proximity encouraged innovation. Members of Langalibalele's Hlubi chiefdom in the Drakensberg reserve, and of the Mphumuza, Nadi and Mfusi chiefdoms in the Zwartkop reserve, diversified their crops to take advantage of the Pietermaritzburg market. Members of Mnini's Thuli chiefdom near Durban even experimented with cash crops such as coffee and sugar. However, coffee cultivation was soon abandoned and, despite the purchase by Mnini of the St George property at Umgababa in 1876, sugar cultivation had ceased by 1880.[30]

With few resident white farmers in south-western Natal other than in Upper Umkomazi, Africans in the area were able to take advantage of the rich soil and the favourable climatic conditions to cultivate large acreages of maize. By the 1870s, African agriculture in the area was flourishing and traders were opening stores to tap homestead production. In 1879 the magistrate of Ixopo estimated that the average hut sold up to eleven muids of maize a year to storekeepers and itinerant traders. Far more grain was grown in Ixopo and Upper Umkomazi than in the rest of the midlands. By the early 1880s it was estimated that over three-quarters of the acreage planted in the midlands were in these two divisions alone, and that each hut reaped far more grain than did huts in the other divisions.[31]

A number of *imizi* were also engaged in long-distance trade. In the 1840s and 1850s, African-grown maize was exported to the Cape and Mauritius. Colonial Africans were also taking goods into Zululand and bartering them for cattle.[32] By the 1860s, and particularly after 1869 when they were encouraged by the demand for goods at the diamond fields, they also became active in transport riding. Africans were employed by white wagon-owners as drivers and *voorlopers*, and the former in particular received wages far above the colonial average, the usual rate being £2 a month. Many recognized the advantages which transport riding could bring and began investing in wagons of their own. Within a decade they were trading throughout the neighbouring territories and undercutting white competition. In 1875 the Byrne settler, Ellen McLeod, complained that 'as they are large growers, and have wagons and oxen, and having so few wants can afford to sell and treck [*sic*] at a much cheaper rate than the English'.[33] Africans were particularly active in supplying grain to arid or drought-stricken areas. Those from more fertile areas supplied the Thukela valley reserves in exchange for livestock, while the inhabitants of Upper Tugela conducted fairly extensive selling and purchasing of grain in the Harrismith district of the Orange Free State. Africans in Inanda seem to have been particularly active in bartering local produce, or goods such as blankets, with Africans in the Thukela valley, in Zululand, and even up-country. These were exchanged for goats or cattle which in turn could be bartered for articles such as tobacco.[34]

Africans were able to trek and sell at cheaper rates than whites. In the 1870s the number of African transport riders steadily increased as farmers began to use their services.[35] The Anglo-Zulu and First Anglo-Boer wars saw the heyday of African transport riding. The profits to be made by conveying goods for the military were high and encouraged growing African participation in the carrying trade.

Despite these examples of entrepreneurship, maize sales remained the most important source of money for almost all *imizi*. The demand for maize and the increased price buyers were prepared to pay for it, combined with the labour-intensive nature of growing most cash crops, discouraged diversification. In the 1850s many *abanumzana* had in fact severely burnt their fingers by following the administration's urgings to plant cotton. The poor quality of the seed with which they had been provided, and the small rewards they received for their efforts, effectively dampened their interest.[36] The failed experiment reinforced the belief of Africans that as long as they had sufficient land to continue establishing new gardens, it seemed pointless to go to the trouble and risk of growing new crops. This concentration on maize, however, created a potentially dangerous situation in which most *imizi* totally depended on maize as a cash crop.

Although there was very little agricultural innovation amongst Africans in general, many were prepared to diversify when it came to stock farming. Interest in woolled sheep steadily grew until it was discouraged by the passing of scab laws in 1865 and 1878.[37] Pigs were bred extensively for sale to the colonists,[38] but the most important innovation was in horse ownership. The loss of cattle through lungsickness and redwater in the 1870s caused many Africans, particularly in the high-lying districts of the colony, to invest in horses. In the late 1870s, the Colonial Secretary's wife, Lady Barker, noted the prevalence of horse ownership among Africans in Zwartkop reserve. Africans also purchased horses after the Anglo-Zulu War and, by the 1880s, there were few *imizi* in the foothills of the Drakensberg without mounts.[39]

Generally speaking, in outlying areas where it was difficult to market a surplus crop, Africans were willing to supply both each other and white farmers with livestock. Elsewhere, until the early 1880s, the majority of *imizi* were able, thanks to the high price of grain, to meet their financial needs through expanded production.

Those Africans who embraced diversification most readily were the *kholwa*, who did so by abandoning the homestead economy altogether instead of adapting it to the changed conditions in the colony. On the lands they had purchased and on the mission reserves, the relatively small number of mission-educated *kholwa* peasants readily abandoned the homestead mode of production and adopted a restructured lifestyle which Western values came to dominate. As a result of the monogamy which conversion entailed, the extended *umuzi* was replaced by the smaller household as the unit of production. This made it far easier for the *kholwa* to adapt to individual tenure and to adopt Western views of commercialized agriculture.

Both on the mission lands and on farms such as Edendale and Driefontein, cash crop production was enthusiastically embraced. On the farms and on many of the mission reserves, particularly those of the American Board Mission at Amanzim-toti, Umvoti, Inanda and Umzinduzi and of the Wesleyans at Indaleni, fruit trees, barley, wheat, potatoes and forage were grown as well as maize and sorghum. European-style houses, schools and churches were built by the converts.[40] Until the 1870s, the towns and villages of the coast and midlands depended for much of their market-garden produce on *kholwa* suppliers, a situation which continued into the early twentieth century in northern Natal. Most of these sales were local, but *kholwa* were enthusiastic transport riders and their wagons could be found throughout the subcontinent. By 1881, the inhabitants of Edendale alone had thirty wagons between them and it was common for thirteen or fourteen wagons to travel upcountry together.[41]

Yet ambitious attempts to grow export crops were seldom successful. On the American stations at Umtwalumi and Umzinduzi the cultivation of coffee was tried, but by the late 1870s it had been abandoned on the former mission while on the latter only sufficient was planted to meet the needs of the reserve.[42] Attempts to grow cotton also failed. The cultivation of sugar was undertaken more extensively than either cotton or coffee, but also with relatively little long-term success. To encourage peasant planters, the government established a sugar mill at Groutville on the Umvoti reserve in the early 1860s. The venture was initially a success and in 1871, 47 African planters cultivated 300 acres of cane and milled 140 tons of sugar. But by the end of the decade, although most of the agricultural plots continued to have sugar-cane, the mill had become an economic liability. By 1880 the government had spent £24 000 on it and had received only £12 000 in return. It accordingly withdrew support from the mill which, in 1882, was leased to four of the planters, Mlau, Mkabani, Mhlonono and Phillip for twenty years.[43] To a large extent, the abandonment of export crops reflects the fact that to the *kholwa*, as to other Africans, maize was by far the most rewarding crop. Many missions had their own maize mills and the rising price of maize until the 1880s meant that maize cultivation remained both a lucrative and safe proposition.[44]

Despite the *kholwa* failure to produce export crops, they were far better adapted to meet the challenges of the late nineteenth century than those Africans who retained the homestead economy. Possibly the greatest way in which they differed from other Africans was that they grew produce for the market specifically to raise money to enable them to evolve a lifestyle based on settler values. To this end, they were prepared to face the risks involved in striking out on their own. This encouraged the development of an individualism which was the very antithesis of homestead communalism. The desire of men such as Stephanus Mini of Edendale and Johannes Kumalo of Driefontein to adapt to European values and to create wealth and authority for themselves as individuals was markedly different from the ambitions of chiefs like Thetheleku and Phakade who used the settler presence to benefit their chiefdoms and who neither accepted nor adapted to white values.

The *kholwa* abandonment of traditional values was particularly evident in their attitude to cattle which they valued in commercial rather than social terms. Their economic dependence on cattle was great, particularly for those who became transport riders.[45] Because of this, few *kholwa* were prepared to accept the missionaries' prohibition of *lobola*. Many saw commercial advantage in marrying off their daughters and fiercely opposed the restrictions imposed by the 1869 marriage regulations on the number of *lobola* cattle.[46]

The *kholwa* break with traditional society was exemplifed by their attempts to obtain exemption from the operation of customary law. In order to encourage *kholwa* acculturation to white values, the colonial administration provided in 1865 that an African who lived in a European-style house, had only one wife, and satisfied certain property and educational tests, could come under the common law of the colony.[47] Many *kholwa* believed that the disadvantages of exemption outweighed the benefits, and that it would weaken both family and group ties and undermine their attempts to consolidate their position as a class.[48] Then, in 1880 the Attorney-General, Michael Gallwey, ruled that all children who were unmarried at the time their father applied for exemption, or who were born after he had become exempted, were themselves exempted.[49] This removed the objection that exemption could undermine family ties and applications steadily increased.

On the mission reserves, where *kholwa* were generally in a small minority, the gradual conversion of other individuals resulted in families with *kholwa* and heathen members living side by side. Although the missionaries on the American reserves claimed that there was little friction between the two, it is possible that they were minimizing hostility. As adherents of an alien value system, the *kholwa* must have been regarded with suspicion. Indeed, the magistrate of Weenen pointed out in 1897, that 'when a Native becomes an *ikolwa* he or she actually loses caste in the eyes of their [*sic*] heathen fellow-creatures'.[50]

Homestead hostility to the *kholwa* is understandable, for the conversion of individuals within an *umuzi* undermined kinship. Although family ties and family enterprise remained as strong amongst the *kholwa* as amongst other Africans, the wider kinship unit was coming under great strain and the accusation levelled at Grout, in the early days of the Umvoti station, was coming true: 'You induce our children to abandon our practices; you break up our kraals and eat up our cattle; you will be the ruin of our tribe.'[51]

Kinship disintegration was hastened by the development of villages with individually owned houses, each with its own enclosed gardens.[52] Although communal labour by no means disappeared, the villages with their individual homes tended to weaken the open, communal nature of African society. Equally importantly, conversion removed the labour services of converts from their *imizi*, undermining them as economic entities. Yet the weakening of kinship ties was not necessarily always the result of the convert's withdrawal from his or her homestead obligations. In many cases, the rupture of kinship ties could as easily have resulted from the action of the converts' lineages in expelling them.

Although the missionaries stressed the importance of the Christian family unit, their refusal to countenance polygamy did much to destroy the stability of the larger homestead family when either the polygamous husband or one of his wives converted. With the notable exception of Bishop Colenso, missionaries steadfastly insisted that polygamous wives should divorce their husbands prior to conversion, while the polygamous husbands had to separate themselves from all but one wife.[53]

Many Africans also believed that the missionaries were using education to undermine and destroy the social and moral basis of African society. Mission schools aimed at converting Africans to Christianity and, in the higher grades, at training teachers, lay preachers, clergy and community leaders. But the emphasis was obviously on inculcating European values and on tightening white control over Africans. Particularly in schools established by the Americans, such as Adams College at Amanzimtoti for boys in 1853, and Inanda Seminary for girls in 1869, traditional African values were attacked and the differences between the *kholwa* and other Africans were stressed. Mission education did not simply equip the *kholwa* to come to terms with the new settler order in Natal, it also, in Stephen Mini's words, made the *kholwa* feel 'that we have interests in common, and are one with the white people'.[54]

Although non-Christian chiefs like Mnini or Mqawe, conscious of the advantages schools could bring to their chiefdoms, encouraged education,[55] the academic education offered by most of the missions did indeed do much to create barriers between *kholwa* and homestead Africans. Education in Natal for white and African children alike took no account of colonial conditions and often had little relevance for the needs of the children. This was particularly true of the syllabuses offered in mission schools. Efforts by the Anglican missionary, Illing, to teach his pupils Latin, Greek and Hebrew could have had little purpose, while those of the Free Church of Scotland to make small children learn 'The Blue Bells of Scotland' and to dress them in Highland costume for recitations of 'Bruce and the Spider',

52   *Betrayed Trust*

could have achieved little apart from alienating them from their own people.[56]

Despite the encouragement by the colonial administration, in the early decades of British rule, of a class of African Christian peasant cultivators, its chief concern was to maintain and support the *umuzi*. Throughout these years and until the end of the colonial period, the thrust of official policy in Natal remained the preservation of the hierarchical and patriarchal nature of African society. Successive governments appreciated that if they were to maintain control of Africans within the colony, they needed to enforce the authority of *abanumzana* over their subordinates. The need to encourage young unmarried men to enter the labour market could also best be met by ensuring their subordination to their fathers. During the early decades of colonial rule the ability of young men to earn money and hold property independent of their fathers seriously weakened the *abanumzana*'s control but did not destroy it. Colonial policy, exercised both by the Native Affairs' Department and through the courts, was to buttress that authority.

The most concerted attempt to enforce the authority of *abanumzana* came with the codification of 'native law' in 1878. This was the first legislative act to codify and legalize the dominant position of elders and males in African society and, particularly, to give legal enforcement to the subordination of women within *imizi*. The clauses relating to the subordination of women acknowledged their crucial position in the survival of the *umuzi*. The nature of the homestead economy meant that while an *umuzi* could function effectively despite the absence of young men, it could not survive without the work of women in the gardens. The colonial presence had given greater scope to women and the Code asserted their subordination to their *abanumzana* and tried to ensure that they remained tied to their households. This process had already begun with the stipulation in the marriage regulations of 1869 that a marriage could not take place unless a woman confirmed her willingness to marry before an official witness. Although the stipulation offered protection from an unwanted marriage, the bride's assent confirmed her acceptance of her subordinate position within her husband's *umuzi*. Now, under the Code, her subordinate status was legally confirmed and, should she try to escape from her situation, the courts were obliged to return her to her father or husband. In this way the Natal government hoped to maintain the *umuzi*, not only as a unit in its own right, but as an integral part of the chiefly system.

Notes

1. For background information, see Wright and Hamilton, 'Traditions and transformations', *passim*. See also A.T. Bryant, *The Zulu people as they were before the white man came*, 2nd ed., Pietermaritzburg, 1967; G.W. Kinsman, *Commentaries on native customs*, Pietermaritzburg, n.d; W.D. Hammond-Tooke, ed., *The Bantu-speaking peoples of southern Africa*, 2nd ed., London, 1974; D.W. Hedges, 'Trade and politics in southern Mozambique and Zululand in the eighteenth and early nineteenth century', Ph.D. thesis, University of London, 1978; E.J. Krige, *The social system of the Zulus*, Pietermaritzburg, 1957; I. Schapera, *Government and politics in tribal societies*, London, 1956; J.B. Wright, 'Control of women's labour in the Zulu kingdom', in J.B. Peires, ed., *Before and after Shaka: papers in Nguni history*, Grahamstown, 1983; W.D. Hammond-Tooke, 'In search of the lineage: the Cape Nguni case', *MAN*, 19, no.1, March 1984, pp.77–93.

2. SNA, 1/1/19, 74/69, Memorandum by Shepstone, 1869.
3. Webb and Wright, eds, *James Stuart archive*, 2, Macebo, 2 November 1898, pp. 42–3, 90–1; Shooter, *Kafirs of Natal*, p. 85.
4. D. Wylie, *A little god: the twilight of patriarchy in a southern African chiefdom*, Johannesburg, 1991, p. 5.
5. Impendhle Administrator of Native Law, 1, 17/92, Mahakanci v. Valulisana. See also J. Iliffe, *The African poor: a history*, Cambridge, 1987, p. 2; L. H. Samuelson, *Zululand, its traditions, legends, customs and folklore*, new ed., Durban, 1974, p. 180; Interview with R. T. Mazibuko, Edendale, 8 August 1979.
6. Shooter, *Kafirs of Natal*, pp. 30, 93; Krige, *Social system of the Zulus*, p. 188.
7. Webb and Wright, eds, *James Stuart archive*, 3, Mkando, 10 July 1902, p. 147; SNA, 1/1/52, 44/82, Magistrate, Umsinga to Chairman, Native Law Board, 19 August 1878; T. Duff, 'First impressions of Natal by a Perthshire ploughman', *Natalia*, 7, 1977, p. 12; Ixopo Magistracy, 3/2/2/2, Untyayo v. Umbofu, 9 May 1889.
8. A. T. Bryant, *A Description of native foodstuffs and their preparation*, Pietermaritzburg, 1907, p. 1; Shooter, *Kafirs of Natal*, p. 28; Stuart Papers, [Killie Campbell Africana Library], 2, 'Place and function of cattle', p. 5; Interview with R. T. Mazibuko, Edendale, 8 August 1979.
9. Bryant, *Description of native foodstuffs*, *passim*.
10. Natal, *Correspondence relative to the eviction of Native occupants from Crown lands . . .*, Pietermaritzburg, 1883, Administrator of Native Law, Lower Tugela to SNA, 27 November 1882, p. 19.
11. Bryant, *Description of native foodstuffs*, pp. 8–9; *NBB*, 1878, pp. JJ1–21; *Natal Witness*, 26 May 1882.
12. *Natal Mercury*, 6 January 1853, 7 September 1853; W. Beinart, *The political economy of Pondoland, 1860–1930*, Cambridge, 1982, pp. 22–3; *NBB*, 1877, p. JJ8.
13. CO 179, 6, Minute of 31st meeting of the Land Commission, 28 June 1848, pp. 119–20; W. C. Holden, *The past and future of the kaffir races*, facsimile reprint, Cape Town, 1963, pp. 138–9.
14. Natal, *Proceedings of the commission . . . 1852*, IV, Peppercorne, p. 9; SNA, 1/3/6, 140/75, Magistrate, Weenen to SNA, 29 May 1875, p. 481.
15. *NBB*, 1869, pp. C2, X12; see also E. H. Brookes and N. Hurwitz, *The native reserves of Natal* Natal Regional Survey, vol. 7, Cape Town, 1957, p. 115.
16. Wright and Manson, *Hlubi chiefdom*, p. 45; Natal, *Report . . . Native population*, 1879, p. 10.
17. *NBB*, 1867, p. X7; 1882, p. X6.
18. Etherington, 'The "Shepstone system"', p. 171.
19. See Hedges, 'Trade and politics in southern Mozambique and Zululand', p. 71; see also W. Allan, *The African husbandman*, Westport, 1965, p. 5.
20. Bryant, *Description of native foodstuffs*, p. 9; Natal, *Proceedings of the commission . . . 1852*, III, Peppercorne, p. 66, VI, Shepstone, p. 85; *NBB*, 1876, pp. J8–9, 1882, p. GG63.
21. E. Le Roy Ladurie, *Montaillou: Cathars and Catholics in a French village, 1294–1324*; tr. by B. Bray, Harmondsworth, 1980, p. 7.
22. Natal, *Report . . . Native population*, 1879, pp. 7, 12, 24, 26, 45.
23. *Natal Witness*, 30 April 1872; Natal, *Report of the Natal Native Commission, 1881–2*, p. 50; *NBB*, 1882, p. X21.
24. Shooter, *Kafirs of Natal*, p. 50; Natal, *Proceedings of the commission . . . 1852*, III, Blaine, p. 32; WMMS, 16, no. 596, Jackson to General Secretaries, 30 September 1863, 17, no. 168, Kirby to General Secretaries, 28 February 1866.
25. Holden, *Past and future*, p. 139; Natal, *Proceedings of the commission . . . 1852*, III, Peppercorne, p. 58; WMMS, 16, no. 605, Pilcher to General Secretaries, 2 August 1864. See also Shepstone Papers, 2, Memo on Law 1, 1869, 5 January 1875; Welsh, *Roots of segregation*, p. 79.
26. See WMMS, 18, no. 689, Akerman to General Secretaries, 11 June 1874.
27. Natal, *Evidence . . . Natal Native Commission, 1881*, Walker, p. 63, J.W. Shepstone, p. 91, Addison, p. 263; Tyler, *Forty years*, pp. 117–8; *Natal Witness*, 21 May 1872; *Natal Mercury*, 25 March 1873.
28. Natal, *Evidence . . . Natal Native Commission, 1881*, J.W. Shepstone, p. 91, Tinta, p. 295; J. Sanderson, *Polygamous marriages among the kafirs of Natal and countries around*, reprinted from the *Journal of the Anthropological Institute*, February, 1879, p. 2; Natal, *Report of the Natal Native Commission, 1881–2*, p. 47. Welsh, *Roots of segregation*, p. 95.

29. *Natal Mercury*, 23 December 1852, 16 June 1853; *Natal Witness*, 30 April 1872; Barker, *Life in South Africa*, p. 71.
30. See A. H. Manson, 'The Hlubi and Ngwe in a colonial society, 1848–1877', MA thesis, University of Natal, 1979; H. D. Kannemeyer, 'The new Bantu society in Natal – its civilisation and culture, 1810–1942', Ph.D. thesis, University of the Witwatersrand, 1945, pp. 116, 124; R. F. Osborn, *Valiant harvest: the founding of the South African sugar industry, 1848–1926*, Durban, 1964, p. 135.
31. Natal, *Report . . . Native population*, 1879, p. 44; 1882, pp. X6, 7; see also *Natal Mercury*, 18 January 1877.
32. Natal, *Proceedings of the commission . . . 1852*, V, Fynn, p. 75; *Natal Mercury*, 1 February 1854; SNA, 1/2/3, 131/54, Government Agent to Magistrate, Tugela, 28 September 1854, p. 403.
33. Gordon, *Dear Louisa*, pp. 188–9.
34. Natal, *Proceedings of the commission . . . 1852*, V, Fynn, p. 75; Welsh, *Roots of segregation*, p. 187. Shepstone Papers, 3, Allison to H. Shepstone, 5 November 1874; NPP, 649, Petition 11, 1890, of members of the Sicali tribe, 5 May 1890; *NBB*, 1882, p. GG11; Natal, *Report . . . Native population*, 1879, p. 18; J. W. Shepstone Papers, 4, 1878, p. 2; *Natal Mercury*, 19 May 1877.
35. Natal, *Evidence . . . Natal Native Commission, 1881*, Unsini, p. 366; Natal, *Report . . . Native population*, 1879, p. 7.
36. SNA, 1/1/10, 26/60, Superintendent of Cotton Cultivation to SNA, 28 March 1860; 1/1/12, 195/62, report by SNA, 4 September 1862.
37. Natal, *Report . . . Native population*, 1879, pp. 6–7; Natal, *Evidence . . . Natal Native Commission, 1881*, Kukulela, p. 234.
38. Natal, *Evidence . . . Natal Native Commission, 1881*, McKenzie, p. 121; see also Holden, *Past and future*, p. 235.
39. Barker, *Life in South Africa*, p. 129; Natal, *Report . . . Native population*, 1879, pp. 53, 57.
40. Natal, *Report on the Native mission reserves*, pp. 4–5, 7.
41. Natal, *Evidence . . . Natal Native Commission . . . 1881*, Allsopp, p. 32; see also SNA, 1/6/10, Applications for exemption.
42. Natal, *Report on the Native mission reserves*, p. 7; see also Kannemeyer, 'New Bantu society', p. 124.
43. C. Bundy, *The rise and fall of the South African peasantry*, London, 1979, p. 180; Natal, *Report . . . Native population*, 1879, p. 22; SNA, 1/1/50, 413/80, Colonial Secretary to Governor, July 1880.
44. See Kannemeyer, 'New Bantu society', pp. 122–3; M. F. Bitensky, 'The economic development of Natal, 1843–1885', MA thesis, University of London, 1955.
45. Kannemeyer, 'New Bantu society', p. 324; Interview with R. T. Mazibuko, Edendale, 8 August 1979.
46. *LC Sessional Papers*, no. 27, 1875, Memorandum from Christian natives to Wolseley, 16 November 1875.
47. Act 28, 1865, *Law for relieving certain persons from the operation of Native law*.
48. See Natal, *Evidence . . . Natal Native Commission, 1881*, Matiwane, p. 145, Mini, pp. 135, 139. This remained a reason as late as 1903, see *SANAC*, 3, Gumede, p. 466.
49. *Natal Witness*, 7 February 1880, Legislative Council debate.
50. Natal, *Report . . . Native population*, 1897, p. 104; See also Switzer, 'Problems of an African mission', pp. 84–5.
51. W. E. Strong, *The story of the American Board*, New York, 1969, p. 281.
52. Natal University, Department of Economics, *Experiment at Edendale*, pp. 2–6.
53. See Natal Wesleyan Mission [Natal Archives], NWM, 1/1/5, 1889 Minutes, p. 240; ABM, A/1/2, Minutes, 4 July 1895, p. 142.
54. *SANAC*, 3, Mini, p. 968; see also Vilakazi, *Zulu transformations*, pp. 123f.
55. SNA, 1/1/14, 99/64, Minute, 17 August 1864; 1/1/33, 44/79, Edwards to SNA, 18 January 1879.
56. USPG, CLR Natal, I, Illing to Secretary, SPG, 3 March 1869, p. 357; *Natal Witness*, 24 December 1885.

CHAPTER FOUR

The Colonial State in the Nineteenth Century

In 1846 the Secretary of State for the War and Colonial Departments, William Gladstone, remarked that Britain would 'spare no pains to secure protection and justice to the native tribes' of Natal.[1] Yet in truth, the Colonial Office did little to secure either during the colonial period. The general attitude of imperial officials was that the annexation of Natal had been a blunder. And when it became obvious that the colony was incapable of benefiting the mother country economically, the Colonial Office began to argue that Natal should expect little in return.[2] The new colony had the misfortune of being annexed to the Crown at a time when economic liberalism was becoming more strongly entrenched in the United Kingdom. Economic liberalism embodied the belief that economic progress could occur only if the state interfered as little as possible in the affairs of its people. As far as the empire was concerned, this meant that all forms of colonial protectionism were abandoned in favour of a policy of free trade. Even old, established colonies, such as those in the West Indies, suffered under the new dispensation, while in the Cape the wine industry was hard hit. The policy was economically disastrous for Natal; it militated against the success of the few attempts that were being made to establish colonial industries and meant that the colony's officials had few resources to pay for the establishment of a sound administrative system.

The political corollary of economic non-interventionism was a growing reluctance by the Colonial Office to be actively involved in the colonies' administrative affairs. In Natal, this policy was evident in the early 1850s when a conflict over African policy developed between Lieutenant-Governor Pine and Theophilus Shepstone. The Colonial Office recognized that the establishment of the reserves, and the administration's failure to provide the mechanisms necessary to control their inhabitants, had in effect created a potentially dangerous situation. The Secretary of State in the early 1850s, Earl Grey, also saw the dangers inherent in Shepstone's obsession with maintaining full personal control.[3] Yet he was reluctant to mediate between the two officials and made no attempt to restrict Shepstone's hold on policy. Although he disapproved of Shepstone's *laissez-faire* approach, neither he nor any of his successors was prepared to initiate change.

Instead, supervision of the chiefdoms increasingly became the preserve of one man, and African policy became shrouded in secrecy.

Despite attempts by later lieutenant-governors, particularly John Scott, to have a greater say in African policy, Shepstone's authority remained inviolate. The Lieutenant-Governor, as Supreme Chief, was technically the paramount to whom all chiefs deferred, but Shepstone successfully interposed himself between the paramount and subordinate chiefs. Because of this, it was difficult for any chief to approach the Lieutenant-Governor without Shepstone's permission.

There was widespread opposition among the settlers to Shepstone's increasingly autocratic exercise of power. Farmers in particular bitterly resented a policy which they believed was fostering African independence and was harmful to the prospect of cheap labour. The growing wealth of chiefdoms such as the Hlubi convinced settlers that drastic action was needed to reform African policy and subject it to their own control. Those who had predicted that Shepstone's policies were potentially disastrous seized on the Langalibalele incident in 1873 as confirmation of their worst fears. Yet the ruthless punishment meted out by the government to the Hlubi and Ngwe chiefdoms, and the subsequent flow of cattle and labourers to the farmers following the dismantling of the two chiefdoms, caused many settlers to look more favourably on Shepstone. The following year, Bishop Colenso's intervention in London to secure justice for the two chiefdoms further rallied public opinion behind the Secretary for Native Affairs. Although the reserve system remained unpopular with settlers, and although their demand for cheap labour never ceased, many white Natalians came to see 'Shepstonism' as synonymous with control and security.

Unfortunately, this was at a time when Shepstone, never the most optimistic of men, succumbed to forebodings of racial disaster. He had been taken aback by the vehemence of African opposition to the marriage regulations in 1869. The regulations had marked a crucial turning-point in African attitudes to the colonial administration and to Shepstone personally. His office was inundated with complaints and accusations of betrayal: 'We thought you belonged to us but you have gone over entirely to your cousins and abandoned us. You have the power of persuading words, and you use that power in the interests of your relatives to ruin us.'[4] Complaints such as this rankled and, when they were followed by the open defiance of the Langalibalele uprising, he became obsessed with the military threat posed by the chiefdoms. After 1873 he continually harped on the need to avoid provoking a further uprising. This, in effect, meant that he was not only unwilling to countenance any administrative changes, but that he was even reluctant to enforce existing laws.[5] As a result, at a time when growing economic interdependence between settlers and Africans was fostering dynamic social changes in the colony, African policy became stagnant and fossilized.

By now, Shepstone's reputation in London as the only man capable of controlling the African population was inviolate. Robert Herbert, a permanent official in the Colonial Office, warned his political superior against interfering with Shepstone's control of policy or awakening his personal distrust.[6] The Secretary of State, Lord Carnarvon, realized that the Langalibalele affair had given the Colonial Office the chance to intervene in African policy, but he deferred to Herbert's warning and the opportunity for reform from London was lost. Consequently, at the same time that Carnarvon insisted on mitigation of Langalibalele's sentence, compensation for his dispossessed followers, and a restoration of the Ngwe lands, he made Lieutenant-Governor Pine the scapegoat for the miscarriage of justice and exonerated Shepstone from blame. The appointment of Sir Garnet Wolseley as Special Administrator to bring order to African policy was little more than a token gesture. He, too, was not prepared to oppose Shepstone. From Natal, he confided to Carnarvon that every change he wanted to introduce was blocked by Shepstone and that he did not feel justified in 'running counter to such advice from so able a man'.[7]

In 1878, two years after Shepstone had resigned as Secretary for Native Affairs to become Administrator of the Transvaal, the High Commissioner, Sir Bartle Frere, gave a penetrating analysis of his policy:

The Shepstone policy . . . on which Natal prided itself, is played out, or rather since Sir Theophilus left, no competent successor to him has appeared. It was a system which was entirely personal and could only endure while there was a great waste to fill up with refugees who were quite content to be let alone. It did nothing to improve or raise them, or to make us known to them or to make them known to us. Everything, in the Native Department, was an official secret and mystery, carefully veiled from non-official eyes, and indeed from everyone but the head of that Department. The great secret of ruling our own natives was to put off every inconvenient or troublesome question, to delay deciding whatever could be postponed. Natal greatly prides itself on things having thus been kept tolerably quiet for many years. But old men, who have been hunted by cannibals, will die, and young men who have never felt the miseries of Zulu rule grow up, and I find no one who knows much about them . . . I meet nobody who can tell me more about the Natives, their wants, wishes or dispositions, than any intelligent traveller might pick up in a few weeks or months.[8]

Despite his resignation, Shepstone retained considerable influence in the formulation of policy until his death in 1893. He was regularly consulted by the Colonial Office and by governors and officials in Natal. Sir Charles Mitchell, Colonial Secretary for the greater part of the 1880s, frequently referred to him for advice and, on becoming Governor in 1889, expressed his intention of continuing to do so in order that 'aided by the "wise-in-Council" I may steer the ship safely'.[9]

This continuing dependence on Shepstone paralysed most initiatives in African policy in the years following his resignation from office. The attitude of the administration to Africans became far more ambiguous than it had been in earlier decades. The small Executive Council, consisting of the Lieutenant-Governor (from 1882, Governor), Colonial Secretary, Treasurer, Attorney-General, Colonial Engineer, Surveyor-General and Secretary for Native Affairs, found itself torn between the colony's continuing dependence on homestead production and the growing crescendo of settler demands for labour. Faced with these conflicting needs, the Executive Council did little to protect African interests. The few steps taken included encouraging land purchases and exemption from customary law, but the official inertia which characterized the implementation of African policy meant that neither bore much fruit, while the recommendations of a Native Affairs Commission which sat in 1881–82 were quietly shelved.

The protection of Africans should have been the governors' major concern, yet both Sir Henry Bulwer (1875–80; 1882–85), and his successor, Sir Arthur Havelock (1885–89), were preoccupied with Zulu affairs and neglected African policy within the colony. Bulwer did try to ensure that Africans were treated justly and fairly, but he received little support from his officials. Of the members of the Executive Council, only the Attorney-General, Sir Michael Gallwey (1857–90), and the Surveyor-General, Dr P.C. Sutherland (1855–87), shared his concern. Yet even they were afraid of innovation, and they were further obstructed by the determination of successive Secretaries for Native Affairs not to introduce any changes at all.

The Shepstone family continued to dominate policy until the introduction of responsible government in 1893. Theophilus's brother, John, acted as Secretary for Native Affairs between 1876 and 1882 and the former's son, Henrique, was Secretary from 1882 until 1893. In 1882, John became Judge of the Native High Court. These men shared Theophilus's aversion to change and were only too willing to follow his policy of non-interference in the affairs of the chiefdoms. But they lacked both his ability and his concern for African welfare. Neither was prepared to visit reserves or to continue Theophilus's personal involvement in the affairs of the chiefdoms. As a result, the contacts Theophilus had assiduously maintained with the chiefs rapidly broke down.[10]

When a deputation of chiefs complained in 1880 that they were no longer consulted, John Shepstone was adamant that he had no time to tour the colony. As a result, despite having an extensive understanding of African law, he had little practical knowledge of the African population. African witnesses to the 1881–82 Native Affairs Commission voiced their dissatisfaction with his failure either to consult them or to represent their interests.[11]

The situation was worse under Henrique, a disastrous choice as Secretary for Native Affairs during a period of marked social change. 'We black people began to complain about the way we were governed when Gebuza ka Somsewu entered office', Madikane of the Qadi chiefdom told James Stuart in 1905.[12] Despite holding office for eleven years, Henrique's knowledge of African society remained negligible, and as late as 1903 he contended that Africans in Natal lived in luxury.[13] In fairness to Henrique, however, the task of administering the African population had become far more onerous than it had been for his father. There was a great increase in the routine work of the department, yet, despite criticizing Henrique's inactivity, the Legislative Council was not prepared to sanction expenditure for additional assistance and he had to make do with two clerks and a handful of African messengers.[14]

As a result, the Native Affairs Department was one of the most inefficient in the colony. It was notorious both for its complacency and its procrastination. In 1879, Frere described it as miserably weak and 'singularly ignorant of all but what is learned from the gossip of the kraals'. He described it as consisting of a 'superannuated old clerk, in a miserable office, full of scrappy, useless reports, and a number of messengers . . . who carry verbal orders and bring back verbal reports'.[15] Seven years later, Sir Charles Mitchell observed to Henrique that there 'must be something wrong in the machinery of your office to account for such serious delays in public business'.[16]

The department was even incapable of ensuring that the Africans were made aware of those laws and regulations which affected them. Theophilus Shepstone had held indabas of chiefs and *izinduna* to explain legislation. These meetings were rarely held after 1876 and information was only made available in notices in English posted in magistrates' offices. After Theophilus's resignation, an unwieldy board consisting of ten members was appointed to frame laws. In 1887, membership of the board was reduced to the Secretary for Native Affairs, Attorney-General, Judge of the Native High Court, and two magistrates or Justices of the Peace. The new board was given authority not only to frame laws, but also to decide on what class of cases should be tried in which of the several courts.

The inefficiency of the Native Affairs Department would have been less serious if there had been an effective system of local government geared to safeguarding African interests. This was not the case. The colonial administration had very little effective power in the countryside and only in the 1870s was a rural police force established to maintain law and order in the divisions. This consisted of 50 mounted white officers and 150 African constables and proved hopelessly inadequate. This number hardly increased before the 1890s. These policemen were under the authority of the magistrates and their duties seldom allowed them to be away from the courts for any length of time. Many of the white officers were from Britain and unacquainted with either the Zulu language or African habits and customs. As late as 1897, less than half even of the colonial-born troopers could speak Zulu.[17] The absence of an adequate police force obviously militated against the effective enforcement of law and order. But it also ensured that the administration had inadequate means of systematically enforcing laws and regulations which would otherwise have borne heavily on the Africans. On the Crown lands and in the reserves the rules of the colonial state could frequently be disregarded.

Should unrest occur, the police could be supplemented by small volunteer forces of cavalry and infantry and by the imperial garrison at Fort Napier. Although the imperial garrison was the ultimate guarantor of settler security in Natal, its actual role in suppressing internal disorder was slight in the nineteenth century. During the campaign against Langalibalele, imperial troops played a secondary role to the volunteers.

The local officials whose presence loomed largest in the lives of Africans were the magistrates and Administrators of Native Law. By the early 1880s, there were nineteen Administrators in Natal whose specific responsibility was for African criminal cases. But only four of these officials were based in reserves and able to devote time to their inhabitants. The remaining fifteen doubled up as resident magistrates with responsibilities to all the inhabitants of their divisions. Few spoke Zulu or had more knowledge of the Africans than had the Secretary for Native Affairs.

As the magistrates were appointed by, and responsible to, the Colonial Secretary, their relationship to the Secretary for Native Affairs was at best ambiguous. Theophilus Shepstone had set the tone for this relationship. Always suspicious of any step which might lessen his authority, he had seen the appointment of magistrates as an undermining of his position. He had only reluctantly advised or supported them and had encouraged African complaints about them. Chiefs such as Phakade, who had their own reasons for resenting the introduction of magistrates into their lands, had accordingly adopted Shepstone's attitude and wherever possible ignored the magistrates' presence.[18] On the other hand, *abanumzana* could use the magistrates to lessen the burdens imposed on them by their chiefs. After Shepstone's resignation, *abanumzana* increasingly bypassed their chiefs' courts and took their cases direct to the magistrates. As Msutu of the Cele chiefdom told the 1881–82 Native Affairs Commission, 'the magistrate is really our chief'.[19]

And this sentiment had been voiced despite the fact that Africans had every reason to be dissatisfied with the treatment they received from magistrates. In general, the ties of social interest and racial sympathy tended to bind magistrates closely to the settler community. Many magistrates were drawn from the farming community, while the Justices of the Peace who supported them were invariably farmers. With this background, the magistracy tended to share farmers' attitudes and prejudices, and to be too preoccupied with the farmers' affairs to pay much attention to African cases.[20] Magistrates had few support staff, often only a Clerk of the Peace who combined the duties of prosecutor and interpreter, an *induna* and a handful of policemen. Consequently, few could cope with their judicial, revenue-collecting and civil functions. Circuit and branch courts were held infrequently with the result that a large backlog of African cases accumulated; in Stanger, for example, cases introduced in 1888 were still waiting to be heard in 1891.[21]

Most magistrates also neglected to promulgate the growing number of laws and regulations affecting Africans.[22] This caused considerable resentment; in 1881, the *kholwa*, Nambula complained that 'the way we see the laws promulgated now is by seeing someone going to prison for disobeying them'.[23] Seventeen years later, the magistrate of Mapumulo acknowledged that the situation was no better:

> Many a Native has been charged with, and severely punished for, contravening some recently-proclaimed Law, about which he knows nothing whatsoever. When he pleads ignorance of the law, he is calmly told 'ignorance is no excuse' by the very magistrate who failed in one of his chief duties, and neglected to acquaint the Native with the law.[24]

Even to a colony in financial straits such as Natal, the publication of laws and regulations in Zulu would not have been inordinately expensive, yet appeals and petitions from chiefs and *kholwa* for such publication were ignored.[25]

Probably the most serious weakness of the whole system of local government was that few magistrates were proficient in either African or Roman-Dutch law. Examinations regulating entrance into, or promotion within, the civil service were only introduced in 1894. Until then, magistrates were not required to have any legal qualifications, and picked up a smattering of law as cases were brought before them.[26] Because of this, their decisions were constantly overturned on appeal to the higher courts. Between 1884 and 1886, for example, only 40 per cent of 357 magisterial decisions which were appealed to the Native High Court were upheld.[27]

The 1878 Code also proved of little use to the magistrates. It ignored the complex procedures and variations in the laws which existed between chiefdoms, and established a new system of 'customary law' in order to bolster patriarchal authority. Yet at the same time it was contradictory and confusing. As the magistrates tried to impose the Code in their divisions, confusion arose and resentment built up amongst Africans. Although they were aware of the problems caused by the Code, few magistrates had either the time or the patience to try to understand the intricacies and local variations within African law. Instead, African bewilderment and resentment were disregarded and dismissed with contempt. This contempt was often mutual, partly because of the magistrates' obvious inadequacies in dealing with African law. In addition, to hereditary chiefs claiming authority over hundreds or even thousands of followers and accustomed to arriving at court with a large retinue, the magistrate's small staff and quarters must have appeared unimpressive.[28]

There were sensible, hard-working magistrates such as John Bird and Dunbar Moodie and, later in the century, James Stuart, T. Bennett and James Gibson. The last three in particular had a thorough knowledge of the Zulu language and of African customs, and were sympathetic to African grievances. They were exceptional, however, and the majority of their colleagues were incompetent and unable or unwilling to resist settler demands. Magistrates such as Captain Johan Struben, John Macfarlane and Thomas Kelly were notorious for their hostility towards Africans and for the harsh sentences they imposed on offenders.[29] Other magistrates proved equally oppressive and avaricious, their conduct being particularly blatant during their visits to *imizi* to collect hut tax. These visits were marked by the *hlabisa* custom whereby a distinguished visitor was provided with a beast. The correct response was for the magistrate to order the beast to be slaughtered and the meat to be distributed to the *umuzi* inhabitants. By the 1880s, Africans were complaining to the Secretary for Native Affairs that magistrates were now demanding that beasts be killed for their own use.[30]

The small salaries received by magistrates made it difficult to attract suitable candidates. Beyond that, the colonial administration did little to ensure that magistrates carried out their duties efficiently. As the years went by the government became increasingly reluctant to act against magistrates, or to express public disapproval when they erred, for fear that such action would lower the prestige of the magistracy even further amongst Africans, consequently undermining law and order in the colony.[31] This disinclination to chastise magistrates became even more acute after the introduction of responsible government in 1893 when the ministries proved reluctant to dismiss inadequate magistrates lest such action fatally harm the prestige of the magistracy.[32]

By the 1890s, few magistrates could cope with the growing pressure of work and in 1892 a commission was appointed to consider reforms. As a result of its recommendations, the number of magisterial divisions was increased to twenty-four, and rules were drawn up for African cases. But in flagrant disregard of the interests of justice, the commissioners solved the problem of ignorant and unjust magisterial judgements by limiting the right of appeal to the Native High Court. Appeals to circuit courts were also discouraged; in future Africans would have to lodge them personally in Pietermaritzburg.[33]

The government also tried to provide the magistrates with a legal code that would minimize the disparity between judgements. It had become obvious that the 1878 Code was a hopelessly inadequate synthesis of African law. To replace it, a new Code of Native Law was issued in 1891. The administration intended that the new Code would strengthen the hierarchical structure of African administration by formalizing the powers of the Supreme Chief and also of the chiefs and *izinduna*.[34] No African under customary law was to be allowed to reside in the colony unless he was a member of a chiefdom. At the homestead level, the *umnumzana*'s legal authority over women and young men in his *umuzi* was strengthened; their position as minors in law was stressed in the Code and they were deemed incapable of alienating property or of making contracts without the *umnumzana*'s consent. Women were forbidden to hold property and sons were required to transfer their earnings to their fathers.[35]

The Code, in its thrust to consolidate the hierarchical nature of African society, sought to reverse the social changes that were taking place within both the chiefdoms and *imizi*.[36] Moreover, ignoring the diversity within customary law, the Code sought to impose rigid uniformity on African life, thus perpetuating one of the main African grievances against the existing system of legal administration. As Dyer Macebo of Groutville pointed out to Stuart in 1898, the Code 'tended to define or crystallize what was indefinite or in a state of flux, or rather it has conveyed a quite false impression' of customs.[37] Equally seriously, it tended to retard the assimilation of customary law into colonial law at a time when African contact with white laws and customs, and innovations such as private landowner-ship, money transactions, urbanization and the migrant labour system, made the perpetuation of a separate body of law for Africans increasingly meaningless and undesirable.

If African administration suffered under the dual disadvantage of ineffective Secretaries for Native Affairs and incapable magistrates, the formulation of policy was paralysed by a continuing conflict between the Executive and Legislative Councils for control of that policy. In 1856, when Natal received representative government, the Colonial Office believed that the new Legislative Council would 'relieve the Home Government from the responsibility of deciding questions of native policy'.[38] Yet from the start, the legislative councillors opposed the administration's policy and sought to gain control of it. The constant conflicts between the Department of Native Affairs and the Legislative Council did much to reinforce Theophilus Shepstone's determination to prevent outside interference in his policy towards the African population.

The main focus of the Council's attack was the sum of £5 000 that was reserved annually for African purposes under the 1856 Charter. The existence of this reserve amount prevented councillors from having a direct say in funding African administration and they correctly saw it as the foundation of the Crown's continued control of African policy. Between 1856 and 1893, when Natal received responsible government, the councillors constantly struggled to gain control of the fund. Although they failed, they were nonetheless able to play an obstructionist role in African policy. The governor's power of veto ensured that councillors could not place racist legislation on the statute book. But under the constitution they had the power to reject any law which came before them, a power which contributed in no small measure to the stultification of policy. Consequently, few laws beneficial to Africans were brought before them. Under the Native Administration Act of 1875, councillors also had to approve any changes which the Native Law Board might wish to make to the 1878 Code. In addition, from 1869 onwards councillors made regular demands for a responsible government constitution which would secure the transfer of the control of the colony's Africans to the legislature. Underlying all these initiatives was the demand for cheap labour and the realization that it could be met only if the Council could enact appropriate legislation.[39] In this regard, Lieutenant-Governor Scott's observations on the councillors in 1858 applied to virtually all their successors:

[They have] no expressed desire to elevate and improve the social position of the native by making him a landed proprietor, an independent cultivator of the soil, a civilized trader in, and a producer of exportable articles, or a mechanic or a skilled labourer. The native population are to be scattered throughout the colony and located on the farms of the white colonists, in the capacity of servants working for wages.[40]

However, many councillors had their own misgivings about the desirability of receiving responsible government. As the Colonial Office pointed out to the Council more than once after 1869, if self-government meant that the settlers would also have to provide the military means to deter rebellion, few councillors would be prepared to accept that responsibility. Until the late 1880s, Natal was too weak to maintain law and order on her own and few settlers were prepared to accept the withdrawal of imperial troops from the colony. This was particularly true of Legislative Council members from the coastal and urban divisions, who did not share the same need for cheap labour as the farmers of the midlands and interior. The continuing dissension in the Council between the coastal and the inland members, therefore, further complicated the formulation of African policy within Natal.

There are other reasons for placing much of the blame for the morass into which African administration was sinking on the councillors themselves. For one thing, the calibre of most of them left much to be desired. Other than a small handful of able men such as the members for Durban borough, John Robinson and Harry Escombe, most were incapable of performing their public duties and sought little else than to protect their own narrow interests. Most were notoriously out of sympathy with African aspirations and their deliberations and decisions reflected their prejudices and their ignorance of African society. Unless the legislation affected their own interests, councillors displayed little concern about the few laws dealing with Africans that were submitted to them. In 1886 for example, a bill to regulate African Christian marriages was thrown out, not because of any objection to it but because the Council had been sitting a long time. 'The impatience felt by some members, and the indifference felt by others . . . seem to have combined to cause its rejection.'[41] When the 1891 Code of Native Law was put before the Council, it was 'galloped through in an hour and before empty benches'.[42]

Although the councillors gained control of African policy only after 1893, the Executive Council became more amenable to their views in the late 1880s. This was partly because the departure of Bulwer from the colony in 1885, and the resignations of Sutherland in 1887 and of Gallwey in 1890, removed those officials most sympathetic to African interests. Increasingly, decisions were now taken by officials with little sympathy for African aspirations. It is virtually impossible to separate changing official attitudes from the growing crisis in African society that will be examined in later chapters. Also important, however, was the spreading influence of white supremacist notions. White consciousness was becoming more widespread in Natal and was particularly influenced by Social Darwinist concepts of the survival of the fittest race, and by the triumph of segregationist ideology in the southern United States. This ideology stressed ethnic differences between the white and black races, and accepted the notion that Africans were ethnically and biologically inferior to Europeans.

The most significant increase in the powers of the Legislative Council came with the passing of the new Code of Native Law in 1891. The preamble to the Act gave councillors the right to introduce amendments. This was to prove one of the Code's greatest defects; it was subject to the whim of men who were often unconcerned with the finer details of African law, but who were certainly interested in tightening its regulations to serve their own ends.[43]

The Code was introduced at a time when the Legislative Council was debating the establishment of responsible government with particular intensity. In 1888, a select committee was appointed by the Council to consider the question, but it took until 1893 for final agreement to be reached and for Natal to receive self-rule. The main reason for the delay was the difference of opinion between the Council and the Colonial Office on the future government of the African and Indian populations. The councillors were insistent that self-rule should include full control over all the peoples of the colony.

This was the demand made by the 1888 select committee. The Secretary of State, Lord Knutsford, rejected it and for the next four years negotiations centred on what powers the Crown should retain to protect the rights of Africans. Agreement was finally reached in 1892, and the new constitution included a number of important safeguards. It provided for a bicameral parliament in which the upper Legislative Council would consist of eleven men nominated for their knowledge of the African population. As further protection for the Africans, the Governor would appoint the members of the first Council. Future members would be appointed by the Governor-in-Council, that is, the ministry. The sum of £5 000 reserved under the old constitution for African purposes was increased to £10 000. The Governor was given the right to reserve bills affecting any particular section of the community; after a suspension of two years, such a reserved bill could be disallowed by the Queen. Furthermore, the Governor retained his powers as Supreme Chief and theoretically could continue to use them without consulting his ministers.[44]

The negotiations for responsible government were led by Sir John Robinson. Although he and the members of his Progressive Party in the Council carefully avoided statements that could be construed as advocating the entrenchment of settler interests, it was obvious from their speeches that control of the African population would be considerably tightened. On the eve of the introduction of the new constitution, Robinson wrote in the newspaper that he owned and edited, the *Natal Mercury*, that in future 'justice and fair dealing to all classes and races in the colony will be combined . . . with the firm exercise of authority and the regular enforcement of law'.[45]

Although Lord Knutsford had tried to safeguard African interests, after 1893 the Colonial Office remained as reluctant to intervene in the handling of African policy as it had been under representative government. The Colonial Office made no attempt to ensure that any of the safeguards bar the royal veto of class legislation was observed. Even before Sir Walter Hely-Hutchinson went to Natal as the first Governor under responsible government, the attitude of the Colonial Office was clear. When he wrote to ask whether he should consult his ministers before he appointed the new legislative councillors, W. Fairfield, a Colonial Office official, minuted on his despatch, 'I think he had better not have asked the question, and hope he will not often raise similar points.' In his reply, the Secretary of State advised Hely-Hutchinson to consult Robinson, privately if possible but otherwise officially. Similarly, in 1896 when the draconian Spoor Law was sent to London, Lord Selborne minuted that, despite its nature 'I see no use in interfering in such matters in self-governing colonies if we can possibly help it.'[46]

The Colonial Office also conceded that the ministry had the right to exercise effective control over the African population. The Royal Instructions of July 1893 laid down that the Governor had to consult his ministers before acting as Supreme Chief.[47] Theoretically, the final choice of action was the Governor's, but in practice no Governor before 1910 exercised these powers independently of his ministers. Consequently, they fell into abeyance. Although the governors were occasionally able to mitigate ministerial severity, they were seldom able to influence ministerial decisions. Hely-Hutchinson only once succeeded in overriding a decision by the cabinet when he refused to allow the use of *isibhalo* labour on the Natal-Zululand railway in 1897. Although he later grew contemptuous of what he saw as his ministers' lack of African policy, initially he accepted the ministry's good faith in matters concerning Africans, and went out of his way to smooth the way to acceptance of legislation in London.[48]

Moreover, he traded away his freedom to influence the government when he not only consulted with Robinson on the appointment of the legislative councillors, but also so placed himself that he had to accept Robinson's suggestions.[49] Consequently, the Council consisted largely of government supporters rather than of men knowledgeable about African society. During the Robinson and Escombe ministries it rejected no bills laid before it.

Prior to 1893, Sir John Robinson had been an outspoken critic of the colonial administration's African policy and had been particularly hostile towards Shepstonism.[50] On taking office, however, he stressed in the new lower house, the Legislative Assembly, the importance of maintaining the status quo: '[The "Native" question] is a question which involves, before all things else, patience, calmness and deliberation. We do not . . . intend to propose to this House violent changes or sudden measures . . .'[51]

Robinson had a reputation for being scrupulously fair and he had a profound regard for observing constitutional principles.[52] But he suffered from ill-health and, despite being Prime Minister, until his early retirement in 1897 he increasingly took a back seat to his fellow member for Durban, the Attorney-General, Harry Escombe. Hot-tempered and impulsive, Escombe was regarded with dislike and suspicion by Colonial Office officials.[53] Despite this, he was genuinely aware of the government's responsibilities towards the Africans and his good faith was accepted by the *kholwa* and by Bishop Colenso's daughter, Harriette, the leading protagonist of African rights in the colony. In the responsible government negotiations he had been more prepared than his colleagues to accept constitutional safeguards to protect African interests. As Attorney-General, he carefully scrutinized legislation affecting Africans.[54]

With their urban backgrounds, Robinson and Escombe were more concerned with commercial than with agricultural issues. But the new constitution had markedly increased the weight of the settler farming community by giving it twenty-nine seats as opposed to the eight allocated to the boroughs. Because of this, neither Robinson nor Escombe could prevent the balance of power swinging to the agricultural interest. Robinson's cabinet of five members included three farmers, Frederick Moor as Secretary for Native Affairs, George Sutton as Colonial Treasurer, and Thomas Murray as Minister of Lands and Works. They presented the farmers' point of view in the cabinet, even if they were never able to dictate policy.

As far as the African population was concerned, the most important man in the new ministry was Frederick Moor. His post of Secretary for Native Affairs placed him in a difficult position. Under the new constitution, the post had to be held by a man representing African interests in the government, yet elected by a white constituency and responsible to it in Parliament. Under responsible government this difficulty was not lessened by the fact that all incumbents of the office between 1893 and 1910 were farmers representing farming constituencies.

Assessments of Moor have been contradictory. Harriette Colenso's sister, Agnes, was of the opinion that he tried to do his best to look after and protect African rights. Sir Matthew Nathan, Governor from 1907 to 1909, also believed that he was sympathetic to African aspirations. Colonel Leuchars, himself Secretary for Native Affairs between 1903 and 1905, likened him to 'one of the most rabid individuals of Exeter Hall'.[55] By contrast, the magistrate, H.J. Colenbrander believed that 'the natives go to the wall by Moor's policy. He may or may not be strong, but he has not sympathy for the interests of the native people as a whole.'[56] In more recent assessments, Dhupelia accepts that Moor was not very knowledgeable about African affairs, but considers that he believed in the necessity for dealing 'fairly, honestly, justly and firmly with the African population'.[57] Marks gives a more balanced verdict in her assessment of him as a white supremacist in the Shepstone tradition, in many ways illiberal and extreme, but less rigid than most of his contemporaries, and opposed to radical measures.[58]

Unlike Escombe, Moor felt strongly that Africans were incapable of 'civilization' and should remain a subject race under their own laws. This belief was to influence official attitudes both to homestead Africans and to the *kholwa*. Moor was particularly hostile to the missionaries' attempts to raise up a distinct class of exempted Africans. He was not prepared to tolerate any political or social equality for the *kholwa*, and was emphatic that until all Africans could be placed on the same footing, it was 'running in the teeth of the laws of nature' to single out *kholwa* for special treatment. In the meantime, the ideal of African government should be to make an African an 'industrious, contented, loyal subject'.[59] He was adamant that the prestige of the government had to be maintained at all times and was even more insistent than his predecessors had been that no chief should approach the Governor without his permission.[60] This insistence may have arisen from his lack of self-confidence. He was incapable of asserting his authority and did not have the strength of will to resist his colleagues. As Nathan was to confide to his mother in 1909 when Moor was Prime Minister, Moor's 'weakness is pitiable – he agrees with my views when with me but goes back on them when he gets with his colleagues'.[61]

In the 1890s, when neither Robinson nor Escombe was prepared to accept all the demands of the farmers, this weakness was not as serious as it would come to be in the early twentieth century when ministries were dominated by the agricultural interest. Yet, even in the 1890s, his weakness told against the Africans; he enthusiastically supported African industrial education, but failed to prevent the Robinson ministry from taking stringent steps against it.[62]

S. O. Samuelson, in the new post of Under-Secretary for Native Affairs, played a more direct role in supervising the day-to-day running of the department. Unlike his political chief, he was a permanent official whose position did not depend on electoral support. The son of a Norwegian missionary, he had had considerable experience of African administration and was believed by the first ministry to be respected by the chiefs and *izinduna*.[63] His appointment was welcomed by the African newspaper, *Inkanyiso Yase Natal*, which commented that no better man could have been chosen and that he was 'the bridge over which Natives will confidently pass to, and contentedly live under, Responsible Government'. The editor believed he combined justice with firmness and would prove a kind and sympathetic friend to the Africans,[64] a belief which was not to materialize for his term of office was marked by negligence of African welfare.

As a result of the Department of Native Affairs' failure to take an active interest in the condition of Africans in the reserves; of the reluctance of the ministry to alienate farmers by enquiring too closely into the position of squatters and tenants on their farms; and of the fact that the Secretary for Native Affairs was the sole channel of communication between the chiefs and the Governor, official contact with Africans became even more irregular than it had been before 1893. Central government officers seldom visited reserves and few councils of chiefs were held. Section 44 of the Code stipulated that the Secretary for Native Affairs should be accessible to, and receive petitions from all Africans. Moor, despite his insistence on being the channel of communication, required Africans to make a deposition before their resident magistrate before going to Pietermaritzburg. By this he effectively reduced the opportunity of meeting even chiefs.[65]

The Robinson and Escombe ministries were to prove to be less acquisitive than their successors. Although these two ministries introduced radical changes in the control of the reserves and stripped the chiefs of many of their few remaining powers, they were reluctant to impose economic burdens on the homestead economy; a reluctance which was not shared by later cabinets. With responsible government they had achieved what they wanted – control of African policy – and they were prepared to move slowly in consolidating the settlers' hold over the African population.

Notes

1. See CO 179, 1, no. 9, Lieutenant-Governor to Governor, Cape, 31 March 1846, p. 105.
2. Ibid., no. 105, Governor, Cape, to Secretary of State, 26 May 1846, Colonial Office minutes, pp. 165f.
3. Ibid., 16, no. 223, Secretary of State to Lieutenant-Governor, 14 February 1852, p. 194.
4. SNA, 1/1/21, 118/69, Promulgation of marriage law, 2 September 1869.
5. Natal, *Evidence . . . Natal Native Commission, 1881*, Shepstone, p. 286; CO 179, 140, Natal 1848, Shepstone memorandum, 1881; see also Sir Evelyn Wood Collection [Natal Archives], III/3/8, Wood to Kimberley, 2 October 1881.
6. Carnarvon Papers [British Library], Add 60792, Herbert to Carnarvon, 1 May 1875.
7. Carnarvon Papers [Public Record Office], 38, Wolseley to Carnarvon, 12 June 1875, p. 84.
8. Sir Michael Hicks-Beach Papers [Gloucestershire Record Office], PCC/1/27, Frere to Hicks-Beach, 27 October 1878.
9. Sir Theophilus Shepstone Papers, 57, Mitchell to Shepstone, 2 September 1889, p. 14; See also CO 179, 140, Natal 1848, Shepstone memorandum, 1881.
10. Sir Evelyn Wood Collection, III/2/22, Colonial Secretary to Wood, 1881.
11. CSO, 2555, c79/80, Report by John Shepstone, 17 December 1880. *Inkanyiso Yase Natal*, 11 June 1891; *SANAC*, 3, J. W. Shepstone, pp. 112–23. Natal, *Evidence . . . Natal Native Commission, 1881*, Mini, p. 137, Teteleku, p. 177.
12. Webb and Wright, eds, *James Stuart archive*, 2, Madikane, 27 May 1905, p. 54.
13. *SANAC*, 3, Shepstone, pp. 75–9.
14. SNA, 1/1/108, 637/88, SNA memorandum, 8 August 1888.
15. Sir Michael Hicks-Beach Papers, Frere to Hicks-Beach, PCC/2/4, 19 January 1879; PCC/2/11, 3 February 1879.
16. SNA, 1/1/88, 801/85, Administrator to SNA, 12 January 1886.
17. Natal, *Report of the commission appointed . . . to inquire into and report upon the sufficiency or otherwise of the magisterial divisions of the colony, 1890–91*, Pietermaritzburg, 1891, pp. 24–5; NPP, 176, no. 98, List of colonial-born men serving with the Natal police force, 23 March 1897.
18. *Natal Mercury*, 21 June 1854, 28 June 1854; see also CO 179, 20, no. 20, Lieutenant-Governor to Governor, Cape, 27 February 1852, p. 300; 35, no. 35, 29 May 1854, p. 167.
19. Natal, *Evidence . . . Natal Native Commission, 1881*, Mawele, p. 200, Tyutyela, p. 362, Msutu, p. 367.
20. S. Marks, *Reluctant rebellion: the 1906–1908 disturbances in Natal*, Oxford, 1970, p. 138.
21. *LC Sessional Papers*, 18, 1891, *Ad interim* report of Magistrates' Commission; *Inkanyiso Yase Natal*, 21 July 1892.
22. SNA, 1/1/103, 1120/87, Puisne Justice to Governor, 21 December 1887; Colenso Collection, 25, R. Samuelson to H. Colenso, 5 November 1888.
23. Natal, *Evidence . . . Natal Native Commission, 1881*, Nambula, p. 175.
24. Natal, *Report . . . Native population*, 1898, p. B11.
25. NPP, 651, no. 21, 1892, Petition for laws and notices affecting Natives to be published in Zulu; *Inkanyiso Yase Natal*, 19 March 1891; *LC Hansard*, XVIII, 24 June 1892, pp. 235–8.
26. *SANAC*, 3, Beaumont, pp. 17–9; *NGG*, XLVI, no. 2701, 16 October 1894, GN 360, 1894, p. 1391.

27. *NGG*, XXXVIII, no.2212, 7 December 1886, p.1357; see also *Natal Witness*, 2 November 1892.
28. Natal, *Report . . . Native population*, 1879, p.B54; *Natal Mercury*, 7 August 1888; *Natal Witness*, 20 July 1893.
29. CO 179, 42, 19, Acting Lieutenant-Governor to Secretary of State, 8 March 1856, pp.351f; no.27, 12 May 1856, pp.559f; 56, no.36, 2 August 1860, p.228.
30. SNA, 1/1/72, 254/85, SNA to magistrates, 8 April 1885; see also CSO, 2572, c34/96, SNA minute, 1896.
31. GH, 229, no.27, Administrator to Secretary of State, 11 May 1904, p.22.
32. See CSO, 2595, c29/05, Colonial Secretary minute, 24 March 1905.
33. *NGG*, XLVI, no.2687, 10 July 1894, Proclamation 19, 1894, p.739; XLV, no.2607, 28 March 1893, GN 161, 1893, p.270.
34. *SANAC*, 3, H.C. Shepstone, p.75.
35. Act 19, 1891, *To legalise the Code of Native law*, clauses 72, 90, 138.
36. See chapter eight.
37. Webb and Wright, eds, *James Stuart archive*, 2, Macebo, 2 November 1898, p.42.
38. CO 179, 43, no.31, Colonial Office minute, 7 October 1856, p.39.
39. John Bird Papers [Killie Campbell Library], 2, Bird to T. Shepstone, 1 August 1885.
40. CO 179, 49, no.36, Lieutenant-Governor to Secretary of State, 8 April 1858, p.462.
41. CO 179, 165, no.193, Governor to Secretary of State, 24 November 1886.
42. See *Natal Mercury*, 21 August 1893.
43. *SANAC*, 3, J.W. Shepstone, p.59.
44. J. Lambert, 'Sir John Robinson and responsible government, 1863–1897: the making of the first prime minister of Natal', MA thesis, University of Natal, 1975, pp.170f.
45. *Natal Mercury*, 17 July 1893.
46. CO 179, 186, Confidential, enclosure, minute by Fairfield, August 1893, p.592; Fairfield to Governor, 31 August 1893, p.605; 195, no.123, enclosure, minute by Selborne, 10 August 1896, p.325.
47. *NGG*, XLV, no.2644, 31 October 1893, pp.1299–1300.
48. SNA, 1/1/263, 2401/97, Minister of Lands and Works to SNA, 29 October 1897; 1/1/290, SNA to Prime Minister, 12 April 1901; Ripon Papers [British Library], LXXIII, Hely-Hutchinson to Ripon, 4 October 1893; Sir John Robinson Collection [Natal Archives], 1, 3/19, Hely-Hutchinson to Robinson, 30 May 1894.
49. GH, 1300, Confidential, Governor to Secretary of State, 14 October 1893, p.378.
50. See *Natal Mercury*, 15 January 1878.
51. *LA Hansard*, XXII, 26 April 1894, Prime Minister, p.13.
52. Lambert, 'Sir John Robinson', pp.5–6, 237.
53. See Ripon Papers, LXXIII, Hely-Hutchinson to Ripon, 6 January 1894, p.48; CO 179, 194, no.123, enclosure, minute by Fairfield, 9 August 1896, p.325.
54. Attorney-General in *LA Hansard*, XXII, 3 May 1894, p.78; XXIV, 12 May 1896, p.217; XXVII, 14 June 1898, p.386.
55. Marks, *Reluctant rebellion*, p.22; see also Colenso Collection, 30, Agnes to Harriette, 11 July 1895. Sir Matthew Nathan Papers [Rhodes House Library], 368, Nathan to Selborne, 15 September 1907.
56. Webb and Wright, eds, *James Stuart archive*, 1, Colenbrander, 20 December 1900, p.81.
57. U.S. Dhupelia, 'Frederick Robert Moor and native affairs in the colony of Natal, 1893 to 1910', MA thesis, University of Durban-Westville, 1980, pp.5–6.
58. Marks, *Reluctant rebellion*, pp.21–2.
59. *SANAC*, 3, Moor, pp.215–24; Welsh, *Roots of segregation*, p.231.
60. *LA Hansard*, XXIX, 4 June 1900, Moor, p.142; GH, 1104, Janivale to McCallum, 17 August 1901, p.19.
61. Sir Matthew Nathan Papers, 119, Nathan to mother, 7 December 1909, pp.86–7.
62. *SANAC*, 3, Moor, p.216.
63. Dhupelia, 'Moor and native affairs', p.7.
64. *Inkanyiso Yase Natal*, 11 August 1893; 20 October 1893.
65. *SANAC*, 3, H.C. Shepstone, p.85; H.E. Colenso, *The problem of the races in Africa*, reprinted from *Asiatic Quarterly Review*, July 1897, p.18.

CHAPTER FIVE

The Deepening Land Crisis

Natal's homestead economy had developed on the basis of free and sufficient access to land. As long as the colony's Africans were able to establish new gardens, and to move their cattle between summer and winter grazing lands, the homestead economy continued to satisfy their needs. Despite the settler presence, most *imizi* had access to sufficient land for gardens and grazing in the early decades of white rule. But, as Africans expanded production to meet the colonial demand for grain, so individual *imizi* needed more land.

By the 1870s it became more difficult to meet this need. The African population had experienced a threefold increase since the late 1840s, with just under half of the approximately 300 000 people living in the reserves. Even in the 1850s, these lands had been overcrowded; now the growing population meant that chiefs were finding it harder to allocate land to *imizi*, and access to grazing was becoming restricted. By the late 1870s many reserve inhabitants were 'at the end of their tether as far as cultivation goes'.[1] Access to non-reserve land was also becoming restricted. Previously the settlers had been so sparsely spread on the ground that their presence had not prevented movement. Now a new generation of settlers was growing up and sons of pioneers were looking for farms for themselves. The Natal government was sensitive to their need and the first sign that it was prepared to meet it came in 1873 in the aftermath of Langalibalele's uprising. In 1857, when the Hlangwini and Sithole chiefdoms had been broken up, their lands had been allocated to other chiefdoms; in 1873 the Hlubi lands were given to settlers.

The 1870s also saw the first real stirrings of white immigration to the colony since the depression of the mid-1860s. Although the price of land away from urban centres remained generally depressed, absentee landowners found it worthwhile to begin selling their better-placed lands. Accordingly, the Natal Land and Colonisation Company began placing on the market some of its lands on the coast and in the mist belt, beginning a process whereby African rent tenants on these lands were evicted, or the amount of land available to them on the farms was diminished. On those lands which were not sold, landowners encouraged more tenants onto the lands to increase their profitability, a process which restricted the amount available to those already there.[2]

In the late 1870s, the colony embarked on a programme of railway construction intended to link Port Natal harbour with the overberg republics. As the railway from Durban steadily pushed towards Pietermaritzburg, farmers in the district became less dependent on wagon transport and agriculture was transformed. This process was hastened by the outbreak of the Anglo-Zulu War in 1879 and the First Anglo-Boer War in 1881. The large imperial garrison in the colony and the increased activity at Port Natal harbour during these years brought prosperity to both Pietermaritzburg and Durban. As the number of inhabitants of both cities increased, their presence had a ripple effect on the surrounding countryside. With the growing demand for produce, owners of the rent-tenancy farms around the two cities began sub-dividing their lands into small garden plots which they sold or leased to Indian and white market gardeners. These market gardeners in turn increased the pressure on tenants, either by evicting them from the land or by increasing the amount of rent they had to pay. It was no longer profitable for landowners to continue charging tenants by the hut, and they were required to pay for every acre they used. As early as 1879, tenants around Durban were annually paying up to £10 an acre. Even as far away as Richmond, rentals of £10 per hut were being asked two years later.[3] Many African families, who had occupied these lands for years, found themselves unable to meet the new rentals and were forced to look elsewhere for land.

Faced with a growing land crisis, demands from Africans for the government to take action reached a crescendo. In the late 1870s, requests to the Department of Native Affairs for assistance show how difficult it was becoming for individual *imizi* or sections of chiefdoms to find new land. The situation was particularly serious in south-western Natal where reserves had been established relatively late and where various chiefs competed to provide sufficient land for their people. As chiefs manoeuvred to find land, hostility between their peoples flared up and the government found itself trying to balance their conflicting needs. The problem was compounded when chiefs from outside the area tried to settle people within it. For instance, the reserve allocated to Mnini on the south coast was bursting at the seams by the 1870s and the chief was engaged in a prolonged battle with the magistrate of Alexandra to settle some of his *imizi* in that county.[4]

The eviction of the Hlangwini, Sithole and Hlubi chiefdoms from their lands had also made chiefs aware that their tenure on the land on which they had been placed was not inviolate. The concept of land ownership (as opposed to land usage) was alien to Africans who understood land as being given into their stewardship by their ancestors: 'Land belongs to a vast family of which many are dead, few are living and countless numbers are still unborn.'[5] Despite this understanding, the dispossession of chiefdoms in 1857 and 1873, and the eviction of Africans when lands were sold, were leading some chiefs to demand tribal titles that would recognize their legal right to the land.[6] By the late 1870s, the pressing need for new gardens and grazing was amplifying these demands and was even causing chiefs to consider purchasing the additional land that they needed.

In this, they were following the example of those *kholwa* who had bought land at Edendale, Driefontein and elsewhere. By the end of the 1870s, individual *kholwa* as well as communities were purchasing. Many were buying small allotments on the north coast for £1 an acre and some were wealthy enough to accumulate larger holdings. For example, Longo rented a small farm from the Land and Colonisation Company for sugar cultivation. With the profit that he made he paid the company a deposit of £300 for Lot 1 of the farm Spitzkop. Similarly, Mxakaza Mngoma bought 100 acres on the Mlazi river and rented a further 100 for grazing, while in northern Natal, William Africa bought half of the farms Lyle and Williams Geluk.[7]

According to a valuation roll of colonial landowners drawn up in 1878, Africans owned 83 104 acres.[8]

Table 1   African-owned land in 1878 (acres)

Coastal counties		Midland divisions		Inland counties	
Alfred	39	Umgeni	15 291	Klip River	49 729
Alexandra	100	Ixopo	735	Weenen	11 167
Durban	921	Upper Umkomazi	1 340		
Victoria	3 782				
Total	4 842		17 366		60 896

Source: Natal Government Gazette, Supplement, March 1881.

In addition to these rural lands, Africans owned seven properties in Pietermaritz-burg, eighteen in Stanger, eight in Ladysmith, two in Newcastle and one in Weenen.

With one or two exceptions, these lands were held by *kholwa*. There were no legal restrictions on African purchases and most of the lands were registered in their owners' names.[9] Homestead Africans who wanted to purchase land were faced with social restraints. In a society which had no concept of individual tenure, men risked either chiefly or lineage disapproval by making individual purchases. However, faced with a growing land shortage, a number of chiefs were beginning to realize that if they were not to lose adherents, they had little option but to consider purchasing land. By 1880, Chief Mqawe had bought 9 000 acres in Inanda, while other chiefs throughout the colony, particularly in Ixopo and Alexandra, were appealing to the Secretary for Native Affairs for permission to purchase Crown lands adjoining their reserves. Some chiefs were depositing 'considerable sums of money' with agents or missionaries in the expectation of purchasing Crown lands.[10]

Since the speculators were releasing only small areas of their lands onto the market, settler and African pressure on the government to open up the remaining 4 620 000 acres of Crown lands grew insistent. To prevent these lands from falling into the hands of speculators, the government had suspended purchases in 1873, but in 1878 the Land and Immigration Board suggested that Crown lands again be offered for sale to meet the growing land hunger. The government drew up rules and regulations based on the board's recommendations and published them in the *Government Gazette* on 16 October 1880.[11]

Apart from lands in Newcastle division and certain forest- and coal-bearing lands, Crown lands were to be placed on the market in freehold lots varying in size from 10 to 2 000 acres. When a lot was applied for, it was to be publicly auctioned at an upset price of 10s. an acre, payment to be made in ten equal annual instalments. The purchaser had to occupy the land 'beneficially', which meant building a suitable house and cultivating not less than one acre in every hundred. After three years, a certificate of beneficial occupation would have to be obtained every following year from the district magistrate, and title to the land would be given on payment of the final instalment.

These stipulations indicate that the administration wanted the sale of Crown lands to benefit bona fide agriculturalists and not absentee speculators, as had happened when Crown lands in the Eastern Cape were sold.[12] And, although its priority was to address the land needs of the settlers, the government was anxious that sales should not exacerbate the land shortage by causing the eviction of the 42 600 Africans squatting on Crown lands.

As has been seen, Africans did not distinguish between Crown and reserve lands; in their opinion both were government land and were equally open to settlement. In the case of chiefdoms which had been placed on Crown lands by Theophilus Shepstone, there was very little alternative suitable land available to them if they received eviction orders. Sir Henry Bulwer was particularly concerned about the consequences of eviction and his fears were fed by Shepstone's dire warnings that the growing land shortage could lead to serious agrarian disturbances.[13]

Although Africans had occasionally purchased Crown lands before 1873,[14] the administration was reluctant to allow individual homestead Africans to buy land as this would endanger the chiefs' powers of distribution. In 1881, Sir Henry Bulwer instructed the Native Affairs Commission to investigate whether such Africans should be allowed to bid for Crown lands. In a majority report, the commissioners pointed out that as landownership tended to enhance cultivation techniques, 'it seems to us unwise . . . to exclude from buying land the very class of persons who it is in some sense specially important should purchase – that is, persons needing most these beneficial influences'.[15] Bulwer and the Acting Secretary for Native Affairs, John Shepstone, agreed with this decision,[16] and in 1882 magistrates were told to advise Africans that they were entitled to bid when local lots came up for auction. The Surveyor-General, Dr Sutherland, was also a strong supporter of African purchases. At his insistence, a government agent, W. Adams, was appointed to explain the terms of sale to Africans and, if necessary, to act for them at the auctions.[17] The government's concern to protect the interests of African squatters on Crown lands was in sharp contrast to the situation in the Eastern Cape where the sale of Crown lands has been interpreted as a deliberate attempt by the Cape government to force squatters into wage labour.[18] In Natal, the Executive

Council remained committed to defending their interests until the 1890s, and often refused to sell lands on which large numbers of squatters resided.[19] This commitment was seldom reflected at the local level, however. Many magistrates ignored the instruction to inform squatters when auctions were pending, while the government agent proved to be equally negligent in carrying out Sutherland's instructions.[20]

Conditions for purchase were favourable in the early 1880s. The army's demand for labour, oxen and transport riders during the wars against the Zulu and the Transvaal had increased the amount of money circulating in Natal. Consequently, many settlers and Africans could afford the initial instalment. As agricultural produce was fetching high prices and stock farming was profitable, 10s. an acre seemed a reasonable price. Within months of the appearance of the notice in the *Government Gazette*, applications began pouring in and by the end of 1883, 528 lots comprising 485 069 acres had been sold for an amount of £267 632 9s. 9d. with prices seldom exceeding 10s. an acre. Just over 25 per cent of these sales were to Africans who bought 200 lots comprising 123 415 acres at a total price of £65 215 18s. 2d. Nearly all the lands purchased by Africans were in south-western Natal, totalling 66 239 acres in Ixopo, 37 507 in Alfred, 8 448 in Alexandra and 5 717 in Upper Umkomazi. The only other purchases were 2 651 acres in Klip River and 2 853 in Umsinga.[21]

A large proportion of the sales in south-western Natal were to those chiefs who had been imploring the Native Affairs Department for additional land. In most cases, these chiefs purchased either lands on which a portion of their chiefdom had already settled, or adjoining lands.[22] These purchases were usually in blocks of 2 000 acres, and the chiefs' followers were expected to contribute to the annual instalments. The government recognized that this could lead to legal conflicts. Under African law the land purchased could not be alienated without the consent of the chiefdom, but the deeds of sale were registered according to colonial law in the name of the chief as an individual.[23] There was thus no legal guarantee that land bought in a chief's name would belong to the people who paid for it. Sutherland urged that a trust deed be devised to protect the latters' interests but was defeated by official inertia. A more pressing problem, however, was that the chiefs might not be able to enforce contributions from their people. This was realized as early as 1882 when a number of chiefs were unable to raise the first instalment and thus forfeited their land.[24]

By 1884, the boom of the wartime years was giving way to a severe depression. Applications for Crown lands dried up and in 1884 and 1885 sales plummeted to 70 225 and 83 371 acres respectively. Of these, only 10 419 were purchased by Africans in sharp contrast to the situation in 1881–83.[25] Those men who had already made purchases were also struggling to maintain their annual instalments. Many of them had expected to meet their instalments either through the sale of agricultural produce or by transport riding. However, the depression was accompanied by a slump in the price of the former and a steady reduction in transport rates.[26] Of the 528 lots sold by the end of 1883, arrears had accumulated on 219. Africans were finding it particularly difficult to raise the necessary money; they had bought 136 of the 219 lots which were in arrears and were responsible for £6 589 15s. 8d. of the £11 861 8s. 0d. of land debt. In other words, although Africans had purchased 25,4 per cent of the lands between 1881 and 1883, they owed 55,5 per cent of the total arrears. Of the 200 lots they had bought, they were in arrears on 136. As the depression deepened, so African debt steadily increased and by January 1887 they owed £15 636.[27]

From 1884, the government was inundated with requests from white and African purchasers for an extension of the time allowed for payment of instalments. The deeds of sale explicitly stated that should a purchaser fail to meet an annual instalment, the sale would be cancelled and all prior payments be forfeited. The Executive Council was only too aware that the whole purpose of the sales would be negated if these terms were enforced. Consequently, it agreed to waive the terms and to grant extensions for all instalments bar the first. (If the first instalment was not paid the land was automatically forfeited.) It was, however, obvious that not even an extension would help all purchasers. To overcome this problem, the Executive Council accepted Sutherland's suggestion that the amount such men had already paid should be credited against a portion of the land that they had bought. This would mean that although their lots would be reduced in size, the purchasers would no longer be in arrears, and their future instalments would be relatively small.[28]

Many African purchasers took advantage of the concession and surrendered a portion of their lands, while no attempt was made by the Surveyor-General to confiscate the lands of those who ignored the offer and remained in arrears. Sutherland also ignored the condition of sale which required purchasers to occupy land beneficially and to build a suitable house. By 1885, realizing that few Africans were in a position to observe this clause, the government accepted that it implied the erection of a building suitable for the purchaser 'as a Native'.[29]

As a firm supporter of purchases by Africans, Sutherland was prepared to bend over backwards to ensure that they retained their lands. But he retired in February 1887 and, because of the continuing economic depression, his office was merged with that of the Colonial Engineer, Col. Albert Hime. With Hime in charge, there was a marked change in official policy. He made it clear that, with the work of two offices to perform, he had no time 'to deal with these complicated Native cases'.[30] His attitude was far less sympathetic than Sutherland's had been. He was, for example, adamant that many Africans were not paying their instalments because they were not being compelled to do so.[31] Certainly, there were cases which proved his point. In 1883, Stephanus Mini bought a 1 250 acre farm, Eden, on the Mkomazi river in Ipolela; by 1888, he had paid no instalments, despite drawing rents from 45 huts on the farm.[32] In cases such as this, Hime vigorously followed up the arrear instalments. Even so, he seldom took the necessary action to enforce payments and cancel contracts of sale, since this required litigation in the Supreme Court, a tedious and expensive process.[33]

By 1889, a total of 812 306 acres of Crown lands had been sold at a price of £444 025 2s. 11d., an average of 10s. 9d. an acre. Of these sales, whites had purchased 664 388 acres at £366 407 6s. 6d. (an average of 11s. an acre) while Africans had purchased 147 918 acres for £77 617 16s. 5d. or an average of 10s. 6d. an acre. African purchases therefore amounted to 18,2 per cent of the total. If surrendered lands are taken into account, a different picture emerges; 80 841 acres or 54,7 per cent of the lands purchased by Africans had been surrendered. By comparison, whites had surrendered 139 448 acres or 21 per cent of their lands.[34] The official figures of purchases for the years 1881 to 1889 are given in table 2.

Table 2   Land purchases from 1881 to 1889

	Acres	£
White	524 940	275 581
African	67 077	36 412
Total	592 017	311 993

The actual figure for African purchases was probably slightly lower, because some Africans sold their land instead of surrendering it. For example, two lots in Alexandra were sold to whites in 1885.[35] This was to become easier after August 1891 when the Supreme Court ruled that unexempted Africans with individual tenure could dispose of their land without any restrictions.[36]

In 1889, the Executive Council accepted that few purchasers would be able to pay off their instalments in ten years and increased the period of payment for new purchases to twenty years.[37] This resulted in a flood of applications from Africans, particularly for small holdings of between 200 and 500 acres. Between 1889 and 1890, the amount Africans purchased increased nearly twenty-fourfold, from 1 519 to 36 284 acres, a good proportion at considerably above the upset price.[38] The conditions under which a purchaser could surrender some of the land, if unable to meet payments, were also widened. Since 1886, purchasers of more than one lot had been allowed to surrender one and transfer the amount paid on it to one or more other properties; now credits could also be transferred from one purchaser to another. For example, Isidumka had bought land in Alexandra and had only paid one instalment. He was allowed to transfer this amount to the credit of D. Makabalo, who in return gave him a share in the farm Meadowlands.[39]

Throughout the 1880s, Crown lands were the most popular source of land for African purchasers. The chance of buying land in interest-free instalments was obviously attractive, as was the low upset price. Yet anxiety about defaulted payments led many prospective buyers to look elsewhere for land. On the American mission stations, the *kholwa* tried to persuade the missionaries to begin selling individual plots again, but the latter were reluctant to do so without a firm guarantee that purchasers would not be able to alienate their plots. As a result, consultations dragged on between the missionaries and the Attorney-General's office until the early twentieth century. As no legal solution could be reached, no mission lands were bought before 1909, when land at Charlotte Dale on the Umvoti Mission Reserve was made available.[40]

The sale of Crown lands had gone a long way towards opening up the remote districts of the colony. Because of this, there was a steady increase in land values and absentee landowners became more willing to offer their lands for sale. Between 1880 and 1890, they sold 200 027 acres. The Natal Land and Colonisation Company was particularly active and the land it held dropped from 545 655 to 443 343 acres between 1880 and 1890.[41] The company also offered lands on an instalment system, although it required an annual interest payment of 8 per cent.[42] While it was usually cheaper to buy Crown lands, absentee-owned farms were closer to markets. These usually went for a higher price than Africans could afford, but the Land and Colonisation Company encouraged both Africans and Indians to purchase its less well-placed lands by sub-dividing them into small plots of 5 to 150 acres each.[43]

Between 1878 and 1890, inclusive of those Crown lands which they had managed to retain, African landowners had increased their holdings from 83 104 to 210 952 acres.[44] As 67 077 were Crown lands, between these years, 60 771 acres of private lands must have been purchased. The position of African-owned land in 1890 compared to 1878 is set out in table 3.

Table 3   African-owned land in 1878 and 1890 (acres)

	1878	1890
Coastal counties:		
Alfred	39	13 928
Alexandra	100	4 782
Durban	921	921
Victoria	3 782	10 460
Total	4 842	30 091
Midland counties:		
Pietermaritzburg*	17 366	84 189
Umvoti	–	1 482
Total	17 366	85 671
Inland counties:		
Klip River	49 729	83 482
Weenen	11 167	11 708
Total	60 896	95 190

*In Table 1 the figures are given by division.

Source: Natal Government Gazette, Supplement, March 1881; A. J. Christopher, 'Natal: a study in colonial land settlement', Ph.D. thesis, University of Natal, 1969.

The marked increase in the amount of African-owned land in Alfred, Alexandra and Pietermaritzburg counties arose from purchases of Crown lands by chiefs. The increase was proportionately less in northern Natal, where the only extensive Crown lands were in Newcastle division and were only available on lease. In general, African lessees experienced greater problems than did African purchasers, mainly because they found themselves in opposition to the entrenched interests of the Afrikaner stockfarmers of the interior.

Fearful that their labour tenants might move onto African-leased lands, these farmers opposed African land leases. They went out of their way to prevent Africans from leasing, a common ploy being to attend sales and push up the bidding. This was not always successful, but it did mean that Africans usually had to pay higher prices than white farmers; in 1886, 5d. per acre compared to 2d.[45] This was not the end of the lessees' troubles, for they were often harassed by neighbouring farmers who disputed their boundaries, refused to accept surveyors' beacons, tried to evict lessees from their lands, or continued depasturing cattle on the leased areas.[46] Yet, by inflating the price an African lessee paid for his land, the farmers realized their own fears of losing labour tenants; many lessees were unable to meet their payments and began encouraging labour tenants to move on to their lands as squatters.[47] The high price of leases also discouraged chiefs in the area from bidding for the land with the result that most of the lessees were *kholwa*. The availablity of Crown-land leases therefore did little to solve the problems of land shortage that faced the chiefdoms of northern Natal.

African lessees were as affected by the depression as were purchasers of Crown lands and in 1887 the government offered to cancel their arrears of £2 947 on condition that each African lessee surrender his lease and pay a rental of £1 per hut for each year that he was in arrears. If he did this he could remain on the land as a squatter until it was re-leased. Many Africans took advantage of this offer and by 1892, twenty-one of the forty-one lots leased by Africans had been surrendered.[48]

If one considers the high incidence of land surrenders, it was clear by the beginning of the 1890s, that the Executive Council had failed in its intention of using the Crown lands to alleviate the growing African land shortage. Not only had Africans failed to become large-scale purchasers and lessees, but where Crown lands had been bought or leased by settlers, evictions had increased and exacerbated the problem. The decade of the 1880s was thus crucial in the process of African land impoverishment, a process intimately tied up with the onset of commercialized settler agriculture.

Crown-land purchases had created new opportunities for white farmers to increase their participation in the market economy, despite the considerable strains experienced by the agricultural community in mid-decade. The years of prosperity between 1879 and 1882 had been accompanied by an over-extension of credit which at one level manifested itself in the purchase of Crown lands. The depression and financial crisis of the mid-1880s caused many men to lose their purchased lands and severely hampered agricultural progress in the colony.

Natal's economy became even more reliant on the overberg trade, a trend which was accentuated by the discovery of gold on the Witwatersrand in 1886.

However, the development of the gold-fields not only made Natal more economically dependent on Transvaal trade, but also created new market and labour opportunities in the colony and encouraged the government to push ahead with the rail link to the republic. The result was an upsurge in immigration and a rise in land values, particularly in the midlands and on the coast. By 1893 the settler population had increased to 43 742 with most of the growth occurring in Durban and Pietermaritzburg and in towns such as Ladysmith, Newcastle and Dundee which expanded as the railway pushed northwards. Until the main railway line reached Johannesburg in 1895, it was given priority over branch lines within the colony. Yet, although the line bypassed the most fertile districts of Natal, the sale of Crown lands and the need to feed the growing urban population encouraged the settlers to begin improving roads and paying more attention to farm management in these districts. By 1890 there was a marked improvement in the position of white agriculture. Land in settler possession had increased from 5 300 000 acres in 1880 to 6 200 000 acres and, of the latter amount, only 772 977 acres, or 12,5 per cent, remained in the hands of speculators, land companies and banks. The number of farmers increased from 1 783 in 1882 to 2 570 in 1893.[49]

Progress was particularly marked in the coastal and midland areas. The development of a market for food, not only in the colony but also on the gold-fields, offered new opportunities for the settlers. It was becoming obvious that homestead agriculture was unlikely to be able to meet any additional demands made on it. Thus merchants were becoming more prepared to assist in the creation of a viable settler farming community capable of meeting food requirements. And, once they were assured of a market, a number of midland and coastal farmers responded by adopting more modern and scientific farming methods.[50]

On the coast, government support stimulated the expansion of the sugar industry. The slow-growing Uba cane was gaining in popularity, but greater acreage had to be planted for it to be economically successful.[51] By the end of the 1880s, virtually the whole coast was in the hands of capitalist planters who were casting covetous eyes on those lands which they did not own, such as the Umnini reserve.[52] In addition, the rapid growth of Durban encouraged the the expansion of fruit and vegetable cultivation around the city.

In the midlands, the grasslands of the mist belt were giving way to plantations of eucalyptus and wattle. Once the commercial value of black wattle (*Acacia mollissima*) as a tanning agent had been ascertained in 1887, its planting advanced rapidly and the country between Pietermaritzburg and Greytown soon became one continuous line of plantations.[53] By the 1890s, the government had also introduced loans for fencing farms which, together with the greater use of winter feeding, made the introduction of better breeds of cattle feasible and encouraged dairy farming. The mist belt was ideal dairy country and the introduction of pasteurization and of the central cream separator stimulated the industry. At the same time, the construction of the railway through Lion's River and the improvement of roads in the midlands made it economically feasible to produce butter and milk, while the introduction of refrigeration meant that dairy products could be supplied further afield than to Pietermaritzburg.[54]

Wattle and dairy farmers needed less land and began subdividing their farms or purchasing smaller Crown-land farms. Even in northern Natal, where commercialization only became significant in the twentieth century, there was a growing tendency for stockfarmers to lease part of their land to white tenants or to place bywoners on their winter-grazing farms.[55]

The development of a plantation economy on the coast and the spread of commercialized agriculture in the mist belt had profound consequences for local Africans. As the settlers began utilizing more land than before, old forms of African tenancy became uneconomic. Because of this, many farmers either evicted tenants from their lands, or restricted the amount of land they could use for gardens and grazing. Labour tenancy was only viable as long as a farmer's own production was limited. On lands where production was increased, farmers began to rely on migrant labour and some of them began emulating the planters by employing Indians or Africans from outside the colony.[56] None the less, few mist-belt farmers were able to rely solely on migrant labourers because they were unable to pay competitive wages. Accordingly, evictions were more common on the coast than they were in the midlands. In 1898 the Revd Bunker was particularly struck by the scarcity of *imizi* on private farms in Inanda.[57]

African access to land was also seriously affected by the increasing number of Indians in the colony. In 1882, there had been 24 865 Indians – located predominantly in the coastal counties. By 1893, their number had grown to 41 208 of whom 3 341 were listed in the 1891 census as self-employed farmers or market gardeners. These Indians tended to be intensive agriculturalists, and by the 1890s many either had bought or were leasing small farms.[58] Indian landowners did not always evict Africans and in many cases encouraged them to remain as labour tenants. Nevertheless, the fact that most Indians adopted intensive agriculture meant that their African tenants had insufficient arable or pastoral land.[59]

Indians were also beginning to squeeze African rent tenants off absentee-owned lands. Speculators such as the Land and Colonisation Company recognized that Indian methods of crop rotation were more beneficial to the land than was African monoculture. In addition, Indians, as successful market gardeners, could afford to pay higher rents. Accordingly, farms were leased to Indian tenants whenever possible, thereby forcing African rent tenants off the land or marginalizing them on less arable ground.[60]

Evictions also took place when Crown lands were sold and the squatters did not come to terms with the new owners. In many cases they were given no option, but were summarily served with notices to leave. In 1882, for example, of the 5 000 squatters on land that was sold in Ixopo, 2 150 were ordered off.[61] The continuing tenure of squatters was threatened as much by African purchasers as by those of other races. This was particularly the case when chiefs bought Crown lands, since they invariably evicted squatters belonging to other chiefdoms.[62]

But chiefs and their people could also be victims. In 1883, Chief Ramncana of the Duma applied to buy the Crown lands on which Theophilus Shepstone had settled his chiefdom. In the auction, however, he was outbid by Stephanus Mini and Stoffel Molife who ordered him to remove his people. As compensation, he was granted 3 000 acres in Ipolela by the government, but the land was useless for agriculture.[63]

Evictions caused more discontent in the 1880s than did any other factor. Not only were Africans faced with the difficulty of finding new land for their *imizi*, but evictions also meant they had to leave their ancestral graves, important sites of ritual observance. Yet when the victims of evictions turned to John Shepstone for help in 1881, they were informed that 'he had nothing to do with the land, and that [they] must go to someone else'.[64] John Shepstone's attitude was typical of the general inertia of the Native Affairs Department. But not even well-disposed members of the Executive Council like Gallwey and Sutherland could prevent evictions. To compound the problem, the government itself became guilty of evicting Africans when it alienated lands at Weenen, Marburg, and Dronk Vlei in Ixopo for immigration settlements.[65] Africans who were evicted, or left their lands to avoid labour services or rentals, had a limited choice of new lands. Where possible they moved onto remaining Crown land or onto private lands, even if this meant moving to different divisions. Alternatively they applied for permission to move out of the colony. As permission for such removals was only sparingly given, very few actually left.[66]

Most Africans were reluctant to move onto reserves because of the limited land available, and because they wanted to avoid chiefly control and *isibhalo* and other services. Despite this, the shortage of alternative land meant that many, particularly on the coast and in Umgeni division, had no other choice.[67] The result was increasing over-population in virtually all the reserves, and forced settlement on lands which could not even provide sufficient crops for their existing populations.[68] In Inanda the situation was so critical that Mqawe, despite having purchased land for his chiefdom, applied for permission in 1890 to move some of his people to Zululand.[69]

Mqawe's application reflects the growing despair gripping chiefs and their people in Natal as access to land became more difficult. It also reflects the failure of Crown-land sales to solve the worsening land shortage. Indeed, as has been seen, these sales were in many cases exacerbating the situation. The government appeared to be incapable of dealing with the problems resulting from these sales. Yet, for as long as it continued to encourage land purchases by Africans, it remained sympathetic to the difficulties which buyers experienced when trying to pay their annual instalments. But by the 1890s official attitudes were becoming harsher. Neither Hime nor the Assistant Surveyor-General, John Masson, shared Sutherland's concern for the rights of purchasers and instead made their position more difficult. The introduction of the twenty-year payment system in 1889 was followed by a tightening of the conditions under which Crown lands were held. In 1890 an Inspector of Crown Lands was appointed to ensure that the very liberal interpretation of beneficial occupation was enforced.[70] Then in 1893, this interpretation was tightened by amended regulations which stipulated the erection 'of permanent homestead buildings, including outbuildings, within two years from the date of sale of a value of not less than one-tenth of the full purchase price of the land' with a minimum value of £100.[71]

When Africans applied to buy lands, these conditions were explained to them and where the Surveyor-General felt that they could not comply with them, he refused to allow the sale to take place.[72] These conditions made it more difficult for Africans other than *kholwa* to purchase or retain Crown lands. The administration was also giving less publicity to Africans of intended sales. There no longer appears to have been an official appointed to do this and the only notification of sales appeared in the *Government Gazette*.[73]

In addition, as the farming community began flexing its muscles, it became more difficult for Africans to purchase lands. The role of the farmers of Newcastle in preventing Africans from becoming leaseholders has been mentioned. But throughout the colony, farmers were becoming ever more aware that if they could deprive Africans of access to land, they could limit their ability to amass cattle and grow crops. This would in turn undermine the homestead economy and force its inhabitants onto the labour market. The influence of the farming community increased markedly after the granting of responsible government in 1893. Although both the Prime Minister, Sir John Robinson, and the Attorney-General, Harry Escombe, favoured individual land ownership,[74] they did little to reverse the already apparent trend or to prevent the Surveyor-General's Office from introducing ever more stringent regulations. Under the new constitution, the work previously done by Hime was handled by the Minister of Lands and Works, Thomas Murray. He was totally opposed to African purchases, an attitude shared by Masson,[75] who was promoted to fill the reinstated post of Surveyor-General. The new Secretary for Native Affairs, Frederick Moor, was more ambivalent; although he approved of the progress associated with land ownership, he was afraid that it would undermine the chiefly hierarchy. With his antipathy to the *kholwa*, he was also afraid that individual land ownership might strengthen their demands for social and political equality.[76]

Although no attempt was made to prevent Africans from purchasing the Crown lands of Newcastle and Dundee when they were offered for sale in 1894,[77] the new attitude was soon felt in other ways. Requests for extensions were not granted as readily and sales were revoked when instalments were not met. In 1896 a new burden was placed on purchasers when interest of 5 per cent per annum was introduced on arrears. African purchasers were also discouraged by the raising of the requirements for beneficial occupation to include the erection of permanent improvements valued at £200 within two years.[78]

The beneficial occupation regulations were enforced with vigour. Purchasers found it difficult to obtain certificates, and even men who never missed paying an instalment had their lands confiscated for contravening these regulations. In 1897, the Inspector of Crown Lands reported that he had granted certificates to only four of the twenty-four Africans who had purchased farms in Newcastle division in 1896.[79] The transfer of money from one piece of land to another was also stopped. This caused considerable losses to Africans such as Lutuli and Nyongo who, in surrendering lot FP 65, had to abandon houses and £52 worth of fencing. Similarly, the Revd Mzamo forfeited £192 when he was unable to pay his sixth instalment on lot 8, Umhlabatyan.[80]

By the 1890s, a new trend appeared of Africans grouping together in syndicates and bidding for Crown lands. These purchases were usually made by *kholwa*, and by the mid-1890s had become common, particularly in northern Natal. If there were sufficient members in the syndicate, there was often very little difference between the annual instalment paid by each member and the rent he would have had to pay as a tenant.[81] Legally there were similarities between purchases by syndicates and purchases by chiefs, for the law did not recognize a syndicate as a purchaser and the sales had to be registered in the names of one or two members. Because of this, the individual members of a syndicate had no legal right to the land. As problems concerning individual rights, access to land and inheritance arose, the syndicates began seeking legal advice on how to protect their members.[82]

In 1896, ostensibly in an attempt to protect the interests of the individual members of the syndicates, Frederick Tatham introduced a bill into the Legislative Assembly to provide for the 'regulation and management of associations of Natives which have acquired, or may hereafter acquire, property'. Had the bill become law, it would have effectively restricted the independent ownership of such lands by empowering the Natal Native Trust to make regulations governing their occupation. Because of this, a group of African landowners petitioned Parliament against the bill and it was withdrawn by Tatham after the ministry announced that it was not prepared to support it.[83] Despite Tatham's rhetoric, the bill reflects the growing concern of farmers and particularly the stockfarmers of northern Natal that syndicate purchasers would threaten their labour supply by encouraging labour tenants to abscond from their farms.[84]

African purchases had been seen as a way of solving the land shortage and of encouraging the spread of European agricultural techniques. The fact that few African cultivators continued to prosper outside areas such as northern Natal where white agriculture remained underdeveloped, raises doubts that the latter aim was ever achieved, even on *kholwa*-owned farms. By 1901 Africans in the colony owned only 382 227 acres,[85] thus land purchases did little to solve the land shortage, particularly in the face of increasing population numbers. By the 1890s, Africans throughout the colony faced a land crisis. At the same time, they had fewer and fewer alternative sources of wealth to draw on, as will be discussed in later chapters. The factor which was to dominate interracial attitudes and relationships in the twentieth century, and which to a certain extent had been present since the start of the colonial period, the interrelationship between land occupation and labour utilization, was now beginning to dominate political and economic conditions. As settler farming expanded and became more commercialized in the late nineteenth century, the seriousness of the impending crisis facing Africans became more apparent.

Notes

1. Natal, *Evidence . . . Natal Native Commission, 1881*, Maweli, p.203, Kukulela, p.232, Madude, p.240, Umsutu, p.367.
2. *Natal Mercury*, 23 November 1875.
3. Natal, *Report . . . Native population*, 1879, p.14; *Natal Mercury*, 7 February 1881; Natal, *Evidence . . . Natal Native Commission, 1881*, Umnini, p.194, Madude, p.242.
4. SNA, 1/3/23, Magistrate, Alexandra to SNA, 11 August 1873, p.727; 1/3/26, 726/76, 10 September 1876.
5. M. Chanock, 'Paradigms, policies and property: a review of the customary law of land tenure', in R. Roberts and K. Mann, eds, *Law in colonial Africa*, London, 1991, p.64.
6. SNA, 1/1/10, 163/60, Memorandum by Shepstone, 15 May 1860.
7. Natal, *Evidence . . . Natal Native Commission, 1881*, Matiwane, p.149; NL&C, 135, Bruce to General Manager, Durban, no.197, 28 June 1881; no.225, 4 July 1881; no.271, 8 July 1881.
8. *NGG*, Supplement, March 1881. Other lands could have been registered in white names.
9. Natal, *Evidence . . . Natal Native Commission, 1879*, Allsopp, p.29.
10. Natal, *Evidence . . . Natal Native Commission, 1881*, Mqawe, p.225; Natal, *Report . . . Native population*, 1879, p.43; 1880, p.JJ121; SNA, 1/1/39, 350/80, Magistrate, Ixopo to SNA, 17 June 1880; CO 179, 134, no.155, Governor to Secretary of State, 7 August 1880.
11. *LC Sessional Papers*, 19, 1878, Bulwer to Legislative Council, 20 July 1878; 32, 1878/9, Rules and regulations for the disposal of the Crown lands, 4 February 1880, pp.197–201; *NGG*, XXXII, no.1849, 19 October 1880, Proclamation, pp.735–37.
12. S. Dubow, *Land, labour and merchant capital in the pre-industrial rural economy of the Cape: the experience of the Graaff-Reinet district (1852–1872)*, Cape Town, 1982, pp.8–11.
13. Natal, *Evidence . . . Natal Native Commission, 1881*, T. Shepstone, p.286; CO 179, 140, Natal 1848, Shepstone memorandum, 1881; see also Sir Evelyn Wood Collection, III/3/8, Wood to Kimberley, 2 October 1881.
14. *Natal Witness*, 3 April 1866.
15. Natal, *Report of the Natal Native Commission, 1881–2*, p.9.
16. GH, 1058, 437/83, Governor to SNA, 28 September 1883, SNA to Governor, 5 October 1883.
17. SNA, 1/1/39, 350/80, Surveyor-General to SNA, 28 July 1882; CSO, 2773, Crown Lands Commission, 1885, Evidence, Surveyor-General; Surveyor-General's Office [Natal Archives] (SGO), III/1/48, 52/81, Surveyor-General to Colonial Secretary, 14 June 1881; *Natal Witness*, 25 August 1881.
18. Dubow, *Land, labour and merchant capital*, p.44.
19. See SGO, III/1/89, 93/93, Minutes, January to August 1893.
20. Natal, *Correspondence . . . eviction of Native occupants from Crown lands*, Attorney-General's report, 10 April 1883, p.7; *Natal Witness*, 13 June 1883.
21. *NBB Departmental reports*, 1884, pp.Z4–6; *NBB*, 1881, p.FF117. Whites purchased 328 lots comprising 361 655 acres at a purchase price of £202 417 5s. 3d.
22. SNA, 1/1/39, 350/80, Surveyor-General to SNA, 28 July 1882; 1/1/75, 530/84, Governor to SNA, 24 March 1884.
23. Natal, *Report of the Natal Native Commission, 1881–2*, p.9.
24. *NBB*, 1882, p.FF106.

25. *NBB Departmental reports*, 1884, p.Z6; 1885, p.Z7.
26. Natal, *Crown Lands Commission, 1886*, p.4. *NBB Departmental reports*, 1884, p.H2; SNA, 1/1/75, 530/84, Magistrate, Alfred to Colonial Secretary, 12 July 1883; SGO, III/1/56, 624/86, Surveyor-General to Colonial Secretary, 19 May 1886.
27. SGO, III/1/53, 2120/84, List of arrear instalments, 1884; III/1/57, 1531/86, Surveyor-General to Colonial Secretary, 20 January 1887. White purchasers owed £23 307.
28. SNA, 1/1/75, 530/84, Governor-in-Council to Colonial Secretary, 24 August 1883, SNA to Magistrate, Alfred, 14 February 1884; CSO, 2773, Crown Lands Commission, 1885, Evidence, Surveyor-General; SGO, III/1/53, 2120/84, Surveyor-General to Colonial Secretary, 21 October 1884.
29. CSO, 2773, Crown Lands Commission, 1885, Evidence, Surveyor-General.
30. SNA, 1/1/99, 441/87, Surveyor-General to SNA, 13 September 1887.
31. *LC Hansard*, IX, 9 November 1886, Colonial Engineer, p.270.
32. SNA, 1/1/112, 77/89, Administrator of Native Law, Ipolela to Magistrate, Ixopo, 16 March 1889; SGO, III/1/77,4587/90, Mini to Surveyor-General, 19 December 1890.
33. *NBB Departmental reports*, 1896, p.H138.
34. *NBB*, 1884–1889; *NBB Departmental reports*, 1890/1, p.H107.
35. CSO, 2773, Crown Lands Commission, 1885, Abstract of unoccupied lands.
36. Kannemeyer, 'New Bantu society', pp.220–1.
37. *NGG*, XLI, 2383, 24 September 1889, Proclamation 48, 1889, p.1221.
38. *Natal Mercury*, 27 January 1893; CSO, 2775, Immigration and Crown Lands Commission, 1891, Masson, p.732; *Natal Witness*, 24 October 1890.
39. SGO, III/1/77, 4308/90, Harris to Surveyor-General, 28 November 1890.
40. Switzer, 'Problems of an African mission', pp.111–4.
41. Christopher, 'Natal land settlement', pp.246, 277, 351.
42. See Parkinson Accession, [Natal Archives], 1, General Manager, Durban, NL&C, to Parkinson, 3 June 1892.
43. See NL&C, 204, no.287, Frances to General Manager, Durban, 7 September 1892; 231, no.108, Essery to General Manager, Durban, 21 April 1898; *SANAC*, 3, Essery, pp.685–6.
44. The figures for 1890 are based on Christopher, 'Natal land settlement', p.276. He gives a figure of 7 148 acres for Victoria and shows that Africans in Durban possessed no land. He appears to have placed land owned by Africans on the American missions with church-owned lands.
45. *NBB Departmental reports*, 1884, p.B34; *NBB*, 1885–1892.
46. CSO, 2557, c80/83, Magistrate, Newcastle to Colonial Secretary, 25 August 1883; c117/83, Magistrate, Newcastle to Colonial Secretary, 28 November 1883.
47. *NBB Departmental reports*, 1886, p.B49.
48. SGO, III/1/60, 845/87, SNA to Magistrate, Newcastle, 22 March 1887; *NBB*, 1885–1892; *LC Sessional Papers*, 33, 1891, Leases of Crown lands . . .
49. Christopher, 'Natal land settlement', pp.248,277; *NBB*, 1882, p.T5, X3; 1892/3, p.T5, X3.
50. *Natal Witness*, 9 July 1889; *Natal Mercury*, 23 September 1889.
51. P. Richardson, 'The Natal sugar industry in the nineteenth century', in W. Beinart, *et al.*, eds, *Putting a plough to the ground: accumulation and dispossession in rural South Africa, 1850–1930*, Johannesburg, 1986, pp.153–4.
52. *LC Hansard*, XIV, 12 June 1890, pp.329f.
53. Ibid., XVIII, Ryley, 6 June 1893, p.113.
54. C.J. Smythe Papers, [Killie Campbell Africana Library], Diary 8, 31 December 1886; *Natal Witness*, 4 July 1891, 5 January 1893, 5 January 1894, 8 June 1894; R.O. Pearse, *Joseph Baynes, pioneer*, Pietermaritzburg, 1983, pp.63–4.
55. See *Natal Witness*, 13 April 1894; Natal, *Evidence given before the Lands Commission (1900–01–02)*, Pietermaritzburg, 1903, Brown, p.347.
56. *LC Hansard*, XIII, 28 May 1889, Symons, p.157; *Natal Mercury*, 13 July 1888.
57. ABM, A/4/59, Circular letter from Bunker, October 1898.
58. *NBB*, 1894/5. p.B21; see also SNA, 1/1/87, 711/85, Answers to circulars on the amount of rent charged, 1885.
59. See Natal, *Report . . . Native population*, 1895, p.108; 1898, p.BB18; 1901, p.B58. Webb and Wright, eds, *James Stuart archive*, 1, Mapeka, 27 December 1898, p.148.

60. *LC Hansard*, VII, 19 August 1884, Robinson and Hulett, p. 485; NL&C, 183, no. 142, Haynes to General Manager, Durban, 13 January 1887.
61. Natal, *Correspondence . . . eviction of Native occupants from Crown lands, 1883*, Magistrate, Ixopo, n.d., p. 26.
62. SNA, 1/1/87, 711/85, Magistrate, Alfred to SNA, n.d.
63. SNA, 1/1/85, 448/82, Mini to Administrator of Native Law, Ipolela, 19 January 1883; 1/1/93, 814/86, Acting Clerk, Executive Council to Private Secretary, Governor, 10 October 1885; Ipolela Administrator of Native Law, 9, Administrator to SNA, 1 September 1881, p. 315; 10, Administrator to SNA, 14 March 1884.
64. Natal, *Evidence . . . Natal Native Commission, 1881*, Representative of Ungangezwe, p. 255.
65. *Natal Mercury*, 26 September 1891; SNA, 1/1/69, 865/84, Magistrate, Alexandra to SNA, 2 December 1884; 1/1/145, 898/91, Magistrate, Ixopo to SNA, 5 and 24 August 1891.
66. *NBB*, 1883, p. GG54; *NBB Departmental reports*, 1884, pp. B16–17; Upper Umkomazi Magistracy, 3/2/2, 109/92, Magistrate to SNA, 26 March 1892; Upper Tugela Administrator of Native Law, 4, 12/83, Administrator to SNA, 18 March 1883, p. 170; SNA, 1/1/139, 333/91, Governor, Cape to Governor, Natal, 24 March 1891; Natal, *Auditor's report on the public accounts*, 1887, p. 9; NPP, 156, 18/91, Return of Natives who received permission to leave the colony.
67. *NBB*, 1881, p. GG8; SNA, 1/1/94, 945/86, SNA to Colonial Secretary, 13 January 1887; Natal, *Evidence . . . Natal Native Commission, 1881*, Walker, p. 69, Teteleku, p. 186.
68. Natal, *Correspondence . . . eviction of Native occupants from Crown lands, 1883*, Acting SNA's report, 18 August 1882, p. 13.
69. SNA, 1/1/134, 1478/90, Administrator of Native Law, Ifamasi to Magistrate, Inanda, n.d.
70. *Natal Witness*, 1 November 1890.
71. *NGG*, XLV, 2611, 25 April 1893, Proclamation 18, 1893, p. 370.
72. SGO, III/1/89, 93/93, Asst. Surveyor-General to SNA, 8 August 1893.
73. For African complaints about this see *Inkanyiso Yase Natal*, 16 April 1891.
74. *LC Hansard*, XIV, 12 June 1890, Robinson, p. 333, 1 July 1890, Escombe, p. 452.
75. CSO, 2775, Immigration and Crown Lands Commission, 1891, Masson, pp. 731–2.
76. *SANAC*, 3, Moor, pp. 213f.
77. *NGG*, XLVI, no. 2656, 16 January 1894, GN 30, 1894, p. 35; 20 February 1894, Proclamation 4, 1894, pp. 117–18. Newcastle division had been divided into two divisions.
78. See SGO, III/1/90, 3190/93, Minister of Lands and Works to Surveyor-General, 16 June 1894; *NGG*, XLVIII, no. 2792, 21 April 1896, Proclamation 21, p. 480; *Natal Mercury*, 16 September 1896.
79. SGO, III/1/120, 3076/97, Inspector of Crown Lands to Surveyor-General, 22 February 1897; see also III/1/111, 2868/96, Minister of Lands and Works to Surveyor-General, 10 September 1896.
80. SGO, III/1/94, 920/94, Surveyor-General to Minister of Lands and Works, 12 March 1894; III/1/96, 2430/94, Surveyor-General to USNA, 11 July 1894, USNA to Surveyor-General, 16 July 1894; III/1/103, 3845/95, Surveyor-General to Minister of Lands and Works, 18 September 1895.
81. SGO, III/1/89, 93/93, Surveyor-General to Colonial Secretary, 6 January 1893; Crocker to Surveyor-General, 22 March 1893.
82. See SGO, III/1/109, 2084/96, Anderson to Surveyor-General, 28 May 1896.
83. *LA Hansard*, XXIV, 16 April 1896, Tatham, p. 65, 7 May 1896, Tatham, p. 189.
84. *SANAC*, 3, Wiltshire, pp. 390–1.
85. *LA Sessional Papers*, no. 3, 1901, p. 25.

CHAPTER SIX

Land and Labour
in the 1880s and 1890s

The development of settler agriculture in the last two decades of the nineteenth century had far-reaching consequences for the homestead economy and for African society as a whole. Sir Henry Bulwer's hope that Crown-land sales would alleviate the growing African land shortage did not materialize. Moreover, the rising value of land prevented many Africans from purchasing privately owned land. This was particularly so on the north coast where there was a chronic land shortage by the 1880s.

Africans most directly affected by Crown-land sales were those who were evicted when the lands were purchased by outsiders. Yet even those who were allowed to remain had their gardens and grazing lands reduced and often had to provide labour to the new owners. The difficulty of meeting annual instalments also encouraged many purchasers to persuade African squatters to move onto their lands as rent tenants.[1]

Rent tenancy was especially prevalent on Crown lands purchased by *kholwa*, many of whom bought lands with the intention of drawing high rents from them.[2] For example, the farm Eden, bought by Stephanus Mini, in Ipolela division reverted to the Crown in 1888 after he had defaulted on his instalments. He successfully bid for the farm again in the subsequent auction and, by encouraging more Africans to move their *imizi* onto it, he was able to meet all his instalments by the end of the century. He charged an annual rental of 30s. if tenants provided labour and £3 if they only paid rent.[3]

African rent tenants on absentee-owned lands also faced new difficulties. The rise in the value of agricultural land encouraged absentee landowners to sell their better-placed lands and to lease the rest to white and Indian farmers. By the 1890s, the Natal Land and Colonisation Company was drawing one-third of its rural rents from white and Indian tenants.[4] And, as it became less reliant on African rents, the company began tightening the conditions under which squatting was allowed. On some of its farms, Africans who used ploughs were charged higher rentals, while on others, tenants were forbidden to own ploughs and had to hire from the company. For a similar reason, tenants were often not allowed to keep bulls and stallions.[5] In the 1890s, additional restrictions were placed on the amount of land tenants could cultivate, particularly on farms about to be placed on the market.[6] Other landowners were also beginning to limit stock numbers, while on the Wilgefontein agricultural settlement outside Pietermaritzburg, tenants were forbidden to graze their cattle on the commonage.[7]

On absentee-owned lands which were leased to white and Indian tenants, Africans who were not evicted were allowed to remain on condition that they restricted their cultivation and grazing and provided the lessees with labour. This did not, however, release them from paying rent to the landowner.[8] The demand for labour caused considerable friction on some Land and Colonisation Company lands, particularly those under the supervision of the agent E. Essery, who in 1892 complained to the general manager that Africans would not work, 'especially if they think they are in any sort compelled or induced to work for the Company'.[9] In order to enforce labour demands, the company began appointing *izinduna* or employing policemen to supervise its tenants.[10]

Some absentee landowners also restricted the amount of land available to rent tenants by leasing gardens and grazing to neighbouring farmers.[11] Although grazing licences were only valid between harvesting in June and planting in August each year, most licence holders ignored the condition, with the result that Africans complained of damage to their crops. There were other causes of friction. On the Land and Colonisation Company farm Faith, for example, tenants complained that lungsick cattle from a neighbouring farm were grazing on their land and infecting their herds.[12]

Despite these disadvantages and restrictions, African tenants were expected to pay steadily increasing rents, with the result that accusations of rack-renting became common.[13] It is difficult to ascertain how widespread rack-renting was, but complaints became more common as the century progressed. Many landowners continued to charge reasonable rents, or even lowered them to attract *imizi* onto their lands. On Oaklands, for example, T. Reynolds charged £1 per hut in 1881 in order to attract *imizi* from a neighbouring Land and Colonisation Company farm where the rent was £2.[14] But the general trend seems to have been for higher rentals and, as agents usually received a commission based on the amount they collected, it was to their advantage to charge as high a rent as possible.[15]

With its enormous holdings, the Land and Colonisation Company incurred most charges of rack-renting, accusations that the general manager's letter books bear out. These abound with complaints that the company's agents were squeezing as much out of tenants as possible. One agent, for example, reluctantly admitted in 1881 that he was afraid of charging more than £2 a hut on the farm Spionkop in case the tenants left. However, he continued; 'I told the kafirs . . . that if they did not locate more kafirs I should either add to the rent or take the farm from them.'[16] Furthermore, by the late 1880s, the company's board of directors in London was complaining that rents were too low and demanded an annual increase in the amount collected. In 1890, the London Secretary ordered the general manager in Durban to increase rentals on all company farms, commenting that he supposed that 'this will not be squeezing the kafirs sufficiently to cause any public notice to be taken of it?'[17] In response, the general manager instructed his agents to increase rents either by 'squeezing' more money out of those Africans already on the farms, or by settling more *imizi* on each. In 1894, Essery instructed the *induna* on the farm Pootje, south of Camperdown, to so increase the number of *imizi* on the farm that the rent would be doubled.[18] Increasing rents meant that despite the amount of land held by the company dropping from 545 655 acres in 1879 to 394 142 acres in 1896, rents from African tenants alone were £7 358 11s. 3d. in the latter year compared to the company's total rental receipts of £9 346 13s. 2d. in 1879. By the early 1890s, the minimum rent appears to have increased from 20s. to 30s. a hut; the average rent was between £2 and £4 a hut, while tenants who built 'square' houses were charged £2 a room.[19]

As alternative land sources dried up, rent tenants often had little option other than to accept the increased demands being made on them. This was particularly so on the coast and in the mist belt where the land shortage was acute and tenants knew that they could easily be replaced if they were unable to pay higher rents. As the commercialization of settler agriculture expanded in these parts of the colony, rent tenants on the few remaining absentee-owned lands near towns and villages saw their rents soaring as high as £10 a hut.[20] In northern Natal where the commercialization of settler agriculture had not yet got underway, rents remained more reasonable as the landowners knew that there were other lands available to which rent tenants could move. Consequently, in the interior the Land and Colonisation Company charged an average annual rent in the early 1890s of only 30s.[21] Local stockfarmers, however, were exacting less labour from their tenants on winter-grazing farms and were instead demanding rent as well as labour.[22]

Because of tightening conditions of occupation, higher rents, and increased population numbers on farms, rent tenancy was becoming less attractive than it had been in earlier decades. It was still preferable to labour tenancy, however, and many rent tenants were still resilient enough to protect their own interests. White tenants on company farms often found this out to their own cost. Many had only leased the farms because of the resident labour supply, yet they found that the tenants often refused to work unless they received stock in payment.[23]

Yet evidence of the general hardship which rent tenants were facing is found in steadily increasing complaints from landowners of how difficult it was to collect rents.[24] Previous rent increases had been offset by the rising price of grain; now the tenants' problems were compounded by the downturn in the price of maize after the early 1880s.

As rentals increased and conditions for homestead production deteriorated, the number of Africans being sued for non-payment of rent steadily increased. In 1887, there were 761 court cases in the colony, 351 in the midlands and 321 on the coast, while 268 of the latter were in Lower Tugela alone. When judgement was given against the rent tenant and he was unable to pay, his cattle were attached, even where their value exceeded the amount owed. For example, in one case in

Upper Umkomazi in 1887, six head were attached as payment for arrears of
£8 3s. 2d. even though cattle in the division were valued at £5 a head. In another
case, ten head were taken for payment of arrears of £15 3s. 7d.[25] Debtors with
insufficient stock were imprisoned, often more than once for the same debt, and
could be evicted after serving their prison sentence.[26] In most court cases, however,
those convicted of defaulting were able to raise the money. Of the 761 tenants sued
for arrears in 1887, property was confiscated in only 73 cases.[27] But in many of
these cases rent tenants had to sell stock in order to pay. The sale of sheep to meet
arrear rents gathered momentum, and by the 1890s there were few African-owned
flocks left in the midlands.[28] Other means of raising money for the increased rents
included Africans selling a larger part of their harvest or sending young men out to
earn wages. With the onset of a drought cycle in 1888, wage labour became the
only viable option for many *imizi*.[29]

On farms where mixed rent/labour tenancy agreements had been common in
earlier decades, more labour was now being demanded and the tenants had to
accept restrictions on the size of their gardens and their use of grazing lands. In
1894, George Sutton pointed out in his weekly agricultural column in the *Natal
Witness*, 'Country Notes', that farmers 'will find they cannot keep natives on their
farms under the existing state of affairs. What natives they keep will have to be
fenced off from the farmer's grazing. Their rent will have to be raised and their
wages accordingly. The stock kept by natives will have to be in proportion to the
rent they pay.'[30]

By the 1890s, a Lion's River farmer, Charles Smythe, was insisting that
Africans who wanted to remain on his farms agree to conditions that severely
limited their freedom.[31] He no longer allowed tenants to cut wood and stopped
accepting responsibility for damage that his cattle might do to their gardens.
Despite the pressures this placed on his tenants to supplement their incomes by
sending young men out to work, even this would in future require his consent.
Although tenants were obviously reluctant to accept such oppressive conditions,
their bargaining power was declining as their difficulty increased in finding land
elsewhere. In accepting these conditions Africans saw their gardens diminished,
their cattle *sisa*'d to those who still had sufficient grazing land, and their
independence as producers reduced.[32]

Had farmers been in a strong enough position to assert absolute power over their
African tenants, the position of the latter would have deteriorated even more
rapidly. Until the mid-1890s, however, few farmers could control their labourers
completely. The farmers were still unable to exert much pressure on the
government, not only because of the continuing influence of the mercantile
community, but also because they were themselves divided by differing
requirements. The needs of progressive farmers such as Smythe, Sutton or Joseph
Baynes were very different from those of the stockfarmers of northern Natal, or of
the struggling purchasers of Crown lands in the colony's outlying districts. In most
divisions, settler agriculture remained backward, and virtually all the progress that

took place was in areas close to the towns. In 1893, the *Natal Witness* pointed out that 'with all our boasting, and the many facilities that we possess, we are, in fact, but little ahead of the Transvaal in agricultural and industrial matters'.[33] Even as late as 1902, a writer to the *Natal Agricultural Journal* lamented that 'it cannot be said that the settlers of Natal rank high as farmers'.[34] Rapid agricultural growth was in fact only to take place in Natal after Union in 1910.

Natal farmers continued to be faced with numerous problems. Very few farms were near the railway and, despite improvements, the colony's roads generally remained in a deplorable condition in the remoter districts.[35] They were also finding it more difficult to find export markets. In 1889 the Cape and Orange Free State formed a customs union which imposed high tariffs on Natal imports, while in the 1890s, the South African Republic imposed border duties on the colony. These obstacles created considerable problems for Natal's farmers yet remarkably few made any attempt to rise to the challenge or, indeed, to meet the demand for produce from the colony's own rapidly expanding urban market. Farmers' Associations deplored the reluctance of the colony's young farmers to work hard on their farms,[36] an accusation given substance by the diaries of Henry Callaway Gold, an Ixopo farmer who left the work of his farm to his labour tenants while he spent much of his time playing tennis and cricket.[37]

Irrespective of whether farmers were trying to meet the new challenges or not, most remained united in demanding 'improved' labour conditions. The old complaint about the unreliability of African labour was becoming more strident and many farmers used it as an excuse for their failure to adapt to change.[38] But different types of farming had different labour needs. On the coast, sugar planters used mainly Indian labour and employed relatively few Africans. In 1888, planters employed 5 985 Indians compared with 2 295 Africans, many of whom were recruited outside the colony.[39] Dependence on Indian labour was also growing in the midlands where farmers who were adopting more intensive farming habits were changing to wage labour as they needed more efficient labour rather than a larger labour supply.[40] On their farms, labour tenancy was a less viable proposition than it had been, and the wattle planters in particular tended to rely more on Indian migrant labourers. Other farmers in the midlands began following their example and, by the end of the century, Indian labourers were commonly employed even in districts like Ixopo which remained predominantly pastoral.[41] These farmers were also less opposed than were labour-tenancy farmers to Africans squatting on Crown or absentee-owned lands, for they were able to draw labour from them.

Despite these changes, there remained a great demand for cheap African agricultural labour throughout the colony. The number of farmers complaining of a labour shortage suggests that few Africans other than labour tenants were prepared to work on farms unless necessity drove them, as was the case during the depression of the mid-1880s or the years of natural disaster in the 1890s. However, an important explanatory factor in African reluctance to work on farms was the practice of wage reduction adopted by many farmers at times when labour was plentiful.[42] In addition, few farmers appreciated Sutton's advice that fair wages would encourage productivity. On the contrary, labourers frequently complained that they could not even get the wages that were due to them.[43]

Unreasonable labour demands on tenants and ill-treatment were also fairly common and help to explain African reluctance to work for farmers. In 1893, *Inkanyiso Yase Natal* pointed out that Africans 'would not so frequently desert if they were justly dealt with by their employers', while in 1895 a correspondent to the *Natal Witness* expressed his belief that 'those who cannot get labour have themselves to blame. There are some farmers who ill-use their boys or make them work beyond the recognised hours.'[44] This comment was echoed by Ezra Msimango who told James Stuart in 1900 that African tenants preferred African landlords to white, 'especially Boers, who compel man, woman and child to work, and freely use the sjambok'.[45] An incident in Weenen County in 1891 reveals the lengths some farmers went to: a young African boy ran away from a farm because he could not cope with the amount of work expected of him. After being captured, he had a seven-kilogram chain shackled to his leg and he was made to cut grass. He was left in this condition for four days and finally had to be sent to a blacksmith to have the chain cut off.[46]

Conditions such as these militated against the reliability of African farm labour. In addition, few farmers attempted to train their labourers. In an examination of labour conditions in 1891, the editor of *Inkanyiso Yase Natal* pointed out that the 'fault lies on both sides – The farmer expects to be well served by his servant, but has not the slightest intention of assisting him to acquire that knowledge of farming which would be useful to him in after life, and encourage him to become industrious, the Native in return works for as short a time as possible, makes as much as he needs and does only what he is compelled to. And why should he do more?'[47]

The fact that more progressive farmers seldom complained of labour shortages bears out these claims. In Richmond district, both Joseph Baynes and William Nicholson were enlightened employers who experienced no problem in drawing labour from nearby farms or reserves.[48]

Farmers would have done well to heed the advice being offered by George Sutton and the editor of *Inkanyiso Yase Natal* for, by the late 1880s, there were increased opportunities for Africans to find work elsewhere. After the discovery of gold in 1886, the rapid extension of railway construction and harbour development created employment openings but, like farming, these were unpopular and few Natal Africans sought them.[49] Urban work as domestics or as *togt* (daily-paid) servants was far more popular. Africans were particularly keen on *togt* labour for it paid more than monthly servants earned and gave the labourers a certain measure of choice in accepting employment. Figures are hard to obtain, but in 1889 the Durban magistrate estimated that there were 7 000 *togt* labourers in the city.[50] Not surprisingly, *togt* labour was unpopular with other employers who, throughout the colonial period, attacked the system as 'subversive of discipline . . . and disastrous to permanent practical industry'.[51]

However, after 1886, the main thrust of the farmers' attacks was directed at Africans working on the mines. There were few complaints at the number going to the diamond mines, or to the coal mines of northern Natal which were at an early stage of development and which were dependent on Indian and foreign African labour as they were reluctant to employ labourers for the short periods that Natal Africans were prepared to work.[52] Many Africans were, however, going to the Witwatersrand gold-fields where, until 1897, wages were steadily increasing. Despite periodic attempts to reduce wages, the need to attract workers for both underground and surface work caused average monthly wages to rise from 42s. in the early 1890s, to 63s. 6d. by 1895.[53] These wages were considerably higher than those which could be earned in Natal and few wage-labour farmers or urban employers could compete with them. Steadily increasing wages tended to outweigh the disadvantages of long hours and hard labour, and there was also the lure of readily found work in domestic service or in offices. This type of work was better paid in Johannesburg than in colonial towns. Natal Africans were particularly valued by employers, and were able to make short-term contracts for as little as one month compared with six months on the mines.

As annual statistics of labour passes were only recorded from 1894, it is difficult to know exactly how many men became migrant labourers outside the colony until then. In that year 25 514 such passes were issued.[54] The increase in the number of Africans paying their hut tax in gold coins after 1886 suggests, however, that a considerable number were going north; before the discovery of the Witwatersrand gold-fields the hut tax had been paid mainly in silver. With the growing number of men going to the mines this changed and in May 1890, of the £5 413 collected in Umgeni, £3 941 was in gold sovereigns or half-sovereigns and only £1 472 in silver.[55]

The mines employed labour agents, or touts, throughout southern Africa in order to obtain a regular supply of labour. Initially, chiefs and *izinduna* were contracted to supply men,[56] but as they fell short of the growing demand, mining houses began relying on traders. These men were ideally placed to supply labourers for they had direct access to *imizi*. Their position was strengthened in times of drought when they encouraged men to contract for mine work by offering them advances of cash or livestock. With conditions deteriorating in many Natal *imizi*, the tentacles of this system spread throughout African society. A man in need of money or cattle for *lobola* would contract with a trader or other tout to serve on the mines for a specific period at a nominal wage. In return, he would receive one or two head of cattle in advance. This was a lucrative arrangement for traders who not only received a premium from the mines of between 20s. and 30s. for each African sent to the Transvaal, but also made a handsome profit on the cattle.[57]

With no agency of their own to recruit labour and unable to match mine wages, both wage-labour and labour-tenant farmers deeply resented the activities of mine agents. During the 1880s, agricultural societies sprung up all over the colony; one of their main concerns, in common with the colonial Farmers' Conference which was founded in 1891, was the shortage of farm labour. Most meetings were dominated by the question of how to increase the supply. But the minutes show that few farmers agreed on the reason for the labour shortage. Beer drinking, polygamy, inadequate punishment for offences under the Masters and Servants Act, and mining competition were the most frequently cited reasons. Not surprisingly, low wages and poor working conditions were never considered.[58]

Prior to the granting of responsible government, farmers repeatedly urged the Executive Council to address their labour problems. One of their main concerns was the frequency with which both wage labourers and the sons of labour tenants were ignoring their commitments and seeking higher wages elsewhere. To prevent this, farmers petitioned the Legislative Council periodically but unsuccessfully to introduce a general registration of Africans.[59] In 1884, the prominent sugar planter, James Liege Hulett, attempted to prevent Africans absconding from farms when he introduced a Registration of Natives Bill. The bill provided for registration tickets to be carried by Africans when they were away from their *imizi*. Yet, despite the support of the farming MLCs, the bill was rejected by fourteen votes to twelve.[60]

The continuing reluctance of the executive and of urban representatives to agree to measures which could undermine homestead production was the main reason for the failure of Hulett's bill and of similar attempts to secure labour for farmers. But, as the maize price dropped and the number of Africans seeking work outside the colony grew, the government was forced to reconsider its *laissez-faire* attitude. While it remained reluctant to curtail an African's right to sell his labour at the highest price, it was not prepared to lose control of those who left the colony.[61]

Consequently, in 1885, the government made it necessary for any African who wanted to leave Natal to obtain a pass from a local magistrate, Administrator of Native Law or field cornet.[62] This regulation was amended, after the discovery of gold, to tighten control of Africans seeking work in the Transvaal.[63] In the first four months of 1889, a total of 3 667 passes were issued. This figure steadily increased during the drought years until by 1894 the number of passes had reached 30 675.[64] Although these figures include passes issued to Africans in transit from the Cape and Zululand to the republic, they also testify to the growing number of Natal Africans who were becoming migrant labourers.

The pass system partly placated those farmers who employed wage labourers, but it was angrily rejected by the labour-tenant farmers of Klip River and Weenen counties who claimed that it was facilitating tenant desertions. In these counties, complaints from stockfarmers of the difficulty of enforcing labour obligations on their farms grew. Yet their continuing reluctance to enter into written contracts made it difficult for the government to help them; if a farmer would not sign a contract, a magistrate had no legal justification for refusing to give one of that farmer's labour tenants a pass.[65]

In addition, under Act 15 of 1871, the breaking of a contract was made a civil and not a criminal offence. Consequently, magistrates were unable to issue warrants for the arrest of a labour tenant who deserted his employer, and the latter had to apply for a summons directing the tenant to appear at the magistrate's court. More often than not, the employer had to deliver the summons himself because the magistrate did not have sufficient messengers, and it was usually impossible for the employer to find the deserter.[66]

Even where they were able to bring a tenant before a magistrate, farmers complained that it was impossible to obtain a favourable judgement.[67] Henrique Shepstone pointed out that this was because of their refusal to enter into proper labour contracts;[68] farmers, however, believed that it was because the magistrates 'stand in such mortal fear of the Attorney-General that they look for any point on which they may discharge the accused, without much regarding the loss sustained by the White man'.[69] Many farmers also felt that, even with a written contract, it would be pointless taking offenders to court. They regarded flogging as 'the greatest and almost only check the law gives us upon our Kafir servants'.[70] In 1876, the Secretary of State, Lord Carnarvon, had drawn Sir Henry Bulwer's attention to the frequency with which floggings were administered in the magistrates' courts. Thereafter, the Governor had to confirm all sentences of flogging under the Masters and Servants Ordinance of 1852. As this caused lengthy delays, magistrates tended instead to fine offenders, a punishment which few farmers regarded as effective.[71]

Not surprisingly, farmers tended to take the law into their own hands. J. Trotter summarily turned tenants off his farm when contracts were broken, while Charles Smythe heard cases between tenants on his farms, thrashed trespassers and fined Africans who let their stock stray on his land.[72] Joseph Baynes also 'held his own court, and dispensed his own brand of justice with firmness and strict impartiality'.[73] These actions may have had a deterrent effect on desertions and disobedience, but they also account in part for the complaints of ill-treatment on so many farms. Moreover, magistrates were usually prepared to turn a blind eye to, if not actively to support, farmers who took the law into their own hands.[74]

After Gallwey's retirement as Attorney-General in 1890, magistrates had less reason to fear official disapproval if they sided with farmers. And, as the settlers' economic power grew, they were able to exert more pressure on both the Legislative and Executive Councils. As a result, when the Magistracies Commission sat in 1892, it recommended that Act 15 of 1871 be amended to strengthen the employers' legal position. Acting on this advice, the government introduced a new Masters and Servants Bill, the most important section of which dealt with magisterial jurisdiction.[75] The terms of the bill reveal the hardening of official attitudes towards Africans by the early 1890s. Under section six, a magistrate was empowered to try any Master and Servant case, even if it had not occurred in his own division. Punishments for desertion, absence from work, negligence and disobedience were £1 or one month's imprisonment for a first offence. A second conviction carried a sentence of £3 or six months' imprisonment. The bill included a number of innovations that seriously undermined the rights of labourers and strengthened those of employers. Arrest warrants could be issued for alleged deserters and a magistrate would no longer have to issue a summons for the accused to appear in court. In future, the employer could notify his servant to this effect, the notice equalling a summons, non-compliance with which would result in arrest. In addition, anyone encouraging a labourer to abscond would be liable to three months' imprisonment or to a fine not exceeding £10. Finally, an offender was bound to complete his contract after paying his fine or serving his sentence.

While the bill met most of the farmers' objections to Act 15, the Executive Council feared that it would be vetoed in London if it was seen as an overtly anti-African measure. It, therefore, included white labourers in the bill's provisions, thus provoking an outcry among the artisans of Durban and Pietermaritzburg.[76] The borough representatives in the Legislative Council withdrew their support from the measure and it was shelved. The following year, Henry Binns moved the introduction of a new bill to include those clauses from the 1892 bill which could be suitably applied to African labourers. Although the Council accepted the motion by twenty votes to nine,[77] the proposed bill was delayed because of the imminent change of government. Thus, the post-1893 ministries were left with the task of tightening the settlers' control over their labourers.

Although John Robinson and Harry Escombe dominated the first two ministries, the cabinets included two of the colony's foremost progressive farmers, George Sutton and Thomas Murray. Sutton, in particular, used his position in the cabinet to encourage settler agriculture. He continued to use his 'Country Notes' column in the *Natal Witness* to urge farmers to unite to further their interests. Referring to the growing influence of the Farmers' Conference, he argued that if it acted with moderation and common sense, its proposals could not be ignored.[78] However, when it became obvious to farmers that Robinson and Escombe were reluctant to grant them greater control over African labour, the resolutions of the Farmers' Conference became more strident. By 1896, delegates were turning the Conference into a political lobby or 'farmers' parliament'. Agricultural 'bills' were published and discussed at its annual meetings and were submitted to the colonial Parliament for consideration.[79]

Not unexpectedly, most Farmers' Conference demands concerned labour. Before the late 1880s, the colonial state's dependence on homestead revenue and produce had deterred it from forcing Africans onto the labour market. But the growing commercialization of settler agriculture and the need for labour, not only of farmers but also of the gold-fields and of urban and industrial interests in the colony, had created stresses and strains that could not be ignored. Donald Denoon has shown that all contemporary southern African governments were committed to economic development and to the 'belief that capitalism was the most promising mode of production for achieving it'.[80] In Natal, the earlier interests of capitalism had been to encourage African homestead production. By the late 1880s, however, the growing importance of settler agriculture and the growing crisis in the homestead economy had made it obvious that future growth lay with settler rather than with African agriculture. In 1890, with an eye to securing farming support for responsible government, John Robinson had stressed the need for official action to increase the colony's agricultural labour supply.[81] With few exceptions, the candidates standing for election to Parliament in 1893 echoed his sentiments.

Despite this, the Robinson ministry soon showed that it had no intention of introducing any important changes to strengthen the farmers' control of labour. Until the fall of the Escombe ministry in 1898, urban, mercantile and mining interests continued to dominate official policy. As both Robinson and Escombe were Durban representatives, they were dependent on urban support and were acutely aware of the power wielded in Durban politics by both merchants and white artisans. The latter class in particular was opposed to urban Indians and *kholwa* whom they regarded as a threat to white dominance in industrial production. This opposition was reflected in much of the legislation of these years.

Official policy under the first two ministries was also coloured by the realization that Natal, cut off from the Cape and Free State markets by the customs union between those two territories, depended for its economic survival on its commercial ties with the South African Republic. The first two years of the responsible government era were dominated by the need to secure the rail link to the gold-fields, and the Robinson ministry exerted itself to conciliate the republican authorities. Consequently, the ministry dared not restrict the outward flow of African labour. Indeed, magistrates were actually encouraged to persuade reserve inhabitants to work in the Transvaal while the only concession to colonial employers was that Africans with registered contracts were refused passes.[82] Since wage-labour farmers identified the reserves as the main source of mine labour, they denounced a policy which reduced their own labour supply and reacted with equal anger to the government's opening in 1895 of a Native Agent's Office in Johannesburg to facilitate the labour flow to the mines.[83] Because of their growing dissatisfaction, a deputation of farmers from Upper Umkomazi met Robinson and Moor in December 1895 to discuss the labour question.[84]

The deputation's main demand was for a government prohibition of labour touting for the mines. It recommended that touting on private property or among labour tenants be made a criminal offence, punishable by imprisonment. The deputation also recommended that no labour tenant be granted a pass to leave the colony without the written consent of the farmer to whom he was contracted and that no African inhabitant on reserve, Crown or absentee-owned lands should receive a pass without the consent of his chief or *induna*. To further tighten control of the movement of Africans, the deputation recommended that a pass should only be granted to an applicant in the division in which he lived, unless his magistrate had given him permission to leave his division to look for work. To regulate the labour supply within the colony, it urged the ministers to establish a government labour bureau in Pietermaritzburg with representatives in each division.

Robinson's reply to the deputation made it clear that the ministry was not prepared to coerce African labour. He reminded the farmers that because Africans were British subjects there were 'limits beyond which we cannot possibly go as a British colony'. He stressed the ministry's determination to make Africans industrious. Yet, in a barbed comment, he pointed out that the tendency of the Africans to look for work in the Transvaal did 'not seem to indicate a growing indisposition to work, although it seems to indicate a growing disposition to go to places where they can get the highest wage'.

The ministry was prepared to meet some of the farmers' grievances, however, and the following year Parliament passed the Labour Tout Regulation Act. This placed a number of curbs on touting: a labour agent would have to apply annually for a £5 licence from the magistrate of the division in which he wished to look for labour; he would require the owner's permission before touting on a farm; and he would be responsible for ascertaining whether an African he engaged was under contract of service or not.[85] To appease the farmers further, the ministry instructed the Natal agent in Johannesburg, J.S. Marwick, not to use the new agency as a labour recruiting centre.[86] These attempts failed to appease farmers who remained convinced of official indifference to their needs.[87] The ministry's whole labour policy was in many ways hopelessly contradictory and reflected its dilemma in attempting to balance the interests of Transvaal and colonial employers.

Yet, while ministers were not able to accede to the farmers' labour demands without offending mining and urban interests, they were prepared to bow to the demands of the stockfarmers for greater control over their labour tenants. With their urban or progressive farming background, they disapproved of labour tenancy, but recognized that it was a fact of life on most farms and that tightening tenancy conditions would not affect the labour supply from elsewhere in the colony. But at Escombe's insistence, ministers refused to concede to the stock-farmers' demands unless they agreed to enter into written contracts with their tenants.

In 1894, Escombe introduced a Masters and Servants Bill in the Legislative Assembly. While the bill provided the means whereby offenders could be punished if a written contract between an employer and labourer were broken, it also tried to protect African interests. When sick, a labourer was entitled to be cared for by his employer, and he could summon the latter before a magistrate if he were ill-treated. The bill also stipulated punishments for employers who withheld wages, failed to provide rations, or detained their labourers' cattle. Yet, despite Escombe's benign rhetoric, the reason for the bill is clear from his speech before Parliament:

If the Natives are discouraged from labour, or are prevented from labour, they will no doubt become unfit for the life in which they find themselves placed and they will have to yield to the competing race [the Indians]. Therefore it is in the interests of the Natives of South Africa, highly necessary that they should not be allowed to be crowded out in the struggle of life. They are to be encouraged to take their part in the work of the world; and the object of this measure is to see that encouragement shall be given to them in that respect . . . The relative rights of masters and Native servants underlie the success, the welfare, and, I may say, the happiness, not only of every home, but particularly of every homestead in the country.[88]

While the bill drew heavily on the abortive 1892 Masters and Servants Bill, many of its clauses were far more stringent. Provision was made for harsher punishments; clause 34, for example, allowed magistrates to impose heavier punishments on labourers who refused to resume service after imprisonment than they could on criminals. Masters were also authorized to order servants to appear at a magistrate's court, and to arrest them if they disobeyed. As far as farmers were concerned, one of the most beneficial provisions was that Justices of the Peace, themselves usually local farmers, could now try Masters and Servants cases.

Despite these advantages for farmers, the bill was fatally flawed and reflected the government's awareness that not all stockfarmers would welcome it. To many farmers, the advantages of verbal contracts of wages and service conditions outweighed the inconvenience of an unreliable labour supply. The bill accordingly included a clause which rendered it virtually useless: it did not make a written contract compulsory.

The ministry also entrenched a situation that had existed on many farms for years. Although both the 1878 and the 1891 Codes recognized chiefly authority over followers on private land, few had been able to exercise this authority. On 19 February 1895, Rule 15a was introduced, under which: 'A judgement of a native chief shall not be enforced on private lands otherwise than on a writ of execution, which the Administrator of Native Law is hereby given a discretion to issue or withhold.'[89] The trying of civil cases on private lands was now legally removed from the chief's to the magistrate's court. Without criminal jurisdiction, and now deprived of his civil jurisdiction, little power remained to the chief whose people resided on private lands. By the same token the hold of farmers over their labourers was strengthened proportionately.

By the late nineteenth century, the consolidation of settler farming was proceeding apace. At the same time, the growing political subjection of Africans, after the introduction of responsible government, was making a more rigid economic exploitation possible. Africans, who had previously received a measure of protection from a government which was prepared to foster peasant production, now found this support withdrawn and were thrown back on their own resources at a time when they were confronted by growing crises.

Notes

1. See CSO, 2773, Crown Lands Commission, 1885, Evidence, Haddon; Natal, *Report . . . Native population*, 1896, p. 61. E. T. Mullens, 'The native question', *Natal Agricultural Journal*, 10, no. 7, 26 July 1907, p. 735.
2. *Natal Witness*, 7 March 1887.
3. SGO, III/1/77, 4587/90, Mini to Surveyor-General, 19 December 1890; III/1/121, 3438/97, Crown Solicitor to Mini, 9 June 1896; *SANAC*, 3, Mini, p. 965.
4. NL&C, 27, no. 142, Secretary, London to General Manager, Durban, 9 April 1897.
5. *LC Hansard*, V, 20 July 1882, Reynolds, p. 219; see also SNA, 1/6/6, 199/76, Magistrate, Lower Tugela to SNA, 26 July 1876.
6. NL&C, 122, no. 81, Walton to General Manager, Durban, 10 December 1874; 26, no. 77, Secretary, London to General Manager, Durban, 2 November 1894; 211, no. 385, Essery to General Manager, Durban, 1 August 1894.
7. Native High Court, II/4/27, CS95/94, Queen v. Umdosi, n.d.; D. W. Bosch, 'The Wilgefontein settlement, 1880' *AYB*, 1964(1), p. 261.
8. NL&C, 28, no. 54, Secretary, London to General Manager, Durban, 19 August 1898; 211, no. 345, Botha to General Manager, Durban, 25 July 1894; 221, no. 385, Essery to General Manager, Durban, 1 August 1894.
9. NL&C, 204, no. 152, Essery to General Manager, Durban, 14 August 1892.
10. NL&C, 124, no. 318, Townsend to General Manager, Durban, 9 July 1875; 204, no. 105, Coutts to General Manager, Durban, 4 August 1892; 209, no. 221, Kimber to General Manager, Durban, 9 December 1893; 211, no. 385, Essery to General Manager, Durban, 1 August 1894.
11. NL&C, 210, no. 246, Essery to General Manager, Durban, 30 March 1894; 215, no. 228, Jackson to Essery, 15 June 1895.
12. NL&C, 155, no. 122, Botha to General Manager, Durban, 16 June 1881; 172, no. 135, Farrer to General Manager, Durban, 31 July 1884; 192, no. 96, Watson to General Manager, Durban, 2 August 1889.
13. See *Natal Witness*, 8 September 1881; NL&C, 15, no. 64, Acting Secretary, London to General Manager, Durban, 24 August 1882; *LC Hansard*, VII, 19 August 1884, pp. 484–8.
14. NL&C, 155, no. 343, Pinder to General Manager, Durban, 22 July 1881.
15. See NL&C, 18, no. 80, Secretary, London to General Manager, Durban, 10 September 1885.
16. NL&C, 155, no. 343, Pinder to General Manager, Durban, 22 July 1881; see also no. 208, Bruce to General Manager, Durban, 30 June 1881; 167, no. 170, Botha to General Manager, Durban, 6 August 1883.
17. NL&C, Secretary, London to General Manager, Durban, 20, no. 51, 10 March 1887; 23, no. 37, 21 August 1890; 23, no. 44, 19 September 1890.
18. NL&C, 211, no. 385, Essery to General Manager, Durban, 1 August 1894.
19. NL&C, Secretary, London to General Manager, Durban, 12, no. 44, June 1880; 27, no. 73, 13 March 1896, no. 142, 9 April 1897; 208, no. 125, Fell to General Manager, Durban, 4 September 1893; 210, no. 22, Colenbrander to General Manager, Durban, 23 January 1894; Essery to General Manager, Durban, 215, no. 385, 1 August 1894; 215, no. 279, 18 June 1895.
20. SNA, 1/1/81, 1155/85, Return showing terms of occupation by natives on private lands, 1885.
21. NL&C, Walton and Tatham to General Manager, Durban, 192, no. 119, 207, no. 185, 22 March 1893.
22. *NBB Departmental reports*, 1894/5, p. B9.
23. NL&C, 209, no. 221, Kimber to General Manager, Durban, 9 December 1893.
24. NL&C, Secretary, London to General Manager, Durban, 20, no. 51, 10 March 1887; 27, no. 54, 20 December 1895.
25. SNA, 1/1/105, 164/88, Return of Natives sued for rent by private owners, 1888.
26. NL&C, 220, no. 71, Walton and Tatham to General Manager, Durban, 14 December 1895.
27. CO 179, 172, no. 142, Governor to Secretary of State, 6 July 1888; see also *Natal Witness*, 13 May 1890; NL&C, 211, no. 313, Howell to General Manager, Durban, 18 July 1894; 213, no. 284, Walton and Tatham to General Manager, Durban, 27 December 1894.
28. Natal, *Report . . . Native population*, 1894, p. 29.
29. NL&C, 20, no. 60, Proposed Directors' report, May 1887; *Natal Witness*, 6 December 1892.
30. *Natal Witness*, 8 June 1894; see also Natal, *Report . . . Native population*, 1895, p. 49.

31. C. J. Smythe Papers, 53, Regulations for Native tenants, 31 August 1896.
32. See Native High Court, II/4/27, CS95/94, Queen v. Umdosi, n.d.
33. *Natal Witness*, 1 April 1893.
34. A. Pearse, 'Agricultural chemistry for beginners', *Natal Agricultural Journal*, 5, no. 3, 11 April 1902, p. 76.
35. *Natal Mercury*, 12 April 1888, 22 June 1888.
36. See 'Malton Farmers' Association presidential address', *Natal Agricultural Journal*, 10, no. 9, 27 September 1907, p. 1137.
37. Henry Callaway Gold Collection [Killie Campbell Library], Diaries.
38. See *Natal Witness*, 5 January 1893, 'Country Notes'.
39. *LC Hansard*, XIII, 28 May 1889, Symons, p. 157; *Natal Mercury*, 13 July 1888.
40. *Natal Advertiser*, 16 April 1891.
41. *NBB Departmental reports*, 1897, p. B15; 1899, p. B29; *Natal Witness*, 15 May 1891; Ripon Papers, LXXIII, Hely-Hutchinson to Ripon, 9 February 1895, p. 102.
42. *NBB Departmental reports*, 1885, pp. B54, 64.
43. *Inkanyiso Yase Natal*, 1 September 1893.
44. Ibid; *Natal Witness*, 11 January 1895.
45. Webb and Wright, eds, *James Stuart archive*, 4, Msimango, p. 47.
46. *Natal Witness*, 2 April 1891,
47. *Inkanyiso Yase Natal*, 9 April 1891.
48. Pearse, *Joseph Baynes, passim*; Natal, *Evidence . . . Natal Native Commission, 1881*, Nicholson, p. 76.
49. NPP, 157, no. 42, 1891, Return showing the number of Natives brought into the colony . . . to work on railway and harbour construction.
50. See Natal, *Report . . . Native population*, 1880, p. 66; *NBB*, 1889, p. T5; See also *SANAC*, 3, H. Shepstone, p. 89.
51. *Natal Mercury*, 24 March 1863.
52. Natal, Department of Mines, *Report upon the coal-fields of Klip River, Weenen, Umvoti and Victoria counties . . . by Frederick W. North*, London, 1881, p. 37; *Natal Mercury*, 12 February 1892; *SANAC*, 3, Wiltshire, p. 385.
53. P. Warwick, *Black people and the South African War, 1899–1902*, Johannesburg, 1983, p. 126.
54. Natal, *Report . . . Native population*, 1894, p. 3.
55. *Natal Witness*, 13 May 1890.
56. *Natal Advertiser*, 19 July 1887, Advertisement by Joseph Pascoe.
57. *Natal Mercury*, 23 November 1896. The system was not confined to Natal but was common throughout southern Africa, see R. Horwitz, *The political economy of South Africa*, New York, 1967, p. 24; Beinart, *Political economy of Pondoland*, pp. 56–8.
58. See e.g. *NBB Departmental reports*, 1885, p. B39; *Natal Witness*, 15 May 1891; 17 March 1892; See SNA, 1/1/108, 607/88, Wood to Governor, n.d.; *Natal Mercury*, 19 December 1892.
59. NPP, 643, no. 33, 1884, 4 August 1884; *LC Hansard*, VII, 6 August 1884, Walton, p. 386.
60. *LC Hansard*, VII, 6 August 1884, pp. 383, 388.
61. *LC Hansard*, XII, 2 August 1888, SNA, p. 66.
62. *NGG*, XXXVII, no. 2139, 9 September 1885, GN 315, 1885, p. 849.
63. *NGG*, XL, no. 2285, 14 February 1888, GN 98, 1888, pp. 102–4.
64. Natal, *Report . . . Native population*, 1894, p. 3.
65. *LC Hansard*, XII, 2 August 1888, Murray, p. 65; XIV, 26 June 1890, Stainbank, p. 416; SNA, 1/1/140, 379/91, Memorandum on LC Address 36, 1891.
66. See *Natal Witness*, 28 April 1892; *LC Hansard*, XIV, 26 June 1890, Van Rooyen, p. 418.
67. See *Natal Witness*, 22 October 1890; 13 July 1891.
68. SNA, 1/1/140, 379/91, Memorandum on LC Address 36, 1891.
69. *Natal Witness*, 9 February 1885, 'Country Notes'.
70. Dr J. C. A. L. Colenbrander Papers, [Killie Campbell Library], Tugela Division Planters' Association, 4 September 1876, p. 20.
71. CO 179, 148, no. 169, Governor to Secretary of State, 5 November 1883; Impendhle Magistracy, 1/2/1/1/1, Criminal record book, 1888–1900.
72. Natal, *Evidence . . . Natal Native Commission, 1881*, Trotter, p. 82; C. J. Smythe Papers, 8, Diary, 21 June 1882, 15 February 1886, 3 March 1886.

73. Pearse, *Joseph Baynes*, p. 240.
74. See for example C. J. Smythe Papers, 8, Diary, 8 March 1886.
75. *NGG*, XLIV, no. 2562, 5 July 1892, Bill 13, 1892, To amend the law relating to master, servants and apprentices, p. 587.
76. *Natal Witness*, 9 June 1892.
77. *LC Hansard*, XX, 30 May 1893, pp. 78–84.
78. *Natal Witness*, 19 October, 9 November 1893.
79. *Natal Witness*, 17 April 1896
80. D. Denoon, *Settler capitalism: the dynamics of dependent development in the southern hemisphere*, Oxford, 1983, p. 8.
81. *Natal Witness*, 28 February 1890.
82. *NGG*, XLVII, no. 2718, 12 February 1895, GN 489, 1894, pp. 150–1.
83. C. A. Gillitt, 'Natal, 1893–1897, the alignment of parties and the fall of the Escombe ministry', BA Hons. essay, University of Natal, 1965, ch. 9.
84. GH, 1545, Deputation to the government to discuss matters concerning the labour question, 12 December 1895, pp. 175ff.
85. Act 36, 1896, *To regulate the system of touting* . . .
86. SNA, 1/1/210, 1346/95, SNA to Agent, n.d.
87. See Mooi River Farmers' Association, 1, Minutes, 3 April 1896.
88. *LA Hansard*, XXII, 5 June 1894, Attorney-General, p. 379.
89. SNA, 1/1/274, 3013/97, Minute, 6 February 1896.

African chiefs at an *indaba* for the Duke and Duchess of Cornwall and York, Pietermaritzburg, 1902.

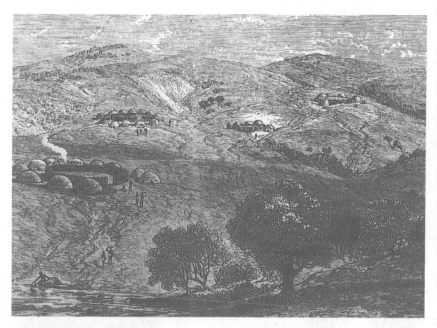

African *imizi*, Zwartkop reserve

Family group in the late 1870s.

African women hoeing in the fields.

A posed demonstration of a faction fight, showing the sticks used as weapons.

A *kholwa* couple photographed in 1865.

Natal Native Police, constable with knobkerrie

The first Natal Ministry under responsible government, 1893–1897.
Standing (left to right)   Harry Escombe, Frederick Moor
Seated (left to right)   Thomas Murray, Sir John Robinson, George Sutton

CHAPTER SEVEN

The Crisis Facing African Production

In the last two decades of the nineteenth century, sales of Crown lands and intensifying utilization by settlers of their own lands, seriously limited African freedom of movement and choice of land. It was no longer as easy as it had been to move between reserve, Crown and private lands; the remaining Crown lands were unsuitable for agriculture or for pasture; and increased rental and labour demands made privately owned lands unattractive.[1]

Africans who were evicted when Crown land lots were sold did have the option of moving their *imizi* onto remaining Crown lands. This led to overcrowding on these lands, and to the degradation of their already poor arable and grazing resources. To guard against overcrowding, the government prohibited any new settlement on these lands in 1884, while in the same year it introduced a squatters' rental of £1 per hut. Further regulations in 1886 imposed a grazing fee on each *umuzi* of 2s. 6d. per annum for ten head of cattle, 1s. 6d. for ten sheep, and 3s. for ten horses.[2] The regulation prohibiting new settlement was, however, evaded; between 1886 and 1889, despite the continuing sale of lots, there was a steady increase in rental receipts from £7 852 to £11 769.[3]

The haphazard way in which Crown lands were sold also created problems for African squatters. Most sales were of small lots which cut up previously large blocks of Crown land in such a way that squatters often lost their best gardens and were cut off from grazing lands.[4] They found it difficult to make ends meet, and after the imposition of the £1 rental in 1886, steadily fell into arrears. By the end of the first year of the new rent, they owed £2 285. Although some of this may have been withheld in protest against the rent, a number of squatters experienced genuine difficulty in raising the money and had to sell stock to meet final demands.[5]

Crown-land squatters could also evade the new rent by looking elsewhere for land. And, with few suitable lands available in the colony, some looked to neighbouring territories. In the 1880s and 1890s, the number of men applying to move their *imizi* to Pondoland, Griqualand East, Zululand or the Transvaal grew.[6] Although most requests came from individual *abanumzana*, there were applications from chiefdoms. That of Mqawe to move some of his people to Zululand has already been mentioned. Similarly, when Chief Ramncana was ordered to leave the Crown land bought by Stephanus Mini and Stoffel Molife, he applied to move with his people to the Umzimkulu division in the Cape. When his request was refused, he moved with ten of his *imizi* to Basutoland in 1889.[7]

In general, the Natal government (and also the neighbouring governments) refused to allow such removals.[8] Africans evicted from their lands, therefore, often had to overcome their reluctance to come directly under chiefly rule, and had to apply to their chiefs for permission to locate their *imizi* on reserve land. Despite overcrowded conditions in many reserves, it was difficult for a chief to refuse land to those *abanumzana* who could claim kinship with his people. Yet few chiefs could do this without diminishing the arable and pasture land available to their existing followers on the reserves. Even in the late 1870s, few coastal chiefs had been able to find room for people moving onto their lands.[9] Their purchases of Crown lands had done little to alleviate the problem. In 1888, the magistrate of Alexandra drew attention to the congestion in his division, and expressed the fear that 'the whole of Natal will, ere very long, be too circumscribed to contain the fast-increasing Native population'.[10]

The growth of the African population in the reserves is evidenced by the hut tax returns. Between 1881 and 1894, the number of reserve huts which paid tax increased from 39 913 to 50 092, while the average number of acres available to each hut declined from 55,1 to 43,9. In the arid Inanda, Umvoti and Tugela reserves the reduction was even more serious, from 42 to 34,9 acres per hut.[11] As early as 1882, the editor of the *Natal Witness* urged that Africans should be compensated for the loss of Crown lands by being given additional reserve land.[12] Yet, apart from slightly increasing the size of the Alfred county reserves by 45 271 acres in 1889,[13] the government made no attempt to address the problem.

The reserves also failed to benefit from railway expansion in Natal. None was close to the main Transvaal route, and the branch lines which were constructed in the 1890s bypassed them as they were too poor and difficult of access to warrant railway expenditure.

During these years official indifference to conditions in the reserves persisted. Henrique Shepstone's apathy was particularly notorious. He seldom visited the reserves and resolutely turned a deaf ear to the chorus of complaints from the chiefs. The £5 000 per annum that was reserved for African administration and welfare under the 1856 constitution was administered by the Executive Council acting in its capacity as the Natal Native Trust. Yet, until 1893, the Trust seldom met and very little use was made of the reserve fund.[14] Hardly any new roads had been constructed to open up the reserves since the 1840s, while existing roads, such as the old military one linking Inanda reserve with the north coast road, had fallen into disrepair.[15] The only initiative shown by the Trust under Henrique was its appointment in 1889 of three supervisors, Thomas Fayle in the Inanda, Ralph Clarence in the Umlazi and J. Balcomb in the Alexandra reserve.[16]

The appointment of the supervisors was in belated fulfilment of the 1846

Locations Commission's intention to provide inspectors to advise reserve inhabitants and to encourage them to irrigate and manure their lands and to cultivate marketable crops.[17] Although the intention behind their appointment was sound, little attempt was made to ensure the success of the venture. The supervisors were poorly paid and were given very little authority. Both Balcomb and Clarence were failures, and by 1891 had resigned and not been replaced. Balcomb had never succeeded in winning the confidence of the Alexandra inhabitants, while Clarence's attentions had been focused on the women of his reserve rather than on agricultural improvement, which had not endeared him to homestead inhabitants.[18] Of the three men, only Fayle conscientiously performed his duties. He earned the respect of the inhabitants of the Inanda reserve, and of the Zwartkop reserve to which he was transferred in 1893.[19] He persuaded the government to repair the old military road in Inanda reserve to allow for wagon transport, and persuaded a number of Africans, including Thetheleku and the Nadi chief, Mzimba kaDibinyika, in the Zwartkop reserve, to manure their gardens, grow trees and plant mealies in rows.[20]

Although important *per se*, Fayle's contributions were little more than palliatives and only benefited a small number of *imizi* in the Inanda and Zwartkop reserves. No matter how tirelessly he worked, he could do little to halt the continuing decline of the homestead economy locally, let alone in the colony as a whole. By 1893, however, his successes seem to have stirred official awareness that some measure of support was essential to prevent the homestead economy in the reserves from collapsing altogether.

Under the responsible government constitution, the £5 000 sum reserved for African advancement was increased to £10 000 per annum. Although only a small proportion of this amount was spent each year on reserves, the normal expenditure of the Natal Native Trust did increase significantly from £531 in 1894 to £23 813 in 1897.[21] By far the greatest part of the money was spent on surveying and fencing the reserves and on building roads and constructing wagon and cart tracks.[22] By the end of the century, five roads had been constructed in the great eastern block of reserves, opening them to the rest of the colony. Whether the government's motives were entirely altruistic is, however, doubtful. In 1895, the Minister of Lands and Works, Thomas Murray, commented that the roads were being built to open them 'for agricultural, mining and industrial use by Europeans'. Evidence given to the South African Native Affairs Commission, in 1903, also suggests that they were intended to provide easy military access to the reserves in the event of trouble.[23] The motives for fencing the reserves were also mixed. By the end of the century 425 miles of fencing had been constructed between reserve and privately owned lands. Although the fences prevented the Africans' cattle from straying onto neighbouring lands and being impounded, they also protected the farmers by cutting off African access to their farms.[24]

The largest work undertaken by the Trust was the construction of irrigation furrows in the reserves. The first was on the Mooi River at Keate's Drift in the arid

Impafana reserve. An area of 240 acres was laid out in lots to be rented to individual Africans. By 1897, the lots had been taken up at an average annual rental of 10s. an acre, and the demand for extra lots prompted the Trust to irrigate a further 60 acres and to start on a second scheme in the reserve, at Smit's Ferry on the Thukela River.[25] The Trust also encouraged individual initiative in building furrows. Fayle was particularly successful in this respect and by the end of 1895 there were at least four irrigation furrows in the Zwartkop reserve.[26]

But these initiatives were too limited to be effective. *Imizi* cultivation had peaked in the 1870s and, by the 1890s, all the signs indicated that the homestead economy was becoming increasingly unequal to coping with the stresses arising from dwindling land resources and growing population numbers.

It is impossible to determine exactly how large the population of Natal was in the nineteenth century. Even for the white inhabitants, figures were inaccurate while those for Africans were particularly unreliable. The first colony-wide census took place in 1891 as part of a wider census of the British Empire. But there were insufficient financial and manpower resources for a comprehensive enumeration of the African population. In addition, the government feared that a census would alarm Africans on the eve of the constitutional change. Instead the African population was calculated on the basis of the hut tax returns, 4,13647 inmates per hut being taken as the colonial average.[27] This figure was based on magistrates' returns and could give no more than an estimate of the population, particularly as *imizi* in the more remote and mountainous reserves probably managed to evade payment.[28] Even accepting that the census figures were an underestimate, they show a remarkable increase in population since the estimated 300 000 of the late 1870s. The census recorded an African population of 455 983 or 22,3 to the square mile.[29] Bearing in mind that there was now less land available to Africans, in real terms the density would have been far higher, particularly in the reserves.

The growing land shortage made it difficult for chiefs to meet the needs of the increasing population. And, as the supply of land dwindled, so shifting cultivation, admirably suited as it was to conditions of abundant land, could seldom be practised. Instead, *imizi* inhabitants had to cultivate exhausted gardens or more marginal lands and the quality and quantity of their crops declined. As early as 1881, Mahobe of the Cele chiefdom in Umlazi had complained that his people were obtaining smaller yields because of soil deterioration. In the same year, Ncapie of the Ngcolosi chiefdom on the north coast lamented that his people were unable for the same reason to raise enough for their own consumption.[30] More *imizi* were raising money through wage-labour to buy ploughs (between 1882 and 1893 the number rose from 8 296 to 17 672)[31] which enabled cultivation of poorer soils and steep slopes, but these lands yielded smaller returns and were rapidly exhausted. The American, W. Allen, points out that it takes anything up to twenty years for the fertility of such soils to be restored.[32]

To compound these difficulties, the colony was devastated by droughts between 1888 and 1893. Maize yields dropped significantly; to an average of 604 997 muids each year during this period from 696 541 in 1882. As the number of huts had increased since 1882 from 93 803 to 110 337, the colonial average of muids reaped decreased from 7,4 to 5,5 per hut.[33] The decline was most marked in the midlands, where the sale of Crown lands and the increase in both the white and African populations had had the starkest impact on the amount of good arable land available to each *umuzi*. As a result, the estimated average harvest of 15,1 muids per hut in 1882 dropped to 8,3 muids. The only exception to the general trend was in Upper Umkomazi whence the Pietermaritzburg market was now drawing much of its grain supply. In this division the number of muids reaped rose from 18,4 to 27,1 per hut.

As sorghum is more drought-resistant than maize, it was cultivated more extensively during the dry years, showing an increase from 85 078 acres in 1882 to an annual average of 106 469 between 1888 and 1893. The amount reaped also increased, from 283 597 in 1882 to an annual average of 381 484 muids between 1888 and 1893, or from 3 to 3,5 muids per hut. Yet taken together, the annual acreage of maize and sorghum cultivated by homestead Africans increased from 255 029 in 1882 to only 276 258 acres between 1888 and 1893 while the number of muids reaped dropped from 5,2 to 4,5 per hut. While this decline by no means constituted an intolerable crisis in African society, it does indicate a trend whereby the *imizi* were increasingly unable to provide for both their own needs and those of the settler community.

Africans, compelled to find new ground for gardens and grazing, were ploughing up young trees and bushes, thereby accelerating the degradation of the environment.[34] The urban demand for timber and firewood also hastened woodland destruction and the attendant deterioration of the soil. By 1891, many Crown forests had disappeared. Although most large timber was removed by white sawyers, young growth was cut by Africans for sale, for use in hut and fence construction, for firewood and wattles, and to provide land for gardens. The situation was particularly serious in the sweetveld areas where the destruction of woodland removed the semi-shade necessary for the veld's survival.[35]

Although all categories of land were affected, the overcrowded reserves suffered most. By the late 1880s, the once heavily wooded Zwartkop reserve was left with only a few isolated clumps of trees. There was also extensive damage on absentee-owned lands, where the government lacked the means to enforce forest regulations. Proclamations to protect forests, which were published in 1853, 1867 and 1882, remained a dead letter. Even when a Conservator of Forests and forest guards were appointed in 1891, they were given jurisdiction only on Crown lands.[36]

Over-cultivation and the destruction of forests and bush cover created perfect conditions for erosion, particularly in the rugged reserves of the coastal interior and the Thukela valley. Ironically, the one innovation widely accepted by homestead Africans, the plough, further accelerated erosion. Palmer and Parsons point out that in southern Africa deep ploughing has had disastrous ecological effects, opening up 'the topsoil (only a few inches deep) to be dried by the sun . . . Few African soils have the chemical properties to sustain continuous cultivation, and continuous deep ploughing has been responsible for turning cultivable soils into sun-baked powder.'[37] In addition, women and children were often unable to hoe and weed the larger ploughed fields properly, with the result that their crops suffered from unavoidable neglect.[38]

The ecological pressures on the reserves were compounded by a sharp rise in cattle numbers. Although lungsickness and redwater had destroyed many cattle in the 1870s, African-owned stock numbers increased during that decade from an estimated 334 563 in 1869 to 384 557 in 1882. During much of the 1880s, the colony was remarkably free of cattle disease and enjoyed relatively wet summers with only localized droughts. Because of this, and despite sales necessitated by the payment of rents and fines, *umuzi* cattle numbers had increased to 494 382 by 1896.[39] Magistrates' reports frequently refer to the difficulties Africans were having in finding suitable pasture lands. Not only were they having to graze a far greater number of cattle on a steadily shrinking land resource, but the herds were also having to compete with a rapidly increasing number of goats, a sign of the growing impoverishment of many *imizi*.

The increase in cattle numbers was not restricted to Africans. The settlers were also having problems finding grazing for their herds. Few farms were fenced or accurately surveyed before the late 1880s and, as the pressure on land grew, so did friction between farmers and Africans. Complaints of trespassing increased during these years and came from both sides, for farmers were often as uncertain as their African neighbours about their boundaries.[40] African complaints of farmers trespassing on their lands were particularly common in northern Natal, where stockfarmers consistently ignored African rights and allowed their herds and flocks to graze on black-occupied lands. For example, in Klip River a farmer, Petersen, regularly drove his cattle onto a neighbouring farm and threatened to assault the African occupier when he tried to prevent him. Although some Africans reported cases of trespass to their local magistrate, most realized that such action would only result in retaliation from the farmers.[41]

The absence of adequate surveys and fences meant that both farmers and Africans could plead innocence when accused of trespass. This became more difficult when a more systematic surveying of the colony's lands began in the late 1880s, and when in 1887 a Dividing Fences Act became law. This measure was permissive and, with a supplementary act in 1889, offered farmers loans for fencing their farms, repayable at 8 per cent over 15 years. By the early 1890s, the colony's farms were rapidly being fenced.[42] Although fences did reduce trespass, they tended to heighten tension between white and African neighbours. The latter often found themselves barred from traditional rights of way, many of which had long been used to drive stock between different grazing lands. The government's haphazard sale of scattered parcels of Crown land, with the resultant establishment of farms straddling paths, also exacerbated the difficulty.[43] Transport riders were also impeded as many farmers ignored the law which required them to provide outspans and either fenced them off or charged riders for the grazing.[44] With rights of way blocked to them and their stock, African anger steadily mounted, particularly in drought years when the need to move cattle became desperate.[45]

By the 1890s, optimum use of seasonal grazing was becoming impossible and over-grazing and grassland destruction was becoming endemic. In more arid reserves much of the sweetgrass cover was beyond recovery.[46] Moreover, the inhabitants of these reserves had to accept more and more *sisa* cattle from kinsmen on farms as the grazing available to them became restricted.

Under these conditions, cattle were becoming a liability. D.I. Bransby calculated that cattle require between 10 and 20 acres of grazing per head to obtain optimum results in the climatic and ecological conditions of the Thukela valley reserves. During a dry season this can rise to as high as 62 acres.[47] No figures are available for cattle holdings in the reserves before 1896, but in that year the 281 399 acres of the Inanda and Umvoti reserves which fell within the Mapumulo and Indwedwe divisions carried 56 000 head.[48] Thus each animal had an average of only 5,02 acres. The result was an unremitting decline of the veld, cattle condition and milk production. Cattle deterioration was worst in winter so that by the planting season oxen were of little use for ploughing. By the 1890s, winter stock losses were becoming severe, a situation which was exacerbated by the encroachment of gardens onto the sourveld as reserve Africans attempted to raise sufficient crops.[49]

During a normal rainfall year, the quality of the grass deteriorates after mid-summer, becoming fibrous, woody and indigestible; the nutritional intake of stock declines and there is an appreciable weight loss. Where drought follows, it is difficult for an animal to recover this loss without supplementary feeding. Even when there are months of heavy rain during a drought cycle, the drought-weakened animals find it difficult to digest the young nutritious grass. These conditions were present during the drought cycle of 1888–93 which included a very wet summer in 1891–92. This resulted in heavy stock losses in both cattle and sheep, particularly in the upper districts.[50]

Confronted by an ecological disaster, the obvious solution was for Africans to cull their cattle rigorously. This they could not do, because of the social importance of cattle and their continuing role as wealth. In addition, despite the overall increase in African cattle numbers, the average number held by each *umuzi* actually dropped. With cows producing less milk and oxen able to do less work, culling would have been out of the question, particularly during the drought years when losses of cattle were highest. *Imizi* where kinship support systems still obtained were better placed to cope with the problems of over-grazing. These families could still *sisa* their cattle but many of them had to do so over increasing distances in order to find adequate grazing; in some cases as far distant as across the colony, or from within the colony to the Transvaal or Zululand.[51]

During the drought years, Africans could not supply grain to the market and were having to buy food for themselves, usually at inflated prices. In 1889, maize cost 35s. a muid in Alfred, 50s. in Greytown and 70s. in the Thukela reserves.[52] By April 1890 there was a complete failure of crops in the thornveld of Weenen county, with maize kernels unobtainable and mealie cobs selling at five for 1s. As a result, the Chunu and Thembu chiefs in the arid Impafana reserve were warning of starvation in their chiefdoms.[53] Although the drought did lead to individual cases of starvation, few Africans succumbed to famine as most *imizi* were able to sell stock to buy food.[54] The worst affected, however, had to rely on roots and herbs; in the coastal divisions many were buying rice from Indian suppliers and in Ixopo, despite the traditional aversion to pork, some were eating pigs.[55] Others were selling stock at ridiculously low prices or pledging labour in return for food. The Frere correspondent of the *Natal Witness* reported an African offering a horse valued at £8 for a bag of mealies, and another entering into a labour contract for one year in return for two bags.[56] In Ixopo a mare and foal were sold for four bags of mealies.[57]

As sorghum was more drought resistant than maize, and more extensively grown during the drought years, *utshwala* became even more important than it had been, becoming the main foodstuff in some reserves. Despite the nutritional value of *utshwala*, the growing dependence on sorghum was creating an unbalanced diet. Sorghum has a relatively low protein and amino acid content and an over-reliance on it can lead to protein-deficiency diseases such as kwashiorkor, particularly in children. In addition, because it ripens later than maize, the period of seasonal hunger became longer and its effects more acute.[58]

The monotony and shortcomings of a grain diet were exacerbated by the serious decline in the colony's game. More intensive grass burning to refertilize the soil drove game birds away from the *imizi*. Buck were not only becoming scarce throughout the colony, but official restrictions virtually prohibited Africans from hunting those that remained.[59] From 1892, only chiefs could apply for permission to hunt in the reserves and few applications were granted: in 1894–96, of 169 permits issued in the colony, only 6 were granted to Africans, and each was restricted to 2 rhebuck. By contrast, permits for hunts in which up to 300 buck were killed at a time were granted to settlers.[60] The hunting regulations were bitterly resented and the number of hunting offences in divisions such as Impendhle indicate the extent to which they were challenged.[61]

Growing financial demands made by the state on homestead Africans also caused bitterness and anger. In times of financial need, the government turned all too readily to Africans for extra revenue. This was as true of the depression years of the mid-1880s as it had been in the late 1840s and late 1860s. The administration of Sir Arthur Havelock was desperately short of revenue in these years of world-wide recession, and saw no way of minimizing its budget deficit except by increasing taxation. Attempts to do this by means of a land tax failed, because of the opposition of both farmers and absentee landowners. With settlers refusing to bail out the government, the Executive Council examined ways of increasing the financial burden borne by the Africans. In addition to introducing charges on Crown lands, it also increased the amount paid in fees and fines. The executive also considered increasing the hut tax and introducing a land tax which would include the reserves. But Havelock was reluctant to approve of any measures which could cause popular unrest and, after consulting Theophilus Shepstone, he rejected both proposals.[62]

The need for tax increases receded when Natal's economy was saved by the timeous discovery of gold on the Witwatersrand. Despite this, an extra financial burden was placed on Africans in the reserves in 1890. A charge of 10s. for cutting wattles for constructing huts had been in force in the reserves for years; now, a new series of charges on reserve and Crown lands was introduced. These included 16s. for a wagonload and 6s. for a cartload of firewood, and £3 for a wagonload of more valuable wood. Bundles of forest wood were charged for at 6d. each and thornwood at 3d. each.[63] As free access to timber was vital to *imizi*, both these charges and the forest regulations struck at the basis of homestead life.

Homestead Africans were finding it difficult to make ends meet under the onslaught of drought, land shortage and increasing financial demands. As long as the demands on their resources could be met by the production of a relatively modest agricultural surplus supplemented by occasional wage labour, most *imizi* had managed to cope with the colonial presence. Now, faced with increased demands and with overcrowding and limited resources, their reluctance or inability to make the required far-reaching adaptations showed up in stark relief.

Homestead Africans could have benefited by emulating Indian cultivators, who used the same gardens for years by rotating legumes and grain crops. Yet few Africans were prepared to follow their example. Le Roy Ladurie, referring to the capitalist development of agriculture in Europe from the fifteenth century, points out that the development coincided with large-scale crop diversification.[64] This made the capitalist expansion of agriculture possible in Europe at a time when it, too, was faced by a rapidly increasing population. Few *imizi* were able to emulate this diversification. A general explanation for this is offered by Eric Hobsbawm, who highlights the extent to which nature's threat dominates peasant communities. To people with few resources, the potential risks of innovation appear greater than the possible gains.[65] In a situation of land shortage and drought, such as in Natal in the late 1880s and early 1890s, these risks became more marked. Yet African reluctance to experiment with other crops ensured their failure to break away from a grain-based economy. And this in turn contributed to the failure of the *umuzi* to nurture capitalist farmers.

The reluctance of homestead Africans to diversify is understandable. Africans who had supplied urban centres with vegetables in earlier decades had seen white and Indian market gardeners capture their markets. It therefore seemed far more sensible to cater to the growing demand for maize from the gold- and coalfields, the railway works and the towns. During these years, despite the fact that white farmers were increasing their sales to the markets, there was an enduring call for grain. Despite the growing commercialization of settler agriculture and competition from Indian cultivators, Africans still reaped three times as much maize as did settlers and remained an important source of supply to most colonial markets. While, in Durban, they lost the market even for grain to Indian suppliers by the early 1890s, and seldom hawked produce in the streets;[66] in Pietermaritzburg they still provided approximately one-third of the produce sold on the Pietermaritzburg market. Now that the produce which they had previously hawked in the streets was available on the market square from white and Indian cultivators, African sales were restricted to maize, forage and wood with maize providing the bulk.[67]

With better quality produce supplied by whites and Indians, purchasers were able to beat down the Africans' asking prices. Between 1888 and 1889, despite generally high drought-induced prices, Africans received an average of 3s. to 4s. per cwt. for mealies and 3s. to 8s. per load for mealie stalks on the Pietermaritzburg market. Yet few could afford to withhold their produce. By the 1890s, despite the drought, they were increasing their supplies to both the market master and grain merchants in the capital. The same position applied to forage and firewood for which they were receiving only 4s. to 8s. per cwt. and 6d. to 1s. 6d. per cwt. respectively. Here too, despite complaints that they were selling at a loss, few Africans had an alternative to continuing supplies.[68] Low prices also discouraged attempts to supply good-quality grain and the Pietermaritzburg market master frequently complained that he was receiving inferior, mushy and dirty mealies. There were also complaints of poor-quality, wet forage and of wet and worm-eaten skins and hides.[69]

Africans were not only contending with low prices, they had also been debarred from selling in the Pietermaritzburg market hall. Furthermore, they had to face the market master's deliberate manipulation of his charges for the produce they sold outside the hall. The average charge paid by suppliers was 4,5 per cent but, on the grounds that they supplied small quantities, Africans were charged a much steeper rate, often as high as 31 per cent. The corporation claimed that these charges were necessary and that high rates on small-volume supplies enabled it to maintain the average charge at 4,5 per cent.[70] This would have been small consolation to the struggling African small suppliers, who were in fact subsidizing the large suppliers.

In the interior divisions, Africans remained more fortunate. As the railway pushed northwards, and as coalmines came into operation, there was a growing demand for produce in Ladysmith, Newcastle and Dundee. Few white farmers could meet this demand, and there were as yet few Indian producers in northern Natal. African prosperity, particularly on *kholwa*-owned lands, was growing and they were supplying not only the growing towns and rapidly developing coalfields, but were also taking grain to the drought-stricken thornveld of the Sundays, Thukela, Mzinyathi and Mooi valleys and exchanging it for livestock.[71]

The colony's continuing demand for grain had created a situation where, despite declining harvests, Africans throughout Natal were selling maize which they needed for their own consumption. A growing number of *abanumzana* were trying to make ends meet by sending their young men out as migrant labourers. Then, knowing that they could use their wages to buy food, the *abanumzana* were selling maize needed for domestic consumption and were using the proceeds to pay their rents and taxes. Most of these fell due between April and June after the harvesting, at a time when there was normally a glut of grain from non-drought areas on the market and prices were low.[72] By the time they needed to buy grain, it was towards the end of the season when prices were high.

The temptation to sell immediately after the harvest was not unique to Africans. White farmers, too, paid little attention to matching their supply of saleable maize to the market and, by selling at harvest time, contributed to the glut. Commenting on this in 'Country Notes' in 1889, Sutton pointed out that without storage facilities it was often better to sell immediately because of the deterioration which occurred if mealies were kept. This problem faced Africans too, for the quality of maize stored in grain pits also declined and there was little demand for it on the market.[73] This had not been a problem in the years of plentiful harvests when such grain was used only for *umuzi* consumption, and when only surplus maize was sold after harvesting.

Africans in more fertile districts were using the growing shortage of grain to build up a trade supplying maize to *imizi* in arid areas. This trade could be very lucrative; in Dundee, Mbonyeni exchanged sufficient grain to accumulate a herd of 150 cattle. The other side of the coin was that as early as the summer of 1889/90, many Africans in the thornveld were left with very little stock.[74]

It was possible for Africans to take provisions to drought-stricken areas because many of them still made a living from transport riding. The Anglo-Zulu and First Anglo-Boer wars had heralded a boom in African transport riding. Many of those who worked as labourers for the military had used their wages to buy army-surplus wagons after the wars, and the number of African-owned wagons increased markedly.[75] By the middle of the 1880s, approximately a quarter of wagon-owner licences were issued to Africans, and because of their low charges, they successfully competed with the railway for freight.[76] Yet transport riding could be precarious and the need to keep prices low to compete with the railway, particularly once it reached northern Natal, meant that profit could be elusive. In addition, particularly in drought years, there was always the danger of oxen dying on the road. As early as 1882, at the height of the African transport-riding boom, the magistrate of Umsinga referred to chronic debt amongst transport-riding *kholwa* in his division.[77] After the discovery of gold there was a great increase in the demand for wagon transport to the gold-fields. In 1890, 27 698 wagons carrying over 80 000 tons crossed the Vaal River. The growing market for produce in colonial and Transvaal centres encouraged white farmers to concentrate on farming and to abandon transport riding, thus creating more openings in that field for Africans. In 1891 Africans in Pietermaritzburg were believed to own three times as many wagons as whites.[78] Philip Kanyele from Inanda offers an example of the profits to be made from transport riding. In 1894 he began trading with a capital of £30. He took tobacco by train to Dundee, and then hired transport from Dundee to Nqutu in Zululand where he traded the tobacco for maize. This was then sold at the Nondweni gold-fields near Nqutu. Within five years he had made a profit of £250 and bought a store in Ladysmith.[79]

Although transport riding helped to keep many homestead and *kholwa* families solvent, it all too often diverted resources from agricultural production. The money earned was seldom ploughed back into improving farming conditions, but went into purchasing cattle, land or a whole range of commodities previously grown or made by the Africans themselves. By the 1880s, the availability of cheap imported goods meant that many traditional artefacts, such as domestic utensils and ironmongery, were no longer being made.[80] This led to growing dependence on traders, a dependence which often included maize and which saw indebtedness spreading throughout African society.

As demand from the *imizi* for grain and white-produced goods grew, so traders opened stores even in remote reserves. Unaccustomed to a market economy, Africans were disadvantaged in their dealings with traders. They had no control over the fluctuations in market prices and, because of their agricultural techniques and monoculture, they were more affected by conditions such as drought than were the more sophisticated commercial farmers. They were therefore at the mercy of the traders, a situation reflected by the number of debt actions being brought against them by storekeepers. Promissory notes were also becoming common throughout the colony, often bearing usurious interest rates.[81]

Records of magistrates' court cases offer a wealth of material on African society from the 1880s, and reflect the difficulties Africans were experiencing in meeting their obligations. The records also vividly illustrate the problems that were arising out of the growing land shortage. Cases against Africans for trespass, and for damage their cattle caused to crops, were becoming common and were being initiated not only by white farmers but also by fellow Africans. These cases became so frequent in Edendale that to reduce the number of lawsuits the inhabitants drew up an agreement that restitution for damage to gardens would be paid in kind.[82]

By the 1890s, the *kholwa* in the midlands and on the coast were experiencing the same difficulties as were *umuzi* Africans. In 1886, a Mission Reserves Commission had exposed this deterioration, particularly on the American reserves.[83] Although the report reflected growing official disillusionment with the results of almost half a century of missionary endeavour, many of its criticisms are borne out by the minutes of the various missionary societies. With Indian and European smallholders usurping the urban markets, few *kholwa* on the coast or in the midlands remained viable peasant farmers.

Conditions on the mission reserves were declining to such an extent that anxious missionaries were having to instruct their tenants on ways of improving their houses and gardens. In 1896, in an attempt to reverse the decline, the American missionaries established a committee on station industries to promote the cultivation of fruit, vegetables, sugar-cane and tea, and the raising of improved stock.[84] In the following year the Groutville missionary lamented that his station's reputation 'as the principle and most advanced centre belongs to departed days'. Many of its sugar lands had become exhausted and been abandoned. Hardly any produce was being sold and 'the few people who are left are in the woeful condition of the poverty-stricken descendents of a great house. They have a great reputation to maintain with nothing to do it with.'[85] In stations such as this, the previous prosperity made it difficult for the *kholwa* to accept their reduced status. They tried to maintain standards by leasing their lands or mortgaging them at exorbitant rates of interest.

In northern Natal, despite the continuing opposition of the stockfarmers, *kholwa* syndicates were steadily increasing their land purchases and were taking advantage of the more favourable opportunities created by the extension of the railway. With little competition from white or Indian cultivators, they remained important suppliers of produce to the towns and coalfields. By the end of the 1890s, many were wealthy enough to have fenced their farms.[86]

Elsewhere, as competition in agriculture became fiercer, so an increasing number of *kholwa* turned from agriculture and tried to retain a semblance of prosperity as a semi-urbanized petty bourgeoisie. With the mainly academic education received at the mission schools, they were well equipped to become school teachers or clerks. By 1894, many mission schools had become dependent on their services, while an increasing number of mission outstations were under *kholwa* supervision.[87] By contrast, very few managed to enter government service. Before 1893, only two succeeded. C. Kunene was appointed clerk and sub-distributor of stamps in Lower Tugela division; John Nambula, who had qualified as a doctor in the United States, was appointed district surgeon of the Umsinga division. By 1891, however, he had resigned because he had so few patients.[88]

A number of *kholwa* became general storekeepers, but their inability to provide credit facilities meant that most Africans continued patronizing white or Indian stores.[89] In the 1880s the government had tried to encourage a broadening of the education offered to Africans by introducing the teaching of basic industrial skills. Under Act 1 of 1884, the provision of industrial education was made a pre-condition for a mission school to receive a government grant. By the 1890s a number of *kholwa* had become carpenters, bricklayers, shoemakers, wagon-makers, etc.[90] Although they were as yet relatively few in number they were already competing for orders with white artisans,[91] and that competition was attracting growing settler hostility.[92] After 1893, as a result of artisan pressure, government measures tended to discriminate against this class of Africans. Regulations were introduced to curb industrial education and a policy was adopted of training Africans to be labourers. Skilled Africans were normally those who had been exempted from the observance of African law. By 1894, there were 1 334 of them in Natal and they were regarded by all Natal ministries as posing the greatest political threat to white rule. From 1893, exemptions were discouraged. In 1894, the Appeal Court ruled that 'a native cannot become a white man' and stressed that exemption only released an African from the observance of 'tribal' customs.[93] By whittling away the rights enjoyed by exempted Africans the responsible government ministries did much to diminish the class differences between the *kholwa* and other Africans.

In the 1890s, most *kholwa* remained, like other Africans, essentially small-scale cultivators facing the same problems of replenishing food supplies and finding money for taxes and rents. When faced with these problems, both homestead and mission Africans usually had little alternative but to become migrant labourers for part of each year. *Imizi* such as those in the Thukela valley reserves could seldom avoid sending their young men out even in years of good rainfall; in the drought years between 1888 and 1893 not only men and boys, but also women, were becoming migrant labourers.[94] The need to provide labour would appear to have remained periodic, however, and in years of normal rainfall the scale of migrant labour dwindled.

Notes

1. *NBB*, 1883, p.GG54; *NBB Departmental Reports*, 1884, pp.B16–17; Upper Umkomazi Magistracy, 3/2/2, 109/92, Magistrate to SNA, 26 March 1892.
2. Act 41, 1884, *To provide for the collection of rent from Native squatters or occupiers of Crown lands*; SNA, 1/1/91, 401/86, Magistrate, Lion's River to SNA, 26 May 1886.
3. NPP, 155, no.83, 1889, Revenue from Crown land rents.
4. See Natal, *Correspondence . . . eviction of Native occupants from Crown lands, 1883*, Magistrate, Alfred, n.d., pp.31–2.
5. NPP, 147, no.126, 1887, Arrears of rents on 31 December 1886.
6. *NBB Departmental Reports*, 1884, p.B16; *Natal Advertiser*, 31 August 1886; SNA, 1/1/94, 945/86, SNA to Colonial Secretary, 13 January 1887; NL&C, 201, no.365, Botha to General Manager, Durban, 25 February 1892; 211, no.272, Essery to General Manager, Durban, 9 July 1894; Natal, *Correspondence . . . eviction of Native occupants from Crown lands, 1883*, Acting Magistrate, Newcastle to SNA, 8 August 1882, p.12; *NBB*, 1882, p.GG54.
7. SNA, 1/1/85, 448/82, Administrator of Native Law, Ipolela to SNA, 18 April 1884; 1/1/121, 1336/89, Administrator of Native Law, Ipolela to SNA, 9 December 1889.
8. See Upper Tugela Administrator of Native Law, 4, 12/83, Administrator to SNA, 18 March 1883, p.170; SNA, 1/1/139, 333/91, Governor, Cape to Governor, Natal, 24 March 1891; Natal, *Auditor's report on the public accounts*, 1887, p.9; NPP, 156, 18/91, Return of Natives who received permission to leave the colony.
. 9 Natal, *Evidence . . . Natal Native Commission, 1881*, Walker, p.69.
10. Quoted in *Natal Witness*, 29 May 1888.
11. Natal, *Report of the Natal Native Commission, 1881–2*, p.50; Natal, *Report . . . Native population*, 1894/5, p.12.
12. *Natal Witness*, 16 January 1882.
13. SNA, 1/1/124, 477/90, Areas of locations.
14. *SANAC*, 3, H. Shepstone, p.81.
15. SNA, 1/1/123, 261/90, Fayle's diary, 19 February 1890.
16. SNA, 1/1/112, 175/89, Appointment of Fayle; 188/89, of Balcomb; 1/1/113, 212/89, of Clarence.

Crisis in African Production 119

17. *LC Hansard*, XIII, 26 June 1889, pp. 382f.
18. SNA, 1/1/123, 396/90, Governor to SNA, 27 March 1890; 1/1/124, 407/90, SNA to Governor, 13 April 1890, Magistrate, Alexandra to Governor, 30 November 1891; 1/1/148, 1260/91, Clarence to Governor, 6 November 1891; Upper Umkomazi Magistracy, 3/2/1, 47/90, Report by Magistrate, n.d.
19. SNA, 1/1/120, 1186/89, 28 October 1889; Kannemeyer, 'New Bantu society', p. 212.
20. See Fayle's diaries in SNA, 1/1/121, 1289/89; 1/1/123, 261/90; 1/1/171, 735/93; 1/1/180, 73/94; 1/1/181, 182/94; 1/1/194, 1428/94; 1/1/198, 257/95.
21. Natal, *Report . . . Native population*, 1894, p. 7; 1896, p. 2; 1897, p. 2.
22. SNA, 1/1/263, 2454/97, Report by Fayle, n.d.
23. *Inkanyiso Yase Natal*, 12 April 1895; *SANAC*, 3, Smith, p. 275.
24. Natal, *Report . . . Native population*, 1901, p. A3.
25. Ibid., 1897, p. 4; GH, 1229, no. 118, Governor to Secretary of State, 12 August 1899, pp. 289f; *Natal Agricultural Journal*, 1, no. 15, 30 September 1898, p. 456.
26. Fayle's diary in SNA, 1/1/201, 456/95, 3 March 1895; 1/1/203, 676/95, 28 May 1895; 1/1/211, 1432/95, 11 November 1895; 1/1/212, 1566/95, 9 December 1895.
27. See Natal, *Report . . . Native population*, 1898, p. A19.
28. *SANAC*, 3, Matthews, p. 891.
29. Natal, *Census of 1891*.
30. Natal, *Evidence . . . Natal Native Commission, 1881*, Mahoba, p. 376, Ncapie, p. 384.
31. *NBB*, 1882, p. X21; 1892/3, p. X21. Incorrectly added as 17 772.
32. Allan, *African husbandman*, pp. 30f.
33. *NBB*, 1882, pp. X6, 7 (statistics for Alfred, 1883, pp. X6, 7); *NBB Departmental Reports*, 1888–1893.
34. Natal, *Report on the Natal forests*, Pietermaritzburg, 1889, pp. 6, 12, 20, 48, 50.
35. See NL&C, 208, no. 85, Weller to General Manager, Durban, 26 August 1893; *Natal Witness*, 29 July 1891.
36. Natal, *Report on the Natal forests*, 1889, pp. 13, 50; SGO, III/1/54, 15/84, Lugg to Magistrate, Alfred, 2 May 1884; 22/84, Duncan to Colonial Secretary, 2 June 1885; III/1/56, 447/86, Crowder to Magistrate, Ixopo, 22 February 1886; NL&C, 172, Townsend to General Manager, Durban, 22 July 1884; *NBB Departmental reports*, 1891/2, pp. F5–6.
37. R. Palmer and N. Parsons, (eds), *The roots of rural poverty in central and southern Africa*, London, 1977, p. 7.
38. T.B. Jenkinson, *Amazulu: the Zulus, their past history, manners, customs and language . . .*, London, 1882, p. 10.
39. *NBB*, 1869, p. X12; 1882, p. xii; *NSYB*, 1896, p. P15.
40. NL&C, 175, no. 74, Botha to General Manager, Durban, 19 January 1885; Colenso Collection, 24, Dulcken to H. Colenso, 12 November 1887; SGO, III/1/83, 716/92, Magistrate, Lower Umzimkulu to Surveyor-General, 22 February 1892; GH, 1545, 209a/85, SNA to Governor, 21 July 1885, p. 87; Impendhle Administrator of Native Law, 3, Administrator to SNA, 29 August 1889, p. 123; *NGG*, XLI, no. 2381, 10 September 1889, p. 1181.
41. NL&C, 204, no. 164, Francis to General Manager, Durban, 17 August 1892; see also Newcastle Magistracy, 3/1/1/8, 457/98 Silgee to SNA, 6 September 1898; Upper Tugela Administrator of Native Law, 4, 46/86, Administrator to SNA, 25 June 1886; 4, no number, Administrator to Crowley, 2 October 1889, p. 418; SNA, 1/1/132, 1244/90, Magistrate, Umvoti to SNA, 18 October 1890.
42. *Natal Mercury*, 19 April 1893.
43. NPP, 152, no. 28, 1889, Annual report, Weenen Agricultural Society for 1888; *Natal Witness*, 16 February 1888; 4 May 1888.
44. *Natal Mercury*, 1 October 1896.
45. See chapter eight.
46. Natal, *Report . . . Native population*, 1894, p. 83.
47. D.I. Bransby, 'The ecology of livestock production in Natal and Zululand', Workshop on production and reproduction in the Zulu kingdom, University of Natal, Pietermaritzburg, 1977, p. 3.
48. *NSYB*, 1896, p. P15.
49. *NBB*, 1894, pp. 78, 83; 1895, p. 46.

50. C.J. Smythe Papers, Diary 9, 31 December 1889; *Natal Witness*, 3 and 9 January 1890; 1 Januar 1891; 3 December 1892; *NBB Departmental Reports*, 1894/5, p.B21; see also J.H. Topp 'Meeting the requirements of cattle in drought conditions', in D. Dalby et al., eds, *Drought Africa*, London, 1977, pp.101f.

51. SNA, 1/1/101, 638/87, Petition of Unklemane for exemption, 15 July 1887; Native High Cour II/4/27, CS76/94, Regina v. Nahlatini; CS95/94, Regina v. Umdosi.

52. C.J. Smythe Papers, Diary 10, 31 December 1891; 31 December 1892; *NBB Department Reports*, 1889, pp.B21, 40.

53. SNA, 1/1/124, 472/90, Magistrate, Weenen to SNA, 13 April 1890.

54. SNA, 1/1/164, 1308/92, Magistrate, Alfred to SNA, 2 December 1892; *Natal Witness*, 5 Decembe 1887.

55. *Natal Mercury*, 26 October 1892; *Natal Witness*, 24 December 1889; SNA, 1/1/156, 502/92, Fayl diary, 2 May 1892.

56. *Natal Witness*, 17 February 1890.

57. SNA, 1/1/163, 1209/92, SNA to Governor, 2 December 1892.

58. *NBB*, 1888–1893; *NBB Departmental reports*, 1888–1893; SNA, 1/1/137, 94/91, Fayle diary 11 January 1891; see also A. Booth, 'Homestead, state and migrant labour in colonial Swaziland *African Economic History*, 14, 1985, pp.107–45.

59. *NBB*, 1882, p.GG13; Natal, *Report on the Natal forests*, 1889, p.15; *Natal Mercury*, 2 Februar 1891; 2 October 1892; Act 23, 1884, *To prevent the indiscriminate destruction of certain valuab wild animals*; Act 28, 1890 and Act 16, 1891, *To make provision for the better preservation game.*

60. *LA Sessional Papers*, no.18, 1896, Return of permits, pp.103–7; *Natal Witness*, 17 July 1896.

61. *Natal Witness*, 29 June 1894; Natal, *Report . . . Native population*, 1901, pp.A48, 50, 52.

62. B.J.T, Leverton, 'Government finance and political development in Natal, 1843–1893', *AYF* 1970(1), Johannesburg, 1971, p.243; Sir Theophilus Shepstone Papers, 54, Governor Shepstone, 11 July 1886, pp.43–5; 11 July 1886, pp.48–9.

63. *NGG*, XLII, no.2355, 30 September 1890, Proclamation 32, 1890, p.1555.

64. E. Le Roy Ladurie, 'Peasants', in P. Burke, ed., *The new Cambridge modern history*, 1. companion volume, Cambridge, 1979, pp.130–4.

65. E.J. Hobsbawm, 'Review of *Peasants, politics and revolution . . .* by J.S. Migdal', *Journal Peasant Studies*, 5, no.2, 1978, p.254.

66. CSO, 2774, Immigration and Crown Lands Commission, 1891, Market Master, p.451; *Nat Mercury*, 15 January 1891.

67. *Natal Witness*, 22 August 1893; SNA, 1/1/189, 977/94, Fayle diary, 31 July 1894; 1/1/205, 815/9 25 June 1895; Welsh, *Roots of segregation*, p.187.

68. *Natal Witness*, 28 April, 15 May 1888; 26 June 1889; CSO, 2775, Immigration and Crown Land Commission, 1891, Market Master, p.627, Mason, p.1113; Maize prices gleaned over a twelve month period.

69. *Natal Witness*, 16 February, 26 April, 17 May, 13 June 1888; 'Natal's hide and skin trade', *Th Colonist*, 1, no.8, 16 January 1904, p.392.

70. *Natal Witness*, 4 June 1888, 'Chamber of Agriculture'.

71. *NBB Departmental Reports*, 1889, p.B51; SNA, 1/1/121, 25/90, Circular, January 1890.

72. See *NBB*, 1895, pp.41, 45.

73. *Natal Witness*, 1 February 1888; 22 June 1889.

74. Native High Court, II/4/29, CS74/95, Regina v. Umbonyeni.

75. *NBB*, 1872, p.X18; 1882, p.X21.

76. *NGG*, XXV, no.2022, 11 September 1883, LC 26, Second interim report, p.809; Natal, *Auditor' report on the public accounts*, 1885, p.9.

77. *NBB*, 1882, p.GG67.

78. CSO, 2776, Immigration and Crown Lands Commission, 1891, Fell, p.1285; R.U. Sayce, 'Th transport ox', in I.C. Peate, ed., *Studies in regional consciousness and environment*, Freepor 1968, pp.72, 74.

79. CSO, 2917, Invasion Losses Enquiry Commission, claim, Kanyele.

80. See Natal, *Report . . . Native population*, 1879, pp.7, 18.

81. *NBB Departmental Reports*, 1884, p.B16; SNA, 1/4/3, c17/86, SNA to magistrates, 5 Novembe 1886. A similar situation existed in the Cape, see Bundy, *Rise and fall*, p.129.

82. *Natal Witness*, 12 March 1885.
83. Natal, *Report on the Native mission reserves*, pp. 2–4. For conditions in Edendale, see S. M. Meintjes, 'Edendale, 1850–1906: a case study of rural transformation and class formation in an African mission in Natal', Ph.D. thesis, University of London, 1988, pp. 364f.
84. ABM, A/1/2, Minutes, 4 July 1895, p. 143, 10 July 1896, pp. 229–30.
85. ABM, A/3/41, Report of Umvoti station, June 1897.
86. *LC Hansard*, XVI, 8 June 1891, Sutherland, p. 175; CSO, 2917, Invasion Losses Enquiry Commission, claim, Celliers.
87. Natal, Native Education Department, *Annual report of the Inspector of Native Schools for 1893–1894*, Pietermaritzburg, 1894.
88. *NBB*, 1889, p. C49; 1891/2, p. C41; SNA, 1/1/150, 1423/91, Nambula to Colonial Secretary, 2 November 1891.
89. Natal, *Auditor's report on the public accounts*, 1885, p. 9.
90. Natal, *Evidence . . . Lands Commission, (1900–01–02)*, Addison, p. 414.
91. SNA, 1/1/105, 196/88, Administrator of Native Law, Mapumulo to Colonial Engineer, 16 May 1888; 1/1/114, 382/89, Clarence diary, 3 April 1889.
92. See *Natal Witness*, 12 June 1889, 28 February 1890; *Inkanyiso Yase Natal*, 9 January 1893, 14 April 1893.
93. *Inkanyiso Yase Natal*, 5 January 1894.
94. *NBB Departmental Reports*, 1889, pp. B40, 51; SNA, 1/1/121, 25/90, Circular, January 1890; SNA, 1/1/139, 320/91, Balcomb diary, 9 March 1891.

CHAPTER EIGHT

The Dislocation of African Society

Despite the crisis facing homestead production in late nineteenth-century Natal, most *imizi* retained a measure of self-sufficiency. Except in years of drought, they were not totally dependent on cash from wage labour, but used it to supplement the money they could earn from produce sales. Yet, due to the growing numbers of African men working as migrant labourers in the colony and the Transvaal, homestead dependence on the cash economy was growing. At the same time, the impact of migrant labour was widely felt at all levels of African society.

Having tasted the freedom of working away from the restraining influence of the *umuzi* and wider kinship group, young men returning to their *imizi* were reluctant to comply with demands made on them by their elders. This had repercussions for the control which elders exercised over their people, and undermined the whole basis of the chiefly patron-client relationship. Because their needs could be met by wage labour, unmarried men were less dependent than they had been on their elders and became reluctant to continue providing services to them. The ability of chiefs to allocate land had already been undermined by the land shortage; now, as men began looking to traders and labour touts for cattle, the *ukusisa* custom came under threat. Since the provision of stock to dependents formed the basis of the patron-client relationship, the decline of the *ukusisa* custom was as destructive to the power base of the chiefs as was the land shortage. Less able than in the past to cement ties of dependence with their people, and less able to distribute and redistribute land, chiefs had few resources with which to shore up their authority.

At the same time, the growing demands made by both government and settlers on their people were making the position of many chiefs untenable. With white landowners tightening control of Africans on their lands, chiefs could seldom call rent and labour tenants out for the *isibhalo* service required by the state. The imposition of rentals on Crown lands in 1884 made squatters on those lands equally reluctant to provide *isibhalo* service. The chiefs were now obliged to rely solely on reserve inhabitants. Besides this, there was the difficulty of finding men who were not already working for part of the year as migrant labourers. Altogether, the ability of the chiefs to fulfil their duties to the state was severely circumscribed. The situation in which Chief Makosini of the Ngwane found himself by 1891 was fairly typical. The sale of Crown lands in Klip River county meant that virtually all of the 154 huts owing him allegiance were now on private lands, yet he was still expected to provide the same number of men for *isibhalo* service. Faced with this dilemma, he tried unsuccessfully to resign his chiefship.[1] Chiefs like Makosini often had little choice but to try to force *abanumzana* on reserve land to provide more men than were expected of them, or even to exert pressure on their followers on private lands to supply labour. As a result, hostility to chiefly exactions became widespread among *abanumzana* as well as among young men.[2]

Despite the continuing determination of the government, as reflected in the 1891 Code, to use the chiefly system to control the African population, official enactments steadily eroded chiefly powers. From 1888, for example, no chief could take an *umuzi* under his authority without the sanction of the Secretary for Native Affairs.[3] After the introduction of responsible government in 1893, the ministry's intention was not so much to bolster chiefly power as to bend it to settler requirements. Amendments were made to those sections of the Code which set out the powers of chiefs and *izinduna*. Not only did chiefs lose their civil jurisdiction over their followers on private lands, but Act 13 of 1894 encouraged the fragmentation of chiefdoms by empowering *izinduna* to try civil cases without reference to their chiefs. But, to tighten official control over *izinduna*, the Code was amended so that a new *induna* could only be appointed with the approval of a magistrate. The new government also tried to blur the distinction between appointed and hereditary chiefs in an attempt to increase the formers' dependence on the administration. Act 40 of 1896 extended to them the *lobola* privileges of a hereditary chief.

Act 37 of 1896 was the most far-reaching attempt to subject chiefs to official control. In place of the authority within the reserves previously vested in the Supreme Chief and lesser chiefs, it substituted the Governor-in-Council, in effect the ministry. The act empowered the ministry to draw up rules and regulations for the administration of the reserves and to delegate its authority to inspectors. The act marked a radical departure in African administration. The Member of Parliament, F.A.R. Johnstone, believed that it would destroy the only power capable of governing the Africans, while the Speaker, Henry Stainbank, warned of the dangers of undermining chiefly authority: 'If we do away with these little matters, which are really the only things in which the chief has any authority, then I say we are striking at the root of our own policy.'[4]

The first rules under Act 37 appeared in the *Government Gazette* in December 1896. They completely undermined the authority of the chiefs, turning them into little more than policemen responsible for ensuring that the rules and regulations were not contravened. By contrast, effective powers were placed in the hands of the magistrates. They became responsible for reviewing the chiefs' allocation of lands and were given authority in all important cases in the reserves including disputes over land.[5]

Caught between the growing intrusiveness of the state and the widespread antagonism of their people, chiefs and *izinduna* throughout Natal were seething with resentment. Many expressed this in growing insolence to government officials and particularly to the magistrates who were usurping their powers.[6] With the breakdown in communication between the Secretary for Native Affairs and the chiefs, official actions often appeared arbitrary and incomprehensible and laid sure foundations for future trouble.

The anger of the chiefs was further fuelled by the growing tendency of landowners and urban authorities to ignore their chiefly authority and to appoint commoners as *izinduna* to control tenants and labourers. These appointments cut across the authority of chiefs and undermined the hierarchical structures of African society. With no traditional foundation for their authority, these men were totally dependent on their employers. In the 1890s, Mazibuko was appointed *induna* of a farm in Upper Tugela and, according to his son, 'when you were appointed headman you always were loyal to the boss – you always supported him'.[7] These men came to be identified with the system of repression and risked ostracism and physical assault. *Izinduna* placed on farms by the Land and Colonisation Company often found rent tenants so hostile that they could not perform their functions.[8] This hostility to African surrogates of white authority was also apparent in the towns, where it took the form of growing conflict between African policemen and young Africans. Although this resistance was usually spasmodic, by the 1890s it was becoming organized.[9]

Resentment was also growing among black Christians. *Kholwa* attempts to identify with European values had antagonized the very class from whom they sought acceptance. As the *kholwa* became landowners and petty entrepreneurs, the settlers began to see them as a threat. Men like Stephanus Mini and Luke Kumalo began complaining of the treatment they received from settlers and officials.[10] These complaints received little sympathy from either Henrique Shepstone or Frederick Moor. Despite this, and despite the introduction of measures undermining their status, the *kholwa* continued to stress the differences between themselves and homestead Africans. In 1888, they formed the Funemalungelo Society, specifically to further their cause. Their interests were also advanced in the newspaper *Inkanyiso Yase Natal* which was started in 1889 at St Alban's College in Pietermaritzburg under the editorship of the Revd F. Greene and taken over, in 1895, by Solomon Kumalo.[11] As the mouthpiece of *kholwa* aspirations, it reflected their ambiguous position, portraying their resentment at their treatment, yet at the same time stressing their distinctive identity.

But as conditions on the mission reserves deteriorated, the real differences between mission *kholwa* and homestead Africans were narrowing. Many residents, particularly of the non-exempted class, became embittered with the failure of the missionaries to fulfil their aspirations. And, just as young Africans generally were questioning and resisting the authority of their chiefs and elders, so young *kholwa* were questioning the authority of the missionaries.[12]

As the African need for land grew more acute, clashes occurred between *kho*
and non-Christian families on the mission reserves and the latter appealed to tl
chiefs for assistance. The chiefs were not loath to intervene on behalf of tl
followers, and to try to prevent them from doing so the American missiona
urged Henrique Shepstone in the late 1880s to extend the system of *kho*
izinduna to their reserves.[13] Job Kambule who had been placed in charge of
Edendale Christians by Theophilus Shepstone before 1861 was the first s
kholwa appointee and by the early 1880s Stephanus Mini had been appoin
When Driefontein was established, Johannes Kumalo had received a sim
position. After 1879, these appointments were extended to the mission static
with both exempted and non-exempted men being appointed.[14] The appointn
of *kholwa izinduna* had not, however, been extended to mission reserves
Henrique Shepstone rejected the missionaries' request as he believed that s
appointments would further divide authority and inflame tensions on the miss
reserves.[15] However, conditions on these reserves continued to deteriorate and
Native Code of 1891 eventually provided for the appointment of *kholwa izind*
over mission reserves. Indeed, the Code went considerably further. It gave to
kholwa izinduna the legal status of appointed chiefs, so enabling them to hear c
cases; they could try homestead Africans according to African law and could
kholwa, in Johannes Kumalo's words, 'as near as I know to White man's law
These measures in effect created distinct chiefdoms on each reserve, a step wh
increased rather than diminished friction and resentment. The non-Christian ch
saw these reforms as an attempt to undermine their authority.[17]

The appointment of Christian chiefs was part of a process whereby
government was blurring the distinction between *kholwa* and non-*kholwa* in
colony. Whereas previously *kholwa izinduna* had exercised jurisdiction only o
fellow *kholwa*, now as chiefs they exercised territorial authority and could acc
men who had changed their allegiance.[18] Henrique's fear that their appointm
would exacerbate factional tension soon proved warranted; in 1898 the magistr
of Ixopo, F.E. Foxon, accused *kholwa* chiefs of showing contempt for heredit
chiefs and of inciting their followers to do the same. This, Foxon wrote, 'is a bi
grievance with some of the chiefs who argue that the land was theirs before it v
given to the missionaries'.[19] At the same time, many *kholwa* were affronted by
change which they regarded as an attempt by government to undermine their sta
and subject them to chiefship.[20] For example, in Edendale in 1891, Stephanus M
found it so difficult to control the unexempted *kholwa* that he tried to resign
chiefship but no one was prepared to take his place.[21]

Government attempts to solve the problems on the mission reserves l
therefore been counterproductive. A dual authority now existed which encoura;
interference by both traditionalist and *kholwa* chiefs in each other's affairs a
complicated the missionaries' task of control.

This dilemma was made no easier by growing official antipathy to miss
work. As long as the missions had been seen as nurseries for a peasantry capabl

providing the agricultural requirements of the colony, there had been a shared interest between the missionaries and the government. In the face of the growing commercialization of settler agriculture and with growing hostility towards any African competition, this community of interest broke down. By the late 1880s, less land was being allotted for mission purposes, and none of it carried full title.[22] The original chiefs on the mission reserves exploited this rift by attempting to recapture their authority and the inhabitants generally challenged the position of the missionaries. The resulting power vacuum, particularly on reserves without resident white missionaries, was something the responsible government ministry in 1893 was not prepared to tolerate. Escombe was determined to assert the ministry's authority over the reserves and under the Mission Reserves Act of 1895 the Governor was empowered to pass regulations for their control. The American missionaries in particular opposed the act and declined to co-operate with the government. Their converts, however, were quick to see where authority now lay; in 1896, for example, the *kholwa* on the Esidumbeni reserve requested the government to draw up regulations for the reserve.[23]

Underlying the problems facing the missionaries were the same pressures of social dislocation that were affecting Africans elsewhere. In general, the complaints of insubordination and youthful disregard for authority were remarkably similar whether they came from missionaries, magistrates, *abanumzana* or chiefs. There was also a markedly similar tendency among both settlers and African elders to impute growing insubordination to increased beer drinking. The consumption of *utshwala* held a prominent place in African society and had a traditional importance both as a form of tribute and as a way of rewarding services. Because of this, control both of the labour required for brewing and of the consumption of *utshwala*, was integral to the maintenance of an *umnumzana*'s power within his *umuzi*. As the power of elders declined during the colonial period, so their control over beer consumption was challenged. By the 1880s, with the growing dependence on sorghum, *utshwala* came to play an enlarged dietary role, while on the coast *utshwala* mixed with treacle was becoming a popular and highly intoxicating drink, *itishimiyana*. As the consumption of *utshwala* and *itishimiyana* increased, many of the social restrictions on young men and women drinking beer were being disregarded. Having tasted the freedom of working away from the restraining influence of the *umuzi* and wider kinship group, returning migrant labourers were proving reluctant to conform to social conventions. Because of age and other restrictions imposed by elders on the consumption of *utshwala*, drinking had associations with masculinity which young men, returning to their *imizi*, were quick to seize on. By ignoring the restrictions they were effectively challenging the authority of the *abanumzana*. Their attitudes influenced both the women of the *imizi* and the youth and saw the formation of new groupings of young men and women which the homestead authorities found difficult to control. Beer drinking was an outward manifestation of their growing independence and, according to Thomas Fayle, *abanumzana* could not even prevent children from drinking.[24]

The most obvious expression of the growing competition among Africans for the colony's dwindling resources was the increase in the number of faction fights, either within or between chiefdoms. Because this increase coincided with the increase in beer drinking, it was commonly held by settlers and African elders that the two were interrelated.[25] Henrique Shepstone shared the view commonly held by African elders that intoxication had a role in African society, providing an outlet for grievances. But few settlers understood either beer's social or its nutritional value in homestead society and they demanded official action to curb its consumption. As a result, in 1884, magistrates were asked to consult chiefs on ways of controlling social gatherings. Aware of the extent to which their dwindling control of these gatherings was undermining their overall control of their followers, several chiefs demanded the introduction of restrictions.[26] Four years later the government responded by allowing *abanumzana* to request the presence of an African policeman to maintain order at *umuzi* gatherings.[27] Few *abanumzana* took advantage of the offer, and in 1892 the Magistrates' Commission advised that such gatherings should be licensed and supervised by police. Instructions were given to magistrates the following year that the chiefs' *izinduna* had to be informed of all gatherings; that these had to be concluded by sunset; that women were to be discouraged from attending; and that only invited young men could attend.[28]

The widespread belief that increased beer drinking led to increased faction fighting is not borne out in official statistics. Between September 1884 and September 1886, 2 703 Africans were tried for faction fighting in the Native High Court, a number which actually decreased slightly to 2 613 between January 1888 and June 1891 when Africans were particularly dependent on sorghum beer.[29] This does not of course mean that drunkenness played no part when clashes occurred. Young men were far more inclined to assert their masculinity when drunk, and chiefs were as convinced as settlers that when people of different chiefdoms convened at social gatherings where large amounts of beer were drunk, it was easy for old animosities to be inflamed.[30]

These animosities were becoming more widespread as competition for gardens and pastures between dispossessed African newcomers and established reserve residents became more intense. As there were no internal boundaries between chiefdoms, it was difficult for chiefs to prevent their followers from trespassing on land belonging to other chiefdoms and disputes over garden sites and grazing frequently escalated into armed clashes. These were particularly common in arid reserves such as the Klip River and Impafana reserves which were to become notoriously violent in the twentieth century. Chronic overcrowding exacerbated the arid and infertile conditions and an intolerable situation developed.[31] This volatility was aggravated by a decline in the position of the Chunu. Under Phakade, the members of the chiefdom had enjoyed a dominant position and had expanded onto the Crown lands abutting on the reserves. As these lands were bought by settlers, evictions began and the chiefdom was increasingly hemmed in. Phakade was succeeded by his grandson, Silwana kaGabangaye, in 1881 and the pressures on him grew as he sought to provide land for his followers and for land-hungry *abanumzana* who had transferred their allegiance to him. Even so, the Chunu and, to a lesser extent, the Thembu chiefs still had a relatively strong position for, with the exception of Ncwadi of the Ngwane in Upper Tugela reserve, they were the only chiefs in northern Natal who were still able to call together *amabutho*. They retained fewer than had been the case in the 1850s and 1860s and were unable to summon them as regularly for the *umkhosi* ceremony.[32] Yet the hold which they could still exert over at least some of their men enabled them to continue building up their chiefdoms, despite the serious problems of growing overpopulation and aridity, in a way that their neighbours could not emulate. As a result, politics in the reserves continued to be dominated by the two chiefdoms. As they manoeuvred to protect their positions, conflict between them and the smaller Mabaso, Qamu and Mbomvu chiefdoms over the limited and sterile resources erupted into increasingly frequent violence.[33]

The situation was also particularly serious in Umvoti reserve, the most densely populated African district in Natal and home to the Qwabe, Mthethwa and Zulu chiefdoms. Both the Qwabe and Mthethwa were historically important chiefdoms and conflict between the two and with the Zulu chiefdom was endemic. Evictions from privately owned lands in Inanda and Lower Tugela divisions was placing great pressure on resources in the reserve and causing intensified friction between the chiefdoms.

In south-western Natal the large number of small chiefdoms, and the insecure position of many of the appointed chiefs, created political conditions conducive to conflict. Upper Umkomazi, Ixopo and Alexandra divisions were particularly affected by the sale of Crown lands and the opening up of the area to white settlement. Despite the purchases made by chiefs, each chiefdom had only a small amount of land at its disposal. It was a common saying that 'there is no law in regard to the occupation of land',[34] and clashes occurred as the men of the various chiefdoms manoeuvred for land. Thus, for example, the Duma chief, Sawoti, a particularly hot-headed and impetuous man, was intolerant of inroads into his lands, but at the same time encouraged his people to encroach on lands belonging to the Mbo chiefs Kaduphi and Mabuna. Followers of the three chiefs regularly clashed, earning for the chiefdoms the reputation of being the most troublesome in Natal.[35] Sawoti believed that he could act with relative impunity; in 1886 he was sentenced to two years' imprisonment for assault by the Alexandra magistrate. This sentence was reduced on appeal from his *izinduna*. After this he became decidedly contemptuous of the government's attempts to control him, publicly boasting that he was stronger than the magistrate.[36]

Like Sawoti, the Mphumuza chief, Thetheleku, was also encouraged by the government's reluctance to stop him from expanding his territory. From the earliest days of the Edendale settlement, his followers in Zwartkop reserve had clashed with the *kholwa* over gardens and grazing and, as the number of *abanumzana* paying hut tax under him increased, so he began encroaching on the

lands of Mzimba's Nadi chiefdom. By 1893, six clashes had occurred betw
them with Thetheleku summoning men from as far afield as Johannesburg
reinforcements.[37] Despite this, Thetheleku still received official backing. '
only chief in the colony permitted to walk into Government House at his leisu
sneered the *Natal Witness*.[38] Thetheleku skilfully used his position to benefit
chiefdom and consolidate his hold over his followers. In 1890 a boundary '
drawn between the Mphumuza and Nadi chiefdoms, yet, in 1893, w
Thetheleku tried unsuccessfully to evict Nadi people from their side of
boundary, he was 'fortunate enough to get the Native Department to assist hin
Despite Mzimba's paramountcy, he was ordered to remove seventeen *imiz*
allow Thetheleku space; eleven *abanumzana* who refused to move were e
sentenced to two months' imprisonment with hard labour.

    The administration, before responsible government, remained remarka
unconcerned about the extent of faction fighting in the colony. The general attit
of the Executive Council was that the clashes were an outlet for 'angry passic
and as such were not an 'altogether unmixed evil'.[40] Theophilus Shepstone l
earlier begun to define boundaries between chiefdoms when clashes occurred,
Henrique seldom followed his example, nor did he seriously attempt to check
causes of disturbances or allow the chiefs sufficient authority to enable them to
so.[41] In reaction to Thetheleku's disregard of the boundary between the Mphum
and Nadi chiefdoms, Shepstone's attitude was that insistence on honouring
boundary would increase tensions because many *imizi* would have to
relocated.[42] In most cases of faction fights, he made little attempt to investigate
causes and punish the guilty; it was easier to punish all involved. This cau
resentment and increased hostility between chiefdoms. As was pointed out a
meeting of chiefs at Zwartkop in 1884, the 'Government punishes all alike a
those who are innocent have it out afterwards'.[43] After 1893, the Robinson minis
tried to end faction fights by defining boundaries between feuding chiefdoms. A
40 of 1896 authorized the defining of such boundaries and gave the government
necessary powers to compel members of the affected chiefdoms to relocate th
imizi.

    Although most fights took place between chiefdoms, clashes also occur
within them. While overcrowding could be the cause of these, many resulted fr
disputed successions. In 1904, Mbovu kaMtshumayeli of Amanzimtoti miss
reserve told James Stuart that succession disputes were 'what tends to dest
tribes, for the members kill one another'.[44] Here the government was prepared
intervene, since control over chiefly succession was crucial to its control o
chiefs. There had always been disputed successions in African society, but
intervention of the colonial state resulted in their becoming both more comm
and more complicated. Before 1875 the Lieutenant-Governor as Supreme Ch
had the final say on chiefly succession. As succession was usually clear becau
the heir would have been nominated by the old chief, he seldom overturned '
choice of the chiefdoms themselves. In cases where it was disputed, the *izindu*

would convene to decide and their nomination generally received the approval of the Secretary for Native Affairs.[45] The Native Administration Act of 1875 deprived the Supreme Chief of his judicial authority and transferred it to the courts. This meant that although he could still appoint chiefs, he could not give judgement on property rights. While Act 44 of 1887 restored his position as Paramount Chief, the division of legal competence was revived by the 1891 Code. Section 58 of the Code upheld the right of the Supreme Chief to decide on chiefship and succession, but sections 98 to 107 gave to the courts the right to decide on property inheritance.

African law did not distinguish between the property and the person of the chief, and the Code created intolerable complexities when the succession to a chiefship was disputed. Despite the appointment of a new chief by the Supreme Chief, rival claimants were now eager to appeal to the Native High Court. A test case occurred in the Umvoti reserve after the death of the Qwabe chief, Musi kaGodolozi, in 1891. The succession was disputed and it was only in July 1892 that the Supreme Chief appointed his son Meseni. The rival claimant, Siziba kaMmiso, appealed to be recognized as Musi's personal heir and in November 1894 the Native High Court ruled in his favour, awarding him the property rights of the chiefly house. Meanwhile, factions had formed behind the rival claimants and bitter fights were taking place.[46]

Disputed chiefships and faction fights were one indication of the deepening crisis in African society; another was the growth of crime and resistance to the settler presence. In 1852, Henry Cloete had confidently asserted that he 'did not believe that the history of man affords a parrallel [sic] to the unprecedented security, both of life and property, which the Europeans have possessed during the last ten years'.[47] In 1879 most magistrates had agreed that crime in their divisions was insignificant and, as late as 1886, Henrique Shepstone and Henry Binns referred to the extraordinarily small amount of crime among the African population.[48] That the situation was changing by the late 1880s is suggested by the increase in the number of cases tried in the magistrates' courts: from 2 416 in the 24-month period 1888–89, to 6 495 in the 30 months, January 1890–June 1892.[49]

Incidents of crime were most visible in the villages and towns where growing numbers of African workers lived in generally squalid slums. From the earliest days of colonial rule, strict steps had been taken to regulate these workers, by the use of such instruments as passes and a curfew.[50] These were seldom effective before the end of the century, however, and young men experienced a freedom in urban life and labour migrancy that encouraged disrespect for established authority. This attitude was carried back to the rural areas to be reflected in the increase in rural crime.

It would be as simplistic, however, to ascribe crime to such attitudes as it would be to attribute it to increased alcohol consumption. By the late 1880s, a pattern can be observed of growing resistance amongst Africans to conditions in the colony.

This resistance did not necessarily take the form of crime; it could be expressed in the relocation by families from farms to escape labour duties or high rentals, or even by chiefs from the colony, such as when Ramncana moved to Basutoland in 1889.[51] Rent tenants could also deliberately delay the payment of their rents. Resistance could also include go-slows by labourers, and even refusal by them to perform certain tasks; the first recorded African strike, in the Umgeni stone quarries, occurred as early as 1867. African workers might even pretend incomprehension of their instructions, reinforcing settler preconceptions that Africans were lazy and incapable of performing the simplest duties.

These were acts of passive resistance and cannot be classified as criminal. But there was also a growing number of crimes being committed on farms, many of them traceable to earlier evictions. In 1882 a Biggarsberg farmer, J.C. Muller, was murdered by an African whom he had evicted, while in 1888 a farmer in Lion's River had his farmhouse burnt down for the same reason.[52] Such acts were by no means only against whites; in Alexandra, a Crown-land purchaser, Somlota, repeatedly had his beacons thrown down and his gardens destroyed by the people he had evicted, while members of Mdindwana's Nyamvu chiefdom, evicted from their land after forty years of settlement, not only threatened to drive the purchaser, Chief T. Joyce, and his people off the land, but also continued planting crops in their old gardens.[53] Throughout Natal, complaints that evicted Africans stole, set fire to grass and stabbed cattle were common. Attacks also occurred on farmers who restricted the acreage of arable and grazing land available to their tenants. The farmers themselves were seldom assaulted, but fence-cutting was a common form of protest.[54]

The absence of a properly organized police force made the detection of crime difficult, and the magistrates were too overworked to pay attention to crime in areas remote from their seats. With few policemen and even fewer Justices of the Peace to assist them, it was impossible for magistrates to combat the spread of crime. In the rural areas, the greatest complaints concerned stock losses. Stock thefts had occurred regularly in south-western Natal from the earliest days of British rule, but were comparatively rare elsewhere. By the 1870s sheep and cattle losses were rising sharply throughout the colony.[55]

Throughout the 1880s, the crescendo of complaints about stock thefts grew, particularly in the district bordering on Griqualand East and Pondoland.[56] Here, kinship links between the chiefdoms on either side of the Natal border were strong and there was a constant movement of Africans across the border so that it was easy for thieves to operate undetected. The Native High Court records suggest that many thefts were by Mpondo and other Cape Africans. In 1885, Mpondo were found guilty of stealing 17 horses in Ixopo and in 1891 they stole 22 cattle, 27 horses and 77 sheep and goats, from Africans alone, in Alfred county.[57] But Cape Africans were by no means the only thieves. In Alfred in 1891, 18 oxen were stolen from T. Webster by Nkomana, a Natal African, to sell in Pondoland, and 8 oxen were stolen by Makemu, likewise from Natal, from N. Boddy for the same purpose. Thefts by Natal Africans south of the border were also numerous enough to cause the Cape government to appeal to Natal in 1895 to take preventive steps.[58]

Between 1876 and 1895 there was a significant increase both in the number of stock-theft cases tried before the magistrates and the Native High Court, and in the number of convictions. The average number of cases before the High Court rose from 70 per annum in the late 1870s to 98 in the mid-1890s, with convictions being given in over three-quarters of the cases.[59] Despite high rates of conviction, farmers complained that insufficient action was being taken to prevent thefts and argued that the Native High Court cases reflected only the tip of the iceberg. George Sutton calculated in 1891 that farmers suffered average losses of from 10 to 15 per cent of their flocks per annum.[60] Yet farmers seldom reported losses to the police, arguing that this was pointless because of the inability of the police to apprehend thieves and the leniency of the sentences, usually imprisonment for between nine months and five years.[61] Many farmers preferred to take the law into their own hands and fined and evicted Africans suspected of stealing stock, while others went further and it was 'commonly reported that . . . two or three natives mysteriously disappeared from some of the up-country districts'.[62] Yet others, like Sutton, employed armed guards. In 1885, Sutton claimed that 276 of his sheep had been stolen by Africans in 1883, but that none had been stolen after he resorted to armed guards.[63]

A word of caution is required. To what extent can these stock losses be attributed to theft? Government officials were sceptical about the farmers' claims. Allegedly stolen sheep often had the habit of turning up later, and even Sutton's diary refers to the return of missing sheep.[64] Many farmers were undeniably careless. Few counted their stock, and cattle and sheep were often allowed to graze without being kraaled at night. It was thus impossible for an accurate tally to be kept, or for the animals to be properly protected. Many farmers continued to allow their stock to graze with African-owned flocks and herds on reserve, Crown and absentee-owned lands. It was, therefore, difficult for them to know where their stock were, or for Africans to distinguish them from their own animals. In several districts sheep were killed by dogs. However, it was popularly believed by farmers that Africans let their dogs fend for themselves when food was scarce. Consequently, farmers demanded that the number of African-owned dogs be curbed and that the 5s. dog tax be amended so that a payment of 10s. could be levied for each additional dog.[65]

Nonetheless, stock losses were so great (for example, one Ipolela farmer's flock declined from 1 100 in 1889 to 700 in 1891),[66] that thefts must have been an important contributory cause. Charles Smythe's experience appears to confirm this – despite fencing his farms and counting his flocks every week, he lost 103 sheep between 20 March and 19 April 1884.[67] In most stock-theft cases only one or two animals would disappear at a time and these were probably stolen by Africans for food, particularly as they occurred more often when grain was scarce. As has been noted elsewhere, beer drinking increased in times of drought because of a greater dependence on sorghum, and many farmers believed that increased beer consumption and increased thefts were intertwined, claiming that beer gave Africans a craving for meat.[68]

Cattle, too, tended to disappear in small numbers and here thefts seem often to have been the cause. One measure taken to try to safeguard settlers' herds, was that Africans were not permitted to drive cattle without a pass. But it remained relatively easy for them to obtain passes, while it was not uncommon for Indians and whites to purchase stolen cattle without checking the seller's pass or its applicability to the animals being sold. The law did not penalize purchasers of stolen stock, so that even butchers such as McFie and Knapp in Pietermaritzburg were prepared to turn a blind eye to the source of their purchases.[69] This loophole was only closed by Act 17 of 1891 which held the purchaser liable if he bought cattle from sellers without passes.

Although most thefts were on a small scale, there were cases where between twenty and fifty sheep at a time were stolen, apparently by organized gangs of thieves. Many such thefts occurred in the south-western border divisions and it is likely that the stolen stock was taken into the Cape. Sheep stolen in the Lion's River division were, it was believed, taken into Basutoland by Sotho working in Natal.[70]

Among the numerous attempts to clamp down on thefts, Act 46 of 1884 tried to enforce homestead responsibility, by which the inhabitants of an *umuzi* who knowingly harboured a stock thief or stolen property could be held liable and fined up to £10. Three years later, Act 44 of 1887 extended homestead responsibility to cases where there was reason to believe that Africans were combining to suppress evidence of stock thefts. This did not really make the enforcement of homestead responsibility any easier. Africans were generally unwilling to risk social ostracism or retaliation by informing on thieves, while chiefs, lacking authority to punish their people, had little incentive to co-operate in the suppression of thefts.[71] Because of the difficulty of proving homestead responsibility in court, few applications were made by farmers to have it enforced. Even where they were made, magistrates were allegedly 'afraid to carry out the spirit of the law, lest their decision should be reversed by the Attorney-General'. Moreover, the Executive Council refused to make the law any more draconian despite demands to this effect from farmers in the Legislative Council or from the Farmers' Conference.[72]

Native High Court files reveal a variety of reasons for stock thefts. In most cases involving cattle and horses, the animals were stolen for resale, while stolen sheep or goats were invariably eaten. Thefts could often be retaliatory and, particularly on labour tenancy farms, were often a form of resistance to oppressive conditions. Mdwebu, for example, stole a sheep from Martinus Potgieter in Klip River because he had been left to mind the farmer's wagons for eighteen days with only mealie meal to eat.[73] On private farms thefts possibly also resulted from the farmers' restricting of their tenants' stock, or were resorted to in order to supplement a monotonous diet.[74]

Native High Court files also suggest that most thefts were committed by men of few means and that just over half of the thefts were by Africans from Africans.[75] The cases may, however, give a distorted picture of the nature and relative incidence of such thefts, especially as an African victim was more likely to receive incriminating information from his fellows. Court records indicate that many stock thefts were perpetrated by young men or boys, a phenomenon which Theophilus Shepstone ascribed to the decline in chiefly authority and the resultant independence of the young.[76]

The growing independence of the young was becoming particularly obvious by the late 1880s. Migrant labour helped undermine existing hierarchical social relations within the *umuzi* and enabled the younger generation to challenge patriarchal authority and even ignore it. African elders complained bitterly about deteriorating social relations and the growing squalor of the *imizi*, a situation which they attributed to the young men's refusal to carry out their expected tasks. Conflict between men and women was also becoming more common as *abanumzana* tried to offset their declining authority by exerting greater pressure on their wives and daughters. Crop production was largely the province of women, and female labour was more crucial than ever at a time when Africans were becoming more dependent on labour-intensive sorghum crops. In arid areas where migrant labour was more widespread, women and girls were having to disregard traditional taboos on working with cattle and were having to plough their gardens themselves.[77] Thus, the survival of the homestead economy depended more than ever on the complete subordination of women to the *abanumzana*, whether they were husbands, fathers or brothers.

As it became more difficult for women to grow sufficient produce to sell, their dependence on their *abanumzana* was reinforced and most had to tolerate the growing demands being made on them. A small number, however, determined to break free from the restrictions. In a study of the effects of migrant labour on women in colonial Natal, Cherryl Walker has indicated the extent to which their very indispensability disadvantaged them.[78] And, as the burdens placed on them increased, so did the temptation to look for an alternative way of life.

There were also those women who sought to escape arranged marriages. Despite the 1869 marriage regulations, a determined father could still insist that his daughter marry the man of his, rather than her, choice. Again, most women appear to have accepted their fathers' dictates, but a small number rebelled and turned to either the towns or the mission stations for refuge.

Most missionaries tried to protect women escaping from forced marriages. *Abanumzana* saw this as blatant interference with their rights and often attempted to force them to return. The result was frequent clashes between homestead men and station inhabitants. Missionaries, by abetting women in escaping from their obligations, were undermining homestead life and patriarchal authority. With the colonial administration committed to bolstering patriarchal authority, friction between officials and missionaries was also inevitable.

The government fully supported the concept of female subordination and encouraged magistrates to uphold patriarchal authority against independent-minded women. In cases where women fled to mission stations, magistrates regularly sided with the *abanumzana* against the missionaries: between 1885 and 1892, of thirty-two girls seeking refuge at the Inanda Seminary from forced marriages, at least eighteen were ordered to return home.[79] Moreover, the subordinate position of women was further reinforced by the 1891 Code which entrenched their position as legal minors under male guardianship. Male control over women was strengthened by clauses giving to *abanumzana* the right to inflict corporal punishment on women, and powers wide enough to enable them to control all aspects of female life.[80]

The growing independence of the younger members of their *imizi* was, in the age-old way ascribed, by *abanumzana* struggling to maintain their authority, to the growing immorality of the young. In support of their contention they pointed to the marked increase in incidents of adultery, seduction and divorce. And the evidence does, indeed, support their view that existing marriage conventions were coming under strain. Not even the efforts of the colonial state to bolster patriarchal authority could stop this trend. Ironically, in the breakdown of family life the missionaries played a major role. Apart from offering refuge to women at their stations, the missionaries demanded that wives in a polygamous marriage should divorce their husbands prior to conversion to Christianity. African responses to this policy can be gauged from the reaction of a group of Groutville *kholwa* who were considering the admission of several of Chief Mqawe's wives to the American Congregational Church. The missionary, H.D. Goodenough, ruled that they could not be admitted until they had divorced the chief. 'The Natives exclaimed that the women, on leaving their husband, would lead immoral lives, as they would then have no-one to depend on.'[81]

Divorce also resulted from men evading their homestead obligations and abandoning their wives and children. As migrant labour became more widespread, such incidents became more common. In most of the divorce cases brought before the Native High Court in the mid-1890s the reason given was that the husband had not returned from Johannesburg.[82]

Adultery and seduction were seen in African patriarchal societies as crimes against the husband and father and had, in pre-colonial days, been punishable by death. With the loss of chiefly power to inflict capital punishment, and the undermining of traditional social values, the seriousness attached to adultery and seduction lessened.[83] Yet both still retained sufficient social stigma to make it difficult for an adulterous woman or a young girl who had been seduced, to face her family, and she would be tempted to seek refuge in one of the towns.

African urbanization was frowned on by both African and white authorities, and women who moved to the towns were regarded as degraded. Because of this, there were relatively few women in the towns before the twentieth century. But their number was growing. If urban conditions for men were poor, for women they were appalling with hardly any provision for accommodation: by 1895 there were only two homes for black women in Pietermaritzburg, and in Durban the first home was opened as late as 1897. Women who moved to a town were almost inevitably lost to their *imizi*, for African elders vehemently denounced their going and stigmatized them as immoral. And indeed, away from the restraints of the family and exposed to the influences of those who had already broken loose from homestead ties, it was difficult for a girl to remain chaste. Not surprisingly, urban African women were accused of being prostitutes.[84] Even accepting that the extent of prostitution was exaggerated, it was none the less widespread in the towns. The *kholwa* landowner, Josiah Africa traced its origins in Ladysmith to the influx of Xhosa and coloured women during the Anglo-Zulu War, although as early as 1876 there were seventy known prostitutes in Pietermaritzburg offering shelter to girls who had left their homes.[85] Because of the lack of alternative accommodation, few girls had anywhere to go but to the brothels.[86] Once a girl had done so it was difficult for her to return home where it was customary for the women of the *umuzi* to examine unmarried girls to ensure that they were still virgins. As a result there was often little option but to 'go on to the streets and die there'.[87]

Despite demands from chiefs and *abanumzana* for the government to prevent women moving to towns and to stamp out prostitution,[88] no action was taken. Municipal officials were prepared to tolerate the existence of brothels, despite by-laws forbidding them, and by 1890 there were about thirty 'houses of ill fame' in the capital, two-thirds of which were of black prostitutes. The police knew where the prostitutes lived but they only took action when there were complaints of rowdiness. Indeed, many white officials looked favourably on African prostitution; as the Pietermaritzburg Superintendent of Police, William Fraser, pointed out in 1890, 'it would be most unadvisable to reduce the number of prostitutes. I think we ought to do everything in our power to increase the number of prostitutes, because by reducing the number, we increase the number of crimes which are certainly most loathsome to us.'[89]

By this 'loathsome crime', Fraser was hinting at the rape of white women by African men, fear of which constantly haunted settler society.[90] By offering an outlet to male sexual energy the prostitutes were believed to be shielding settler women. But by the 1890s the authorities were forced to reconsider their tolerant attitude to prostitution. Not only was there the renewed emphasis on bolstering homestead authority, but the growing promiscuity was seen as raising new threats to white society. Returning labourers from the gold-fields who visited the brothels were spreading syphilis and venereal disease in the towns – in Pietermaritzburg in 1889 alone, 174 such cases received treatment as outpatients at Grey's Hospital, while the number of more serious cases necessitated the opening of two syphilis wards in the hospital.[91] Few domestic servants in the towns were safe from the disease and it was spreading into the countryside as *togt* and other urban labourers returned to their *imizi* after being infected. But the authorities' main concern was that syphilis would be passed on to white men. Sexual relations between African women and white men were far more common than most settlers would have admitted, and an African woman had far more reason to fear rape by a white man than a white woman had to fear rape by a black man.

Urban domestic servants were frequently raped in the homes in which they worked. Superintendent Alexander of the Durban Police referred to the number of African women who were infected with venereal disease by their 'young masters', while in 1894 the *Natal Witness* reported that the person mainly responsible for raping black women in the towns was 'your lah-di-dah man-about-town'.[92]

By the 1890s, the deteriorating social condition of African society was creating tension between black and white Natalians in both rural and urban areas. Fears among settlers of the spread of syphilis and of epidemics such as smallpox, combined with alarm at what was regarded as growing African insolence and insubordination. These fears were exacerbated by the settlers' continuing view of Africans as economic competitors. For despite deteriorating conditions in parts of Natal, particularly the Thukela valley reserves, the African population continued to show remarkable economic resilience. In the colony as a whole, both homestead Africans and *kholwa* remained buoyant enough to continue organizing their way of life and the amount of time they spent as migrant labourers. Most Africans continued to resist settler pressures to force them onto the labour market and destroy their independence.

Notes

1. Klip River Magistracy, 3/3/10, Magistrate to SNA, 10 February 1891.
2. See SNA, 1/1/105, 220/88, Magistrate, Alexandra to SNA, 12 March 1888.
3. SNA, 1/1/111, 1056/88, Magistrate, Inanda to SNA, 27 November 1888.
4. *LA Hansard* XXIV, 2 June 1896, p.347; 9 June 1896, p.433.
5. *NGG*, XLVIII, no.2844, 15 December 1896, GN 697, 1896, p.1766.
6. See for example *Natal Witness*, 20 July 1893.
7. Interview with R.T. Mazibuko, Edendale, 8 August 1979.
8. See NL&C, 214, no.355, Essery to General Manager, Durban, 20 April 1895.
9. *Natal Mercury*, 2 April 1889, 23 May 1889; *Natal Advertiser*, 18 and 20 May 1889, 20 May 1889.
10. *Natal Witness*, 23 March 1880, 9 June 1882; *Natal Witness*, 10 September 1889.
11. Welsh, *Roots of segregation*, p.243; *Inkanyiso Yase Natal*, 4 January 1895.
12. See ABM, A/3/41, Report of the Amanzimtoti station, June 1895.
13. ABM, A/1/2, Minutes, 16 December 1886, p.138.
14. Etherington, *Preachers*, p.113; SNA, 1/1/290, 1447/1900, Memorandum by USNA, 20 February 1901; Natal, *Evidence . . . Lands Commission, (1900–01–02)*, USNA, p.13.
15. SNA, 1/1/125, 640/90, Petition of Verulam Kholwa, 30 May 1890.
16. Natal, *Evidence . . . Natal Native Commission, 1881*, Kumalo, p.323.
17. ABM, A/2/22, USNA to Goodenough, 14 May 1898; Natal, *Evidence . . . Lands Commission (1900–01–02)*, Kilbon, p.69.
18. See *Inkanyiso Yase Natal*, 28 October 1892; Ipolela Magistracy, 4/1/4, 253/98, Magistrate to SNA, 7 July 1898.

19. CSO, 2576, c13/98, Report by Magistrate, Ixopo, 20 January 1898.
20. ABM, A/2/22, Report by USNA, 14 October 1896.
21. SNA, 1/1/146, 1017/91, Mini to Magistrate, Umgeni, 2 October 1891.
22. Kannemeyer, 'New Bantu society', p. 217.
23. ABM, A/2/22, Report by USNA, 14 October 1896.
24. SNA, 1/1/169, 441/93, Fayle diary, 8 April 1893; See also NPP, 146, no. 111, 1886, Report of SNA, 16 July 1884.
25. See SNA, 1/1/145, 897/91, Circular *re* beer drinking.
26. NPP, 146, NO. 111, 1886, Report of SNA, 16 July 1884; SNA, 1/1/75, 507 and 508/84, Replies to circular, July/August 1884.
27. NPP, 150, no. 74, 1888, List of applications.
28. NPP, 168, no. 55, 1894, Circular 15, 1893.
29. NPP, 146, no. 109, 1886, Return of faction fights; *NBB Departmental reports*, 1888–90/1.
30. *Natal Advertiser*, 1 April 1891; SNA, 1/1/145, 897/91, Circular *re* beer drinking, evidence of Duzindela and Teteleku.
31. SNA, 1/1/48, 437/81, Magistrate, Umsinga to SNA, n.d.
32. Natal, *Evidence . . . Natal Native Commission, 1881*, Sibankwa, p. 329, Paterson, p. 346, Mganu, p. 350.
33. *Natal Witness*, 3 May 1895; *NBB Departmental reports*, 1896, p. B18.
34. Stuart Papers, 30, 'Land occupation under the Zulu tribal system', p. 6.
35. SNA, 1/1/105, 199/88, Magistrate, Alexandra to SNA, 8 March 1888; *Natal Mercury*, 2 October 1888, 12 March 1892.
36. *Natal Mercury*, 7 August 1888.
37. See *Natal Witness*, 11 November 1891; 23 November 1892; *Inkanyiso Yase Natal*, 22 September 1893; SNA, 1/1/162, 1161/92, Perry to SNA, 17 October 1892; 1/1/247, 1191/97, Johannesburg Agent to SNA, 5 July 1897.
38. *Natal Witness*, 24 November 1892.
39. *Inkanyiso Yase Natal*, 22 September 1883.
40. See *LC Hansard*, IX, 23 November 1886, Acting Colonial Secretary, p. 380.
41. SNA, 1/3/24, SNA to Magistrate, Inanda, 26 March 1874, p. 759; *Inkanyiso Yase Natal*, 5 November 1891, 25 November 1892.
42. SNA, 1/1/160, 914/92, Petition of Umzimba, August 1892; 1/1/148, 1295/91, Magistrate, Umgeni to SNA, 4 April 1892; SNA to Governor, 12 June 1892.
43. SNA, 1/1/145, 897/91, Circular of 1884 *re* beer drinking.
44. Webb and Wright, eds, *James Stuart archive*, 3, Mbovu, 25 September 1904, p. 42.
45. SNA, 1/1/36, 38/80, Magistrate, Inanda to SNA, 17 January 1880; 1/1/37, 154/80, SNA to Lieutenant-Governor, 15 March 1880; 1/1/56, 414/82, SNA to Magistrate, Inanda, 30 October 1882.
46. *Natal Witness*, 2 November 1894; *Natal Mercury*, 13 July 1894.
47. Natal, *Proceedings of the commission . . . 1852*, 1, Cloete, p. 39.
48. Natal, *Report . . . Native population*, 1879, pp. 1f. *LC Hansard*, VII, 6 August 1884, SNA and Binns, pp. 384–5.
49. *NBB Departmental reports*, 1888–91/2, SNA reports.
50. See *Ilanga lase Natal*, 11 January 1907; *SANAC*, 3, Clarke, p. 612; M. W. Swanson, 'The urban factor in Natal native policy, 1843–1873', *Journal of Natal and Zulu History*, 3, 1980, p. 11.
51. SNA, 1/1/121, 1336/89, Administrator of Native Law, Ipolela to SNA, 9 December 1889.
52. *Natal Witness*, 21 October 1882, 29 May 1888.
53. SNA, 1/1/116, 609/89, Balcomb diary, 27 May – 3 June 1889.
54. *Natal Witness*, 16 March 1894; NPP, 144, no. 58, 28 September 1886; 655, no. 28, 10 June 1896; SNA, 1/1/102, 881/87, Magistrate, Ixopo to SNA, 30 September 1887; Upper Umkomazi Magistracy, 3/2/2, 54/93, Magistrate's report, 24 February 1893; *Natal Mercury*, 8 October 1894.
55. *LC Sessional Papers*, no. 31, 1877. Report of the select committee; *Natal Witness*, 21 May 1872, 14 June 1872.
56. NPP, 145, no. 77, 1886, Return of convictions for stock thefts, 1881–1886; *Natal Witness*, 2 and 5 December 1887; *NBB Departmental reports*, 1896, p. F6.

57. Native High Court, II/4/20, CS12/91, Supreme Chief v. Manziegudu; SNA, 1/1/147, 1116/91, Magistrate, Alfred to SNA, 26 September 1891.
58. Native High Court, II/4/21, CS93/91, Supreme Chief v. Nicomana; CS90/91, Supreme Chief v. Makemu; NPP, 174, no. 147, 1896, Correspondence from the Cape on the lack of a spoor law in Natal.
59. Native High Court, II/4/20–30, Cattle stealing cases.
60. *Natal Witness*, 26 November 1891; see also SNA, 1/1/196, 1634/94, Report by Sub-Inspector Clarke, 19 January 1895.
61. *LC Hansard*, VIII, 1 September 1885, Walton, p. 402; NPP, 145, no. 84, 1886, Return of sentences passed; 650, no. 18, 1891, Memorial of the Nottingham Road Farmers' Association, 1 June 1891.
62. *Natal Witness*, 21 May 1885, 'Sheep Farmers' Congress'.
63. Ibid., 20, 21 and 29 May 1885, 8 March 1895.
64. *LC Sessional Papers*, no. 12, 1890, Report of the Select Committee on thefts and destruction of stock, p. 151; *LC Hansard*, VIII, 1 September 1885, Colonial Secretary, p. 402; Sutton Collection, 4, Diary, 29 November 1883.
65. *Natal Witness*, 21 May 1885; SNA, 1/1/128, 854/90, Stewart to SNA, 16 July 1890; *LC Hansard*, XIV, 22 April 1890, pp. 60f.
66. *Natal Witness*, 25 April 1891.
67. C.J. Smythe Papers, 8, Diary, 20 March – 19 April 1884.
68. *LC Sessional Papers*, no. 12, 1890, Report of the Select Committee . . . stock, p. 150; *Natal Witness*, 6 February 1890; *LC Hansard*, IX, 23 November 1886, Yonge, p. 380.
69. *LC Hansard*, VII, 19 June 1884, Colonial Secretary, p. 20; Native High Court, II/4/20, CS26/91, Supreme Chief v. Utshikwana; *LC Sessional Papers*, no. 12, 1890, Report of the Select Committee . . . stock, p. 151; *Natal Witness*, 6 February 1890.
70. *Natal Witness*, 2 December 1887, 1 October and 11 December 1890; NPP, 650, no. 18, 1891, Memorial of the Nottingham Road Farmers' Association, 1 June 1891; see also *LC Sessional Papers*, no. 12, 1890, Report of the Select Committee . . . stock.
71. *LC Sessional Papers*, no. 23, 1891, Report of the Select Committee on agriculture, European immigration, irrigation and industries, p. 206.
72. *Natal Mercury*, 2 December 1891, 17 March 1892.
73. Native High Court, II/4/20, CS18/91, Supreme Chief v. Mdwebu.
74. Natal, *Native Affairs Commission, 1906–7, Evidence*, Mnyango, p. 714.
75. A selection of Native High Court files between II/4/20–30, 1881–1895 were consulted. See particularly II/4/26, CS77/94, Queen v. Tulebu, CS79/94, Queen v. Ndinga, CS11/95, Queen v. Utshopi and Umcetwa.
76. Cape, *Report and proceedings with appendices of the government commission on Native laws and customs*, Shepstone, pp. 5f.
77. See Natal, *Report . . . Native population*, 1894, p. 54.
78. C. Walker, 'Gender and the development of the migrant labour system, c.1850–1930' in C. Walker, ed., *Women and gender in southern Africa to 1945*, Cape Town, 1990, pp. 168f.
79. Inanda Seminary Papers, 1a, Cases illustrating the forced marriages of Native girls.
80. Act 19, 1891, *To legalise the Code of Native law*; SNA, 1/1/196, 1621/94, Bruce to SNA, 20 December 1894.
81. Webb and Wright, eds, *James Stuart archive*, 2, Macebo, 2 November 1898, p. 43.
82. *NBB Departmental reports*, 1894/5, p. E7.
83. Natal, *Report . . . Native population*, 1879, p. 5.
84. Natal, *Report . . . Native population*, 1879, p. 61; *Natal Mercury*, 11 August 1893.
85. Webb and Wright, eds, *James Stuart archive*, 1, Africa, 16 December 1890, p. 236; SNA, 1/6/6, 256/76, Magistrate, City to SNA, 20 June 1876.
86. *Inkanyiso Yase Natal*, 2 August 1895; *Natal Mercury*, 7 August 1897; *Natal Witness*, 16 August 1895.
87. Kinsman, *Commentaries*, p. 9.
88. *LC Sessional Papers*, 27, 1875, p. 2; Natal, *Evidence . . . Natal Native Commission, 1881*, Mawele, p. 202, Madude, p. 241.
89. *LC Sessional Papers*, unnumbered, 1890, Report . . . on the Contagious Diseases Prevention Bill, no. 19, 1890, pp. 22–3.

90. See N. Etherington, 'Natal's black rape scare of the 1870s', *Journal of Southern African Studies*, 15, no. 1, October 1988, pp. 36–53.
91. *LC Sessional Papers*, unnumbered, 1890, Report . . . on the Contagious Diseases Prevention Bill, no. 19, 1890, pp. 2–9, 21, 23.
92. *Natal Witness*, 11 May 1894; *LC Sessional Papers*, unnumbered, 1890, Report on the Contagious Diseases Prevention Bill, no. 19, 1890, pp. 22–3.

CHAPTER NINE

Locusts and Rinderpest, 1894–1898

In the early 1890s, despite population and land pressures and the growing antagonism of the colonial state to African aspirations, most *imizi* retained sufficient resources to maintain their way of life. Before 1893, the state possessed neither the power nor the will to destroy their independence. But the situation was to change dramatically within a few years. A succession of natural disasters undermined the homestead economy's ability to fend off renewed political assaults, thus enabling the responsible government state to consolidate settler hegemony in the colony.

After 1894, Natal was crippled by a series of calamities. Droughts and pestilence were, of course, nothing new to the colony. In the past there had been cycles of drought and crop failure, a particularly serious cycle having occurred in the late 1870s. Despite relatively good rains in the 1880s, the drought cycle of 1888 to 1893 had destroyed crops and caused widespread African hunger. Livestock, too, had fallen prey to occasional epizootics. During the colonial period there had been periodic outbreaks of redwater and foot-and-mouth disease among cattle, but the only serious epizootic was lungsickness which had ravaged herds in the 1870s. The droughts of 1888 to 1893 had also diminished stock numbers, nearly 10 per cent of cattle having died during these years.

The first of the new disasters was a locust plague. For thousands of years such plagues have been one of the scourges of Africa and between 1826 and 1854 Natal was ravaged by swarms on seven separate occasions.[1] Locusts then disappeared until, in October 1894, new swarms arrived over the coastal divisions, settling on sugar and maize crops. By December, vast numbers were seen throughout the colony; one report mentions a swarm extending in breadth for one and a half miles and taking an hour and a half to pass overhead, while another records a swarm thick enough to obscure the sky.[2] Despite the extent of crop destruction, the government delayed taking action until June 1895, when the locusts had already laid eggs throughout Natal. As there was insufficient money to employ paid locust exterminators, the ministry introduced a Locust Extermination Bill in the Legislative Assembly that would enable it to co-opt assistance. When passed, the act gave the government wide-ranging powers to proclaim locust areas; to compel local inhabitants to assist in carrying out instructions for exterminating the locusts; and to authorize the Governor-in-Council to 'make, repeal, alter and add to the rules and regulations, and . . . all things necessary for the extermination of locusts and for carrying out the provisions of this Act'.[3]

The act also provided for the appointment of locust officers. Cultivators noticing swarms were obliged to report them to an officer and to carry out his instructions. Failure to comply entailed a maximum fine of £20, or three months' imprisonment with or without hard labour. Under the terms of the second provision, the government could order *abanumzana* on reserves to provide men to combat the plague on white-owned as well as on their own lands. This caused widespread resentment, but the government sweetened the pill by paying 6d. for every pound of locust eggs or each muid sack of mature locusts collected.[4] Africans responded with alacrity to this financial incentive and, by 10 January 1896, the government had purchased 8 304 muid sacks of locusts and had paid £5 712 for eggs.[5] The incentive paid off. For example, the inhabitants of Alfred county saved on average 35 per cent of their grain crop in 1896 compared to a virtual total loss in neighbouring Griqualand East.[6]

The money ran out in early January 1896, and without this incentive the collection of eggs and locusts stopped. Unfortunately, this coincided with a renewed invasion of locusts from both Zululand and Basutoland. Swarms began laying on arrival and by March eggs were being hatched in vast numbers throughout the colony. Faced with this renewed invasion, the government virtually abandoned the struggle. It was left to a sugar planter, A. G. Wilkinson, to discover an antidote to locusts, an insecticide combining arsenic with sweet potatoes or treacle. The plague could now be effectively prevented from spreading, and by the end of 1896 only isolated locust flights were reported.[7]

Apart from sugar, maize was the crop most commonly attacked by locusts. Consequently, *imizi* gardens suffered seriously, the African maize crop in 1896 being less than 40 per cent of that in 1895. Losses were particularly heavy in the Thukela valley and in south-western Natal. In these two areas, over 75 per cent of the grain crop was lost with the average in Ixopo and Upper Umkomazi being over 90 per cent.[8] Fayle reported famine conditions in Zwartkop reserve with Africans stealing maize cobs from their neighbours' gardens, while around Bulwer many Africans were living on herbs.[9] Conditions were often worse on private farms, for many farmers tried to recoup their own losses by demanding increased labour or higher rents from their tenants.[10] The attitude of the Land and Colonisation Company was particularly harsh. The Durban Manager refused either to assist tenants with money for purchasing grain, or to allow more than a limited extension of time for rent payments. The manager's unsympathetic attitude was approved of by the London Secretary who observed that 'we cannot be expected to bear other people's misfortunes as well as our own'.[11]

Few chiefs or *izinduna* were able to provide their people with maize as hardly any of them still retained the grain pits formerly used for storage against times of famine. Unable to turn to their elders for help, many Africans inundated Pietermaritzburg with pleas for assistance. The ministry, however, showed remarkably little sympathy for their plight.[12] Moor brushed aside all pleas other than that of Thetheleku, and he was given a mere 62 muids.[13] But, faced with a critical shortage which affected the whole colony, the government did assist the merchant community to import 466 507 cwt. of maize from the United States in mid-1896. Yet, of this amount, only 3 105 muids were earmarked for sale to chiefs at 25s. per muid.[14] Despite the shortage, maize could be bought for less than 25s. in the towns while, even taking the cost of transport into account, a muid cost between 22s. 6d. and 25s. in the Thukela valley reserves in September.[15]

Because of this, the government could not find a market for the maize it had set aside for relief. In late 1896 it lowered the price of the remaining 2 468 muids to between 16s. 6d. and 22s. 6d. per muid and sent them to the worst-affected divisions. As few Africans in these divisions could afford even this reduced price, the government was obliged to supply maize on credit. Thus the Mbomvu chiefdom in the Krantzkop and Umsinga divisions received maize worth £1 069 on credit in December.[16] Even had the government been more lenient it could have done little to relieve distress with a mere 3 105 muids. Many Africans were understandably bitter at the paucity of aid, particularly after the assistance they had given in collecting locusts and eggs. Chief Mlungwana complained bitterly in Lower Tugela division that his Amanziba people were facing starvation, while representatives of the Ipolela chiefs expressed dissatisfaction at the aid they had received and unsuccessfully asked the government to convene a general meeting of chiefs to discuss relief.[17]

Faced with official indifference, Africans had to depend on their own resources. In general they showed great adaptability. *Umuzi* inhabitants in Indwedwe, Lower Tugela and Umlazi divisions planted sweet potatoes and *idumbe*, which were less vulnerable to locusts than was grain. In Upper Umkomazi, many Africans raised the wherewithal to buy grain by selling pigs, while others sold cattle in the main stock-farming areas of Klip River and Weenen counties.[18] This latter strategy, however, had its drawbacks for it was difficult to get fair prices for stock which had been weakened by the drought years. Moreover, both farmers and butchers in Natal had been buying reasonably priced cattle from Griqualand East and Barkly West in the Cape since the early 1890s and showed little interest in buying stock from Africans unless they were prepared to sell 'not only their "fatted calf," but also the "bell-wether," or in other words their show ox, usually the fattest and the pride of the kraal'.[19]

In contrast to its tardiness in providing aid, the ministry eagerly seized on the Africans' distress to urge chiefs to persuade young men to enlist as migrant labourers. The magistrates were also instructed to inform destitute Africans that they would be advanced six sacks of maize for each person who volunteered for six months' work on the harbour.[20] Not even hunger, however, could make harbour work attractive.

Africans were more prepared to work on the gold-fields. Faced with the need to repay the £1 069 advanced by the government, the *izinduna* of the Mbomvu chiefdom met at Chief Mawele's *umuzi* where they decided that the chiefdom's able-bodied young men should go to Johannesburg to work. Most of the men in Chief Swayimana's Ganya chiefdom in New Hanover were also sent to Johannesburg,[21] while men from Ixopo, Upper Umkomazi and Krantzkop sent remittances from Johannesburg, through the Natal Agent, to their *imizi* to buy grain. In 1896, £30 314 was remitted through the agent, the bulk of which was used to alleviate distress.[22] The response of chiefdoms such as the Mbomvu and Ganya to the food shortage shows that in times of crisis chiefs and elders still had sufficient authority to have their instructions carried out.

Despite cash remittances, suffering was rife in most of the colony, and particularly in the more remote areas, until the harvesting of the new season's crops in the autumn of 1897. The elderly and children were particularly hard hit; there were reports from Ipolela in October 1896 that children 'with bloated bellies and crooked limbs are fast becoming a common sight'.[23] There were, however, remarkably few reports of Africans dying of starvation and it would appear that, despite the hardships experienced, most *imizi* were able to cope with their losses. There was a slight reduction in the amount of hut tax paid in 1896 – to £76 847 from £84 868 in 1895, but this resulted from magistrates collecting the taxes after June and sending them into the Treasury later than usual. No reports of difficulties in drawing rents are mentioned, not even by the Land and Colonisation Company.[24]

Some Africans were, indeed, able to turn the plague to their advantage. Those in less-affected divisions sold mealies to *imizi* elsewhere in the colony or bartered them for cattle and goats. The Driefontein *kholwa* were particularly active in this regard and in September 1896 took more than fifty wagonloads of maize into Zululand to barter for oxen.[25] A side-effect of the plague was, therefore, that it increased the disparity between those who had the resources to prosper from the misfortune of their fellows and those who were helpless. Not only were the former able to ask high grain prices, but the purchasers often had little option but to barter stock at a loss.

The harvest of 1897, welcome relief though it provided, only partially erased the legacy of the locust plague. This was because it was not a good harvest, partly because of a drought during the previous summer, and partly because cattle were often too weak to be used for ploughing.

And then, on top of these calamities, rinderpest struck in 1897 at precisely the time when cattle were still weak and vulnerable. Rinderpest has had a long history since it was first recorded in biblical and Homeric accounts. Epizootics occurred in Eurasia throughout the Christian era, but there are no records of the disease in sub-Saharan Africa until the 1880s. In 1889 it appeared in Somalia whence it rapidly spread south, arriving in Rhodesia in March 1896 and in the South African Republic a month later.[26] Rinderpest is an acute and highly contagious disease which spreads very rapidly among ruminants, particularly cattle. Within a week of infection, an animal shows symptoms of fever, diarrhoea and dehydration, and within the following week it dies.

Early measures against rinderpest were seldom successful and few cattle survived its onslaught. In the early 1890s when it became obvious that rinderpest would eventually reach southern Africa, Natal's Colonial Veterinary Surgeon, S. Wiltshire, urged the colonial government to take preventive steps.[27] After consultations with the other southern African administrations, the government passed an Animals' Contagious Diseases Act in Parliament in 1894 which authorized measures to segregate stock suffering from contagious diseases and to prevent the importation of diseased animals.[28]

By June 1896, stock was no longer allowed into the colony from Rhodesia, the Transvaal or Bechuanaland, while men driving cattle from the Orange Free State had to have a certificate from a landdrost stating that the animals had not been off their owner's land during the previous six months. In the same year a conference of southern African representatives was held in Mafeking to plan joint preventive measures, such as the fencing of borders and the destruction of all infected cattle.[29] Under an amendment to the Animals' Contagious Diseases Act, the Natal government began erecting a double barbed-wire fence along the colony's borders with the Orange Free State, Transvaal and Zululand. The border counties were divided into districts, each under three rinderpest commissioners responsible for preventing the spread of the disease.[30] In October, the commissioners began supervising the construction and maintenance of fences and the isolation of suspect cattle. At the same time, the quarantine regulations were extended to livestock other than cattle. The government employed 883 white and black guards to patrol the colony's borders with Basutoland and the two republics and, as an additional safeguard, dynamited sections of the Drakensberg passes to make them impassable.[31]

The government tried to secure the co-operation of the rural community in its attempts to keep rinderpest out of Natal. It was difficult to construct the border fence with Zululand because of the absence of roads in the Thukela valley reserves. Because of this, S.O. Samuelson met reserve chiefs in September and October 1896 and extended the *isibhalo* system to make them responsible for conveying fencing material to the border and for ensuring that no cattle crossed the river into the colony. He warned the chiefs that stock should not be moved within their reserves and specifically instructed them to stop *sisa*'ing cattle. He also accepted the chiefs' suggestion that official witnesses and district *izinduna* be made responsible for isolating suspect cattle in their own districts.[32]

The Transvaal, Free State and Zululand borders had all been fenced by May 1897, and a number of internal fences had been erected. No attempt was made to fence the south-western border as the government believed that the Cape was capable of preventing rinderpest from spreading into that colony.[33] This confidence was misplaced. By April 1897 rinderpest had appeared in Herschel in the Cape and was also in Bethlehem just over the Free State border. With the danger to Natal now imminent, the government was given even greater powers to control the movement of cattle.

It proved impossible, however, to keep rinderpest out of the colony and the disease broke out in an African *umuzi* near Dundee on 15 July 1897. Within 36 hours the police had destroyed and buried every animal belonging to the *umuzi* and had fenced off the infected area. In addition, 50 policemen were stationed around it to isolate it from its neighbours.[34] These precautions were useless for within a fortnight nine divisions stretching as far south as Alfred county had been infected.[35] There was consternation throughout the colony. In many divisions farming operations came to a standstill while farmers in uninfected areas demanded that the government ruthlessly exterminate diseased stock.[36] But, realizing the futility of such action and afraid of driving Africans into revolt, the government abandoned extermination in favour of inoculation.

Bile inoculation had been used elsewhere in southern Africa, but had not proved particularly effective. Consequently, the Transvaal Veterinary Surgeon, Arnold Theiler, and H. Watkins-Pitchford, Natal's Principal Veterinary Surgeon, conducted experiments with serum inoculation in early 1897 with satisfactory results.[37] But, while the Natal Department of Agriculture built up sufficient stocks of serum, bile inoculations continued. Inoculation stations were established at various centres and cattle were purchased to provide bile and, later, serum.[38]

Before rinderpest broke out in the colony, many Africans had ignored government warnings of the dangers posed by the disease and had continued moving cattle.[39] Their reaction when the epizootic broke out was mixed. Some, quickly realizing the implications of the disaster, either slaughtered their cattle before the disease reached them, or sold stock to butchers or to the inoculation stations for as little as £2 for oxen and 10s. for cows.[40] Others, such as the Xolo of Lower Umzimkulu, kept quiet when rinderpest broke out in their *imizi*, hoping that they could save at least some of their cattle.[41] Despite the urgency of the situation, the government was afraid to force Africans to inoculate their herds as, in 1890, attempts by the previous administration to make Africans comply with lungsickness inoculation regulations had been fiercely resisted.[42] Moor, instead, appealed to missionaries, farmers and landowners to use their influence to persuade their tenants to inoculate.[43]

Inoculators were appointed for the reserves, and magistrates were instructed to call chiefs and *izinduna* together to urge them to have their chiefdoms' cattle inoculated. But persuading Africans was no easy task; during the early months of the outbreak many Africans believed either that inoculation *could* spread the disease or that it was being deliberately used by the authorities to do so. Because of this, they were understandably determined to await proof that white-owned cattle benefited from it.[44]

Consequently, the government's inoculation attempts bore little fruit in the early months of the outbreak. Farmers, landowners and missionaries were unable to persuade their tenants to inoculate, while reports from the reserves indicated a similar refusal.[45] The only exception among reserve Africans was in the Upper Tugela reserve where Ncwadi's Ngwane were among the first Africans in Natal to ask for inoculators.[46] This widespread refusal strengthened the government's reluctance to enforce inoculation and also necessitated the provision of police escorts for inoculators in isolated areas.[47] Yet, although there was considerable unrest in neighbouring Griqualand East and the possibility of trouble spilling over into Alfred county and Ixopo, the only people to offer physical resistance to inoculators were the Xolo in Lower Umzimkulu.[48]

It is not difficult to understand why Africans were reluctant to inoculate. Those white and black stockowners who agreed to use bile inoculation found it gave their stock very little protection.[49] Indeed, the President of the Umvoti Agricultural Society accused the Veterinary Department of misleading farmers over its efficacy and acknowledged that Africans were justified in believing that the farmers' use of bile was spreading the disease.[50] Yet even serum, when it was eventually introduced, proved ineffective. When first used in Richmond in September it was a complete failure.[51] Stockowners were also charged for the inoculation of each beast at a rate of between 6d. and 1s. for bile, and 1s. 6d. for serum. Africans were understandably reluctant to pay to have their beasts inoculated when the chances of survival were so slim. In an attempt to surmount this problem, they were allowed to hand over 10 per cent of their surviving stock in lieu of the fee.[52]

By late 1897, the Veterinary Department was obtaining better results with serum and, as it had become obvious that rinderpest was not going to die out of its own accord, Africans were more prepared to inoculate. The major problems were now a lack of serum and too few government inoculators. Because there were so few official inoculators, the government had to rely on the help of volunteers whose charges, particularly to Africans, were often exorbitant. Africans in Lower Tugela were paying half of their surviving stock while in Ipolela, reserve Africans were charged up to 5s. a beast for serum which was being sold for 1s. at the inoculation station outside the reserve.[53]

The Natal government's efforts to stamp out rinderpest had not proved very effective. In this, however, it was not unique, since few colonial administrations in Africa had enjoyed any greater success. No colonial government had the resources necessary to contain the disease or to prevent its spread through the continent. The southern African governments were better able to combat the disease than their more recently established counterparts in central and east Africa yet even their efforts bore little fruit. There are no statistics for most of the continent, but herds were devastated throughout east Africa while it was estimated that between 90 and 95 per cent of all cattle south of the Zambezi, approximately 5 500 000 head, died.[54] The amount spent in fighting rinderpest throughout the continent is unknown; the Natal government alone spent £193 221 2s. 10d. by the end of 1898 yet managed to save only 232 323 head of cattle. Even the far wealthier Cape government which spent £1 146 911 could only save 1 063 571 head.[55]

The Natal government did, however, do very little to aid stockowners whose herds had been decimated. In addition, the little assistance it did give tended to be directed to the settlers. In 1898 the Department of Agriculture spent £527 on fifty oxen to lend to nine farmers who had lost all their oxen. They were later able to purchase these at £10 a head which was considerably lower than the prevailing price of between £14 and £20 a head.[56] The government also imported 1 000 mules and 1 000 donkeys from South America for ploughing. While there was no bar to African cultivators buying them, they were too expensive, at £16 per head for mules and £8 for donkeys, for most *imizi* to afford them.[57] The only concession which benefited both African and white farmers was a relaxation of the conditions under which Crown lands were held and a two-year suspension of payments.[58]

Elaine Unterhalter argues that the Natal government hoped that the loss of their cattle would force more Africans onto the labour market, but that it did not want to see a complete destruction of the homestead economy since that would force whole families into the towns. Certainly, the ministry was reluctant to do anything which could 'deprive the people of all energy and self-reliance'.[59] It was also determined that, despite their losses, Africans should continue paying their hut tax. In 1897 the Chunu chief, Silwana, was reprimanded for seeking a reduction in the amount of tax his people owed for the year. When he asked the governor whether he could be blamed for interceding on behalf of his people, Hely-Hutchinson replied; 'Yes, you did wrong.' The following year the new Secretary for Native Affairs, James Liege Hulett, again refused to agree to any deferments.[60]

Silwana, unable to get his people's taxes reduced, had also asked the government to persuade landowners to reduce their rents.[61] Apparently his request was not considered, but the Land and Colonisation Company's files suggest that landowners would have rejected requests for lower rentals. The company's London Secretary in fact believed that tenants should pay for any rinderpest expenditure which the company had incurred on their behalf.[62] Although the company collected rents with little difficulty in 1898, by early 1899 they were £2 344 or 30 per cent in arrears. This seriously alarmed the board of directors in London which demanded action from the general manager, pointing out that 'if they are starving, as you now maintain, it must be because they decline to work, and they must be taught that it is no more than the common law of nature that starvation follows idleness'.[63]

Official and settler refusal to heed their pleas for assistance caused considerable bitterness among Africans. Rinderpest further exacerbated relations between settlers and Africans in Natal, and increased African alienation from white rule. Throughout southern Africa, indeed throughout the continent, Africans and settlers blamed each other for spreading the disease.[64] In Natal, the Commissioner of Agriculture expressed the view of many farmers, particularly those in the northern districts, when he accused Africans of deliberately introducing and disseminating rinderpest.[65] Even more charitably inclined settlers believed that Africans unwittingly spread the disease by moving stock.[66] Racial tension over rinderpest became so acute that some farmers opened fire on African trespassers on their lands.[67]

For their part, many Africans believed that settlers were deliberately spreading the disease in order to destroy their herds, prevent them from marrying, and force them into labour.[68] Many Africans refused to inoculate because of these suspicions and even the sight of white-owned cattle dying did little to shake their conviction for, 'it is nothing to the white man . . . if his cattle die, because he has money wherewith to purchase fresh cattle, but the natives have no money'.[69] Although many settlers who still had stock ploughed their tenants' land or lent them oxen, others contributed to the growing African alienation by charging them up to 10s. a day for ploughing.[70] The regulations requiring entrants into the colony to be disinfected were also a cause of great resentment. These regulations were on the whole applied with greater vigour to Africans than to whites in that only the former had to undergo complete dipping.[71]

In Rhodesia, the belief that settlers were deliberately spreading rinderpest contributed to the outbreak of the Chimurenga rebellion in 1896.[72] In Natal, fear of a similar uprising was a factor in the government's reluctance to enforce cattle extermination or compulsory inoculation.[73] Although rinderpest fuelled rural unrest amongst Africans in neighbouring Griqualand East,[74] the only obvious unrest in Natal was that mentioned earlier amongst the neighbouring Xolo chiefdom. Even on Land and Colonisation Company farms, there was no trouble despite the company's insensitivity in choosing the height of the disaster to prohibit its tenants from keeping more than one dog per *umuzi*.[75]

With their lives and customs so intimately bound up with cattle keeping, few Africans could at first comprehend the magnitude of the disaster caused by the destruction of their stock. Magistrate Ritter of New Hanover reported that Africans in his division were suffering from a state of temporary shock,[76] while the magistrate of Weenen, George Adamson, wrote that

old headmen and fathers would cry like children, as I saw them, at the sight of their cattle and calves, their sole asset upon earth which they had watched for years grow and increase before their eyes, drop down and die by scores before them, cleaning out the coveted collection of a lifetime in fewer hours than it had taken them years to acquire them, the food for their children, and the wives for their young men taken from them without power to rescue . . . To say that the consequences of this scourge have been the disorganization of their social system and the disaster of their domestic is only to briefly compass the evils which its advent has entailed. Cattle being the basis of all their social contracts and ceremonies, and money being in their eyes an impossible substitute, I do not think it can be adequately appreciated by Europeans what the force and effect of these enormous losses to the Natives really mean.[77]

The most immediate problem Africans faced was a shortage of food, a hard blow to bear after the earlier locust and drought-ravaged years. There was, however, little hunger in 1897. Firstly, although the crops were poor that year, they had to be consumed in the *imizi* since there was no way of transporting produce to the market. Second, the carcasses of diseased animals were boiled with germicidal plants and so provided an abundant amount of meat.[78] In the long term, however, the situation was more dire. The drought continued during the summer of 1897/98. That summer also saw a recurrence of locusts in some areas which exacerbated the scarcity of food and saw the average price of maize again reach 25s. per muid. Even so, there were few requests for grain and many *imizi* still seem to have had sufficient cash from migrant-labour wages to enable them to buy food from traders and stores. In Tanganyika, estimates of Masai deaths from starvation during the rinderpest period ranged from two-fifths to three-quarters of the entire people. In Natal, by contrast, the only talk of famine was in Ixopo division.[79]

Yet rinderpest had serious repercussions for African children because cattle losses reduced the availability of *amasi*, a staple article of a child's diet. Mothers had to rear their babies on a porridge made of pulped sweet potatoes and finely ground maize and sorghum.[80] This dietary change was often disastrous. In 1898, district surgeons reported that cases of gastro-intestinal complaints had increased throughout the colony and that infant mortality was growing in all divisions.[81]

The only positive result of rinderpest was that cattle losses relieved the pressure of over-grazing, particularly in the reserves. With more grazing the condition of the surviving cattle improved.[82] The process of rebuilding herds was painfully slow, however, especially in light of the high price of new stock. In 1896, before rinderpest entered the colony, cattle could be purchased for slightly more than £5 per head on average; this figure rose rapidly to £14 in 1898, and to just under £20 in 1900.[83] Africans who were able to sell cattle before the disease reached their area did not benefit as the glut of slaughter cattle on the market in mid-1897 kept the price increase to three-farthings a pound over 1896. By the time the price began rising in late 1897, few Africans had cattle to sell. They tried to dispose of the dead animals' hides and horns once the restriction on sales of these items was lifted in October 1897 but they seldom received good prices, for the hides were usually poorly tanned.[84]

The decline in African prosperity since the 1870s is clearly shown by their inability at this stage to replace cattle with other livestock. In that decade, cattle killed by lungsickness in the Zwartkop and Drakensberg reserves had been replaced with horses. Few Africans remained wealthy enough to do so in the late 1890s, especially as there had been a sharp increase in the price of horses, from £17 18s. 0d. in 1896 to £28 6s. 0d. in 1897.[85] For example, although the price of cattle had soared by 1898, Ngani in Klip River had to give three head of cattle in exchange for a horse.[86]

A comparison of African and settler cattle losses shows how disastrous rinderpest was for Africans. Despite their losses, those white farmers who had inoculated suffered proportionately far less than did Africans; Joseph Baynes lost only 50 per cent of his 1 000-head herd while Charles Smythe's herd dropped from 183 to 120 head.[87] By late 1897 when the effectiveness of serum inoculation had become apparent, some white farmers bought cattle cheaply from Africans and, by inoculating them, were able to recoup their losses.[88] A total of 114 873 head of cattle belonging to settlers (approximately 47 per cent of their stock) was lost in 1897 whilst 379 576 (over 76 per cent) of African-owned stock died during the same period. During 1898, however, the number of white-owned cattle increased by 29 164 (23 per cent) whereas Africans suffered a further decrease of 38 997 (34 per cent) of their surviving cattle. By the end of 1898, whites owned 155 456 cattle valued at approximately £1 725 800 or £11 per head, while the number of cattle owned by Africans was 75 809, value unknown.[89]

African cattle losses were spread evenly over the colony, but the suffering was greatest in the interior and midland divisions which were more dependent on cattle. For example, the Sithole chief, Mbande, one of the richest chiefs in Klip River division, lost 760 head and was left with only 29.[90]

But the impact of rinderpest was also social. In his report for Weenen division for 1898, George Adamson commented on the subject thus:

> Socially the Natives have been turned topsy-turvy by the wholesale loss of their cattle. All their social customs, contracts and status, practically being bound up in their stock, the consequences of this calamity are of necessity far-reaching. The chief difficulty created is in reference to the delivery of *lobola* . . . and this appeared insuperable to them in the first force of the blow dealt them by the depredations of the plague. Confronted with this stoppage of the first essential of union, they set to work to deal with the difficulty and devise some means of its solution; and the result has been all manner of marriage contracts, of which the feature appears to be present trust and future fulfilment. I fear in all this that there is some sowing of seeds whose fruit will ripen into difficulties and dissensions in time to come, for the real trouble has been less generally met than postponed.[91]

Marriage difficulties began as early as mid-1897 when *abanumzana* began refusing to allow their daughters or sisters to marry because the *lobola* cattle might die.[92] By the end of the year, long-term marriage problems were emerging. The main difficulty arose from the 1891 Code's stipulation that *lobola* had to be paid in full before a marriage could take place. Thus, an *umnumzana* could not legally allow a female dependant to marry on the understanding that her prospective husband would pay all or part of the cattle after the marriage. And if he did disregard the law, he had no legal claim to payment once the marriage had taken place. Because of rinderpest it was usually impossible for *lobola* to be paid in full before marriage. Throughout late 1897 chiefs urged their magistrates to ask the government to intervene. Silwana suggested to Adamson that the prohibition against actions for the recovery of claims be dropped, pointing out that most men were prepared to allow their daughters to marry on the understanding that they would receive the cattle at a future date.[93]

The magistrates asked the government for a ruling. The Secretary for Native Affairs, Liege Hulett, proposed that payment of *lobola* be delayed, or that a money payment be accepted in lieu of cattle. His colleagues agreed to implement both suggestions and introduced legislation in Parliament.[94] In February 1898 an SNA minute was circularized to magistrates asking them to inform Africans that they were at liberty to make what arrangements they pleased to meet their *lobola* difficulties. But to avoid a repetition of the claims which had proliferated before the passing of the marriage regulations in 1869, the government refused to allow *lobola* payments to be legally enforceable, or to recognize any promissory notes which might be given for *lobola* debts.[95]

The returns for marriages under customary law in the 1890s clearly show the effect of rinderpest. The total number of marriages (excluding those of widows and divorcees, and *ukungena* unions) dropped from 4 349 in 1896 to 3 736 in 1897; 3 792 in 1898; and 2 211 in 1899.[96] Although the number of marriages had returned to their pre-rinderpest level by 1902, this was still a relative decline because of population increase. The figures do not indicate whether *lobola* was given or not, but in 1903 Hulett told the South African Native Affairs Commission that he knew many Africans were doing without it.[97]

For most Africans in Natal, the consequences of rinderpest were far reaching. Although conditions improved for those who retained sufficient stock to enable them not merely to weather the storm but to profit by it, it became even more difficult than before for most Africans to participate in the distribution of resources. Dahl and Hjort point out that in a pastoral society a large herd is necessary to protect the household against drought and epizootics. They argue that to enable the household to continue while the herd is being rebuilt, a sufficient number of animals must survive a disaster.[98] For many *imizi* in Natal, rinderpest made the fulfilment of this condition impossible.

In Tanganyika, the ecological disasters which began in the late 1880s 'set in motion a long process of environmental deterioration which still complicates cultivators' efforts to regain subsistence security'.[99] James Giblin draws a link between this and the impact of the colonial presence in East Africa, arguing that the latter prevented the recovery of African cultivation. In Natal, there was a similar link between the disasters of the 1890s and the undermining of African social patterns. Because of the settler presence, the traditional network of support which had buttressed homestead society had been undermined. In the early colonial years there had been a patron-client relationship designed to cope with any disasters that took place. The chiefs' powers to distribute resources and the prevalence of the *sisa* custom had provided a safety net, but this net had been significantly weakened by the end of the century.

Yet the settler presence itself also provided a safety net which was absent in East

Africa. The deaths from starvation and the wars between chiefdoms which accompanied rinderpest in East Africa[100] were noticeably absent in Natal and, at that level at least, the colonial state performed a valuable function. At the same time, however, the ecological disasters served to cement Africans more firmly into a position of dependency on the settlers. With little left to receive from their chiefs, many Africans had no choice but to turn to farmers, traders or touts for the resources they needed to begin rebuilding their herds. In the process, the ties binding members of chiefdoms and kinship groups were further weakened, while the ability of *imizi* to function independently of migrant labour was made wellnigh impossible. This struck at the very basis of the *umuzi* and accelerated a process of proletarianization in African society.

Notes

1. A. T. Bryant, *Olden times in Zululand and Natal*, London, 1929, p. 305.
2. *Natal Witness*, 7 September 1894, 23 November 1894.
3. *LA Hansard*, XXIII, 13 June 1895, pp. 379f; Act 33, 1895, *To provide for the extermination of locusts*.
4. *Natal Witness*, 6 December 1895.
5. Natal, *Report . . . Native population*, 1895, pp. 22,58; *NGG*, XLVIII, no. 2778, 28 January 1896, GN 59, 1896, p. 101.
6. *Natal Witness*, 22 August 1896.
7. C. Ballard, '"A year of scarcity": the 1896 locust plague in Natal and Zululand', *South African Historical Journal*, 15, 1983, pp. 50–1.
8. *NSYB*, 1894/5, p. N7; 1896, p. P7.
9. SNA, 1/1/215, 125/96, 23 January 1896; 1/1/222, 832/96, Fayle diary, 3 June 1896; 1/1/215, 173/96, Police report, 13 February 1896.
10. NL&C, 223, no. 5, Lund to General Manager, Durban, 24 July 1896.
11. NL&C, 27, no. 75, Secretary, London to General Manager, Durban, 27 March 1896; See also NL&C, 27, no. 79, Secretary, London to General Manager, Durban, 12 June 1896.
12. Sutton Collection, 4, Diary, 12 March 1895; SNA, 1/1/225, 1157a/96, Minister of Lands and Works to SNA, 8 August 1896; 1/1/234, 2011/96, Minister of Lands and Works to SNA, 2 December 1896.
13. SNA, 1/1/221, 712/96, Tetelegu to SNA, 19 May 1896.
14. See H. J. Choles, 'Some effects of the rinderpest plague', *Natal Agricultural Journal*, 9, no. 11, 23 November 1906, p. 1058; *Natal Witness*, 24 July 1896; NPP, 177, no. 160, 1897.
15. SNA, 1/1/229, 1539/96, Magistrate, Mapumulo to USNA, 11 September 1896; 1540/96, Sub-Inspector, Natal Police to Magistrate, Lower Tugela, n.d.
16. SNA, 1/1/237, 168/97, SNA to Minister of Lands and Works, 22 January 1897.
17. Welsh, *Roots of segregation*, p. 190; SNA, 1/1/225, 1157a/96, Magistrate, Ipolela to SNA, 4 August 1896.
18. Natal, *Report . . . Native population*, 1896, pp. 75, 93, 107, 118; 1897, pp. 64, 166; ABM, A/3/41, Report of Esidumbeni station, June 1897.
19. *Natal Witness*, 31 October 1896.
20. SNA, 1/1/216, 204/96, Circular 4, 1896, 12 February 1896; 1/1/225, 1157a/96, SNA to magistrates, 29 July 1896.
21. SNA, 1/1/229, 1575/96, Request by Swaimana, 21 September 1896; 1/1/233, 1997/96, Application by Mawele, 26 November 1896.
22. Natal, *Report . . . Native population*, 1896, pp. 20–1, 48, 55, 89.
23. SNA, 1/1/231, 1774/96, Royston to SNA, 22 October 1896.

24. *NSYB*, 1896, p.D1; Natal, *Auditor General's report*, 30 June 1896, p.iii; NL&C, 27, no.132, Secretary, London to General Manager, Durban, 12 February 1897. Ballard's assertion that 'hundreds or even several thousand blacks . . . probably died of starvation' ('Year of scarcity', p.46) is unsubstantiated.
25. Natal, *Report . . . Native population*, 1896, pp.84, 93; *Natal Mercury*, 21 September 1896.
26. J.N.P. Davies, *Pestilence and disease in the history of Africa*, Johannesburg, 1979, p.12; A.S. Chigwedere, 'The 1896 rinderpest disease and its consequences', *Heritage*, 2, 1982, p.30.
27. See CSO, 1942, 1529/96, Colonial Veterinary Surgeon to Prime Minister, 17 March 1896.
28. Act 38, 1894, *For preventing the spread of contagious and infectious diseases amongst animals*.
29. *NGG*, XLVIII, no.2788, 2 April 1896, Proclamation 17, 1896, p.385; *LA Sessional Papers*, no.2, 1896, document 74, pp.9–10; 82, p.11; *LC Hansard*, IV, 30 June 1896, Treasurer, p.138.
30. *NGG*, XLVIII, no.2827, 22 September 1896, GN 528, 1896, p.1477.
31. *NGG*, XLVIII, no.2831, 13 October 1896, GN 575, 1896, p.1541; no.2835, 28 October 1896, Proclamation 106, p.1604.
32. SNA, 1/1/229, 1557/96, Report by USNA, 21 September 1896; NGG, XLVIII, no.2827, 22 September 1896, GN 528, 1896, p.2827.
33. *NBB Departmental reports*, 1896, pp.B141–2; 1897, p.H159; *Natal Witness*, 17 April 1896.
34. *Natal Witness*, 24 July 1897; *NBB Departmental reports*, 1897, pp.H159–60.
35. *NBB Departmental reports*, 1897, pp.H159–60.
36. *Natal Witness*, 24 July 1897.
37. *NBB Departmental reports*, 1897, p.H161; *LA Sessional Papers*, no.2, 1897, Report by the Principal Veterinary Surgeon, 19 March 1897.
38. *NBB Departmental reports*, 1897, pp.H161–2.
39. See Natal, *Report . . . Native population*, 1896, p.90; *Natal Mercury*, 30 July 1897.
40. Natal, *Report . . . Native population*, 1897, pp.138,168,184; *NBB Departmental reports*, 1897, p.H162; NL&C, 229, no.314, Garland to General Manager, Durban, 28 November 1897; Agriculture (AGR) [Natal Archives], 2, 587/98, Richardson to Minister of Agriculture, 17 October 1898.
41. Natal, *Report . . . Native population*, 1897, p.190.
42. SNA, 1/1/123, 278/90, Clarence diary, 18 February 1890; NL&C, 228, no.272, SNA to General Manager, Durban, 21 August 1897.
43. NL&C, 228, nos.244 and 265, SNA to General Manager, Durban, 16 and 19 August 1897; *Natal Advertiser*, 12 August 1897.
44. *NBB*, 1897, pp.143, 172; *NBB Departmental reports*, 1897, p.B38; *Natal Mercury*, 20 August 1897.
45. C.J. Smythe Papers, 11, Diary, 15 July 1897, 29 August 1897; *Natal Witness*, 28 August 1897; SNA, 1/1/251, 1570/97, General Manager, Durban, NL&C to SNA, 6 September 1897; SNA, 1/1/254, 1801/97, Bridgeman to SNA, 26 August 1897; *NBB*, 1897, p.125.
46. *Natal Mercury*, 19 and 20 August 1897.
47. GH, 1301, Confidential, Governor to Secretary of State, 11 September 1897, p.297; *NBB*, 1897, p.125; Ipolela Magistracy, 4/1/4, 572/97, Magistrate to SNA, 20 October 1897.
48. GH, 1301, Confidential, Governor to Secretary of State, 11 September 1897, pp.296–7; 23 October 1897, p.314; Natal, *Report . . . Native population*, 1897, p.190.
49. *Natal Mercury*, 24 and 28 August 1897, 4 September 1897; *Natal Witness*, 11 September 1897, 25 November 1897.
50. NPP, 181, no.84, 1898, *Annual report of the Umvoti Agricultural Society for 1897*, p.3.
51. NL&C, 228, no.16, Essery to General Manager, Durban, 15 September 1897; 229, no.279, Essery to General Manager, Durban, 19 November 1897; 230, no.59, Stedman to General Manager, Durban, 31 January 1898; *Natal Witness*, 18 September 1897.
52. *Natal Mercury*, 26 August 1897; SNA, 1/1/259, 2080/97, SNA to Allan, 4 November 1897; 2288/97, Thornhill to SNA, 20 November 1897.
53. *NBB Departmental reports*, 1897, p.B38; Ipolela Magistracy, 4/1/4, 572/97, Magistrate to SNA, 20 October 1897.
54. Davies, *Pestilence and disease*, p.14.
55. *NSYB*, 1898, pp.P10–15; Choles, 'Effects of rinderpest', p.1061.

56. AGR, 1, 266/98, Blomayer to Minister of Agriculture, August 1898; 288/98, Commissioner of Agriculture to Minister, 16 August 1898; *NBB Departmental reports*, 1898, p.H71.

57. SNA, 1/1/254, 1838/97, Notice, 4 August 1897.

58. SGO, III/1/120, 4115/97, Cooper to Surveyor-General, 16 November 1897; III/1/122, 3832/97, Molefe to Surveyor-General, 16 November 1897; and generally III/1/124; *NGG*, L, no.2940, 22 March 1898, GN 177, 1898, p.350; See SGO, III/1/132, 5449/98, Gallwey to Surveyor-General, 17 November 1898.

59. E. Untherhalter, '"The natives appear contented and quiet": the Nqutu district of Zululand under British rule, 1883–1897', University of London, Institute of Commonwealth Studies, Collected seminar papers, 8, 1976–77, p.67.

60. SNA, 1/1/254, 1830/97, Precis of memorandums, 2 September 1897; 1/1/282, 1990/98, Notes of meeting, 8 September 1898.

61. SNA, 1/1/254, 2159/97, Magistrate, Weenen to USNA, 4 October 1897.

62. NL&C, 27, no.174, Secretary, London to General Manager, Durban, 17 September 1897; no.184, 10 December 1897.

63. Ibid., 28, no.12, 18 February 1898; no.85, 3 March 1899; no.93, 14 April 1899.

64. Davies, *Pestilence and disease*, p.17; C. van Onselen, 'Reactions to rinderpest in southern Africa, 1896–97', *Journal of African History*, 13, no.3, 1972, p.478.

65. *NBB Departmental reports*, 1897, pp.H160–1.

66. Ibid., p.B86; *Natal Advertiser*, 30 July 1897; *Natal Witness*, 31 July 1897.

67. *Natal Mercury*, 7 August 1897.

68. Natal, *Report . . . Native population*, 1897, p.127; Ipolela Magistracy, 4/1/4, 437/97, Magistrate to SNA, 28 August 1897.

69. *Natal Witness*, 18 September 1897.

70. Natal, *Report . . . Native population*, 1898, pp.B2,17,43,46.

71. Van Onselen, 'Reactions to rinderpest', p.480.

72. Chigwedere, '1896 rinderpest disease', p.30.

73. See *Natal Witness*, 10 April 1896, 31 July 1897, 9 and 16 October 1897; *Natal Mercury*, 28 October 1896.

74. Beinart, *Political economy of Pondoland*, p.47.

75. NL&C, 228, no.175, Blaney to General Manager, Durban, 5 August 1897. This was done in the interests of sheep farmers.

76. Natal, *Report . . . Native population*, 1897, pp.85,90,94,200.

77. Ibid., pp.104–5.

78. Interview with Mrs Ruth Kubone, Umlazi, 5 March 1979; See also Bryant, *Description of native foodstuffs*, p.1.

79. J. Iliffe, *A modern history of Tanganyika*, Cambridge, 1979, p.124; Natal, *Report . . . Native population*, 1898, pp.B1, 14, 24, 25, 46, 67.

80. Interviews with Mr H.M.S. Makhanya, Umbumbulu, 6 March 1979 and Miss Bertha Mkize, Inanda, 4 August 1979; Bryant, *Description of native foodstuffs*, p.8.

81. Natal, *Report . . . Native population*, 1897, pp.120,136,152; 1898, pp.B38, 42, 58.

82. Natal, *Report . . . Native population*, 1898, pp.B26, 48, 61, 63.

83. Choles, 'Effects of rinderpest', pp.1055, 1059.

84. *Natal Witness*, 20 November, 18 December 1897; *The Colonist*, 1, no.8, 16 January 1904, p.392.

85. Choles, 'Effects of rinderpest', p.1058.

86. CSO, 2919, Invasion Losses Enquiry Commission, Nugani, p.29.

87. Pearse, *Joseph Baynes*, p.83; C.J. Smythe Papers, 11, Diary, 13 March 1897, 7 April 1898.

88. *NBB Departmental reports*, 1898, p.B32.

89. Choles, 'Effects of rinderpest', p.1061. *NSYB*, 1898, p.P15 gives 75 842 for Africans. In addition, Indian stock keepers were left with 1 025 head.

90. *NBB Departmental reports*, 1897, p.B86.

91. Natal, *Report . . . Native population*, 1898, p.B32.

92. Ibid., 1897, p.55.

93. SNA, 1/1/254 2159/97, Magistrate, Weenen to USNA, 4 October 1897.

94. Ibid., 1830/97, Precis of memorandums, 2 September 1897.

95. Natal, *Report . . . Native population*, 1898, p.A50; SNA, 1/1/268, 2858/97, SNA circular 13, May 1898.

96. Welsh, *Roots of segregation*, p. 95. The figures exclude Zululand.
97. *SANAC*, 3, Hulett, p. 157.
98. G. Dahl and A. Hjort, *Having herds: pastoral herd growth and household economy*, Stockholm, 1976, p. 17.
99. J. Giblin, 'Famine and social change during the transition to colonial rule in northeastern Tanzania, 1880–1896', *African Economic History*, 15, 1986, p. 85.
100. Iliffe, *Modern history of Tanganyika*, p. 124.

CHAPTER TEN

War, Recession and Impoverishment, 1899–1905

By the end of the nineteenth century, African society in Natal was reeling under the cumulative impact of overpopulation and natural disaster. In addition, the colonial state had been more rigorously enforcing its authority over its black subjects since the advent of responsible government in 1893. However, official policy under both Sir John Robinson (until ill-health forced his resignation in February 1897), and Harry Escombe, had continued to be dictated by urban and mercantile concerns, and the need to retain the trade of the South African Republic. The settler farming community had been infuriated by the government's reluctance to accede to its land and labour demands, and by 1897 there was barely concealed hostility between the ministry and the Farmers' Conference.

In September 1897 the Escombe ministry was defeated at the polls and a ministry was formed under Henry Binns. Binns died two years later and was succeeded as Prime Minister by Colonel Alfred Hime whose accession to power marked the end of the influence of the merchant community. Thereafter, until 1910, every ministry was dominated by farming representatives determined to protect and advance settler agriculture. Under these ministries there was a general tightening in the enforcement of the restrictive and harassing laws introduced by their predecessors, a tightening which added to the growing climate of uncertainty and distrust among Africans.

As the 1890s drew to a close, officials were frantically trying to cope with the rinderpest epizootic. No sooner had the disease subsided, than war clouds began to gather on the horizon. By mid-1899 it was obvious to most Natalians that the impasse between Great Britain and the South African Republic, ostensibly over representation for British subjects in the republic, was likely to be resolved on the battlefield. By October, Natal, as part of the Empire, found herself at war with her republican neighbours. The South African War began disastrously for the colony and within weeks the small imperial force in northern Natal had been trapped in Ladysmith or swept back south of Colenso. The whole of northern Natal was occupied by republican burghers who were assisted by many of the Afrikaner stockfarmers of the district.

With republican forces entrenched in northern Natal, the British army's first priority was to muster its resources for a counter-attack. This had considerable repercussions for both whites and blacks in the colony. Local resources and labour were mobilized as rapidly as possible and the colonial population was involved actively in the war effort. There was a great need for transport riders, wagons and oxen. Africans with wagons and oxen hired them out to the army, often at prices as inflated as £2 a day.[1] There was also an increased need for labour. As Africans strongly resisted attempts to use *isibhalo* labour for war work, the government established a Native Labour Corps under J.S. Marwick. This consisted of volunteers, many from Ncwadi's Ngwane chiefdom. During the first summer of the war there was a drought throughout the colony which drove Africans onto the labour market. The army's presence more than compensated for the closure of the gold- and coal-mines; military wages were far in excess of the colonial rate. Many Africans found employment as riders and *voorlopers*, while at least one thousand volunteered for work in the Native Labour Corps at £2 a month. The scope of work was wide, ranging from loading wagons, digging sangars and building gun pits to cutting grass and wood, and heaving coal.[2] There was also a growing demand for produce to which most Africans responded by contracting directly with the military rather than working though agents or traders.

The war obviously did not benefit all Africans equally. In northern Natal its effects were often devastating. During the republican occupation, many Africans fled behind the British lines, abandoning their crops and livestock. Those who stayed faced being press-ganged by the invaders to provide labour, or saw their crops requisitioned and cattle and horses stolen. As the imperial army advanced (and particularly after the relief of Ladysmith on 28 February 1900), there was further destruction and theft, both by British soldiers and by retreating burghers.[3]

But once the invaders had been driven from the district, those on rebel farms used their owners' absence to recoup their losses and there was a fair amount of looting and stealing of stock on these farms. The Natal government was determined to prevent Africans from using the war to overturn rights of property, and instructed magistrates to call out labour tenants on all rebel farms for *isibhalo* service with the military.[4] Africans in the area were, not surprisingly, bewildered by a turn of events which they saw as favouring the interests of rebel farmers, despite their own loyalty and losses.

The war did much to further racial tension in northern Natal. Even before hostilities began the colonial government had urged Africans to volunteer as scouts and had provided Chief Ncwadi with guns to patrol the Drakensberg passes.[5] Yet once the danger to the colony had passed, narrow settler interests again asserted themselves and there was a determined official onslaught on all attempts by Africans to improve their position. Clashes between the colonial government and the military over labour conditions and wages were endemic until 1902 when the army agreed to lower its wage rate. Yet, despite the annexation of Zululand to Natal in 1898, the Natal government was unable to prevent the army from recruiting from the area to raid into the Transvaal to capture cattle although it was able to keep Natal Africans out of the conflict.[6]

The end of the war in May 1902 saw a return to the *status quo ante* in northern Natal. As compensation for her losses during the war, Natal received the Transvaal districts of Vryheid and Utrecht in 1903. The annexation of these districts increased the number of Afrikaners in Natal and deterred the government from taking steps that would alienate them from British rule. In Klip River county, rebel farmers returned to their farms and no attempt was made by government to protect labour tenants on these farms from reprisals. Many homestead inhabitants were summarily evicted from the farms while others were subjected to tighter labour conditions. Africans who had suffered losses during the invasion also found difficulty in obtaining adequate compensation. An Invasion Losses Enquiry Commission assessed claims, but it was more difficult for Africans than for settlers to prove their losses. Even those whose claims were accepted as bona fide, usually received only 75 per cent of each claim. This, and the fact that those who were paid were seldom advised that the balance would not be forthcoming, heightened feelings of alienation.[7]

For Natal's population as a whole, however, the war brought opportunities rather than hardships. The military presence and increased activity on railways and harbour works provided jobs for large numbers of men. In the towns the boom conditions brought greater employment prospects for African women, as well as men, and resulted in the growth of permanent black communities, particularly on the outskirts of Durban. And, as the price of agricultural produce soared, Africans planted extensively to meet the demand for vegetables and maize; in Ixopo, Africans even invested in mealie tanks to store their surplus.[8] The import figures of goods specifically for African use indicate the increase in African prosperity. They rose from £159 910 in 1899 to £271 450 in 1902.[9]

The wartime boom continued until 1903. In that year, the return to peacetime levels of expenditure, accompanied by the removal of all but a small imperial garrison, caused a decline in the inflow of funds and the onset of a recession which lasted until 1909. The start of the recession coincided with a return of drought and locusts and a minor recurrence of rinderpest. Then, a year later, in 1904, a new tick-borne disease, east coast fever, began to attack colonial cattle herds and threatened to destroy the stock increases of the previous few years. Much of the wartime earnings of Africans had to be spent on buying grain instead of restocking herds. By 1905 the number of African-owned cattle had risen to only 276 997 head, still far short of the 494 382 of 1896.[10] Africans were now believed to have less than two head of cattle per hut, a marked drop from the estimated five per hut of 1869.

The crisis Africans faced as a result of the disasters of the 1890s and early 1900s was compounded by the continuing rapid rise in population numbers. The colonial census of 1904 included, for the first time, an enumeration of the African population. While earlier population estimates, based on hut tax returns, were not very reliable, the comparative statistics none the less suggest marked population growth. According to the census, the number of Africans in Natal (excluding Zululand and the recently annexed Vryheid and Utrecht territories) had increased since 1891 from an estimated 455 983 to 607 229, giving an average of 29,7 Africans per square mile compared to 15,72 in 1891. This was a considerably denser population ratio than in Zululand where the average was 17,1 to the square mile.

The spread of settler agriculture meant that few lands remained in Crown or absentee hands. With fewer farms, the Natal Land and Colonisation Company tried to maintain the level of rural rentals by crowding more huts onto each farm without regard to carrying capacity.[11] And as absentee-owned and Crown lands were sold, evictions caused more overcrowding on the reserves and remaining Crown lands. By 1906, the reserve inhabitants had to make do with an average of 36,19 acres per hut compared to 55,1 in 1882. It was calculated that there were six acres per person in the reserves compared to eight in those of the Cape.[12]

As congestion increased, reserve inhabitants became even more determined to prevent newcomers from encroaching on their lands. At the same time, continuing eviction of *imizi* from white-owned farms forced chiefs to find land for their people, thereby aggravating tensions and overcrowding in the reserves.[13] Destruction of the natural vegetation and soil erosion increased. And, despite rinderpest and east coast fever, over-grazing remained a problem since many *abanumzana* tried to recoup their losses by allowing neighbouring white farmers to graze cattle on their lands.[14]

With traditional farming methods and resources too limited to irrigate or fertilize gardens, grain cultivation was no longer sufficient to maintain the viability of the homestead. Soil exhaustion and erosion had seriously hampered African grain cultivators, and they no longer dominated the colony's maize production. Between 1902 and 1904 they reaped only 38 per cent of Natal's maize crop, an estimated annual 388 634 muids whereas whites reaped 479 891 muids and Indians 139 764. Africans were now reaping an annual average of 2,8 muids per hut, only half of the crop reaped by the average African household in the early 1890s. This deterioration was particularly marked in the midlands where the decline since the early 1890s was from 8,3 muids per hut to 3,3. Although the decline in the sorghum crop was not as marked, from an estimated 3,5 to 1,8 muids per hut, the increased reliance of so many *imizi* on sorghum meant that there were serious shortages of this grain as well.[15]

These statistics reflect the growing impoverishment of African society. In the earlier colonial period, the market economy had encouraged homestead cultivation in areas close to markets. As the maize statistics indicate, this situation had now changed. Once the increased wartime demand for produce ended, African sales slumped. In *imizi* where boom conditions had been exploited to restock herds, there were still opportunities for rebuilding a semblance of prosperity. Owners of oxen hired their stock out for ploughing and there were still *imizi* throughout the colony where lands were irrigated and where cash crops were grown.[16] But these were no longer the norm. On the whole, restricted access to land prevented Africans from owning much stock, while the expanding commercialization of settler agriculture and the rapid growth of Indian market gardening, deprived many of their main urban markets.

Overcrowding in the reserves, and the restrictions on the size of gardens on white-owned farms in the coastal and midland divisions, meant that few Africans in these divisions could continue to supply the market. Numerous witnesses to the Natal Native Commission in 1906–7 complained that there were Africans who no longer had land of their own, while witnesses to both this commission and to the South African Native Affairs Commission in 1903 referred to the decline in African supplies to markets. While some producers still supplied towns with beer or a few fowls or eggs, the supply of maize showed a marked drop. In 1903 Hulett told the South African Native Affairs Commission that he knew of no Africans on the coast who continued to sell maize, while a maize contractor, John McKenzie, reported that he no longer bought even half-a-dozen bags from African suppliers. The chairman of the Pietermaritzburg Chamber of Commerce, S.J. Mason, estimated that Africans around the capital could still supply 50 000 bags of mealies to the market, but that they had to repurchase later in the season.[17]

But, as Natal witnesses to the South African Native Affairs Commission pointed out, since the rinderpest, Africans were also finding it difficult to meet their own food requirements.[18] With grain, meat and milk now in short supply, and with the depletion of traditional stand-bys such as natural vegetation and game, Africans throughout the colony were experiencing food shortages. Zbigniew Konczacki points out that the required daily food-intake for a moderately active male is 3 000 calories, and for a female, 2 400. He calculates that by 1904 Africans in Natal were reaping an average of only 4,75 lbs per head of maize and sorghum per week, or a daily intake of 835 calories.[19] Depleted natural vegetation, and infrequent meat and milk would have been insufficient to make good the calorific shortfall. In general Africans had too little to eat, and what they did eat provided a starchy and unbalanced diet.

Purchases of food only partially remedied the imbalance. The District Surgeons' reports reflect a deterioration in health caused by overcrowding, bad diet and malnutrition. As overpopulation reduced access to fresh water, typhus and dysentery spread, while cramped conditions in many huts encouraged tuberculosis. Intestinal complaints and enteritis were also becoming common.[20] Children continued to suffer the most and malnutrition undermined their resistance to disease. In 1905 the District Surgeon of Estcourt reported on the number of infant deaths caused by the milk shortage and estimated that African mothers lost on average two out of three babies through abdominal complaints. The average life expectancy was low – in 1905, 67,8 per cent of African deaths were of people under thirty.[21] Migrant labourers suffered as seriously through bad diet as did other Africans. Neither *isibhalo* workers, nor the coal miners and railway workers, received a meat ration or fresh vegetables. Many returned home suffering from scurvy, a disease which was made more prevalent by the growing consumption of American maize which, because it was kiln-dried, was vitamin-C deficient.[22]

Despite the setbacks they had received during the war, inhabitants of African-owned lands in northern Natal were able to use the return to peacetime conditions to consolidate their position. Because so many white-owned farms remained in the hands of rebel Afrikaner stockfarmers and bywoners who had been impoverished by the war, there were still opportunities for African agriculturalists. The inhabitants of Driefontein and of the Crown lands purchased by *kholwa* syndicates still found a ready market for wheat, maize and vegetables in the district.[23] Conditions remained particularly favourable in Newcastle and Dundee divisions where Africans had bought 72 417 of the 497 944 acres sold since the opening of the Crown lands in 1894.[24] The return of peace and the reopening of the coal-mines brought an influx of people into the area and created a demand for produce in the towns of Newcastle and Dundee, and on the coal-mines themselves.

Yet, as the stockfarmers struggled to recoup their losses by tightening control of their labour tenants, it was usually only the *kholwa* who were able to take advantage of the opportunities offered. And, as their own position deteriorated, labour tenants tried to escape their obligations by moving onto syndicate-owned lands as rent tenants. This threat to their labour supply alarmed the stockfarmers. Even before the war they had demanded that African purchases of Crown lands be prohibited, arguing that since Africans had lands set aside for them, they should not be allowed to purchase in 'white' areas.[25] This demand now became particularly insistent and in 1903 the government bowed to the pressure and barred all Africans, including exempted *kholwa*, from further purchases of Crown lands.

The closure of Crown lands did not deny Africans access to private lands and many *kholwa* syndicates purchased or rented the farms of impoverished Afrikaners in northern Natal.[26] The *kholwa* centre of gravity in the colony was thus shifting to the interior. By 1905, of *kholwa* births registered in the colony, 38,9 per cent were in Klip River county.[27]

Throughout Natal, however, a small number of *kholwa* families, particularly those which had been appointed to chiefships, continued to prosper. Despite the decline of Groutville, the Luthuli family had consolidated its position after being appointed as chiefs over the Umvoti mission station, and Martin Luthuli had become an important sugar planter cultivating his cane with wage labour. Inland, Stephanus Mini's son, Stephen, who had succeeded him in the Edendale chiefship, and Johannes Kumalo at Driefontein also hired their labour requirements. These men, and many of the more affluent *kholwa*, had taken on the trappings of a petty bourgeoisie living largely off the rents they drew from their tenants.[28]

But, for most coastal and midland *kholwa*, conditions continued to deteriorate. Transport riding was no longer very lucrative and agriculture seldom paid now on mission lands. Even in Edendale and Groutville it had become easier to raise money by letting lots to whites and Indians than through agriculture.[29] The extent to which overcrowding was occurring on the missions is evident from the hut tax returns which show that between 1882 and 1906 the number of huts paying tax increased from 571 to 5 776.[30] The social friction which had been developing from the late 1880s was undermining the economic viability of the mission reserves. By the beginning of the twentieth century only the inhabitants of Inanda and Amanzimtoti are mentioned as selling produce or stock.[31]

The government's receptivity to farmers' demands for ending African Crown-land purchases reflects the changes that were occurring in official policy. With farmers in a majority in all cabinets, the Farmers' Conference, now called the Natal Agricultural Union, became far more influential. The Conference had always demanded restrictive legislation but, as noted above, the Robinson and Escombe ministries had resisted its demands. After a brief spell during which Binns was Prime Minister and Liege Hulett was Secretary for Native Affairs, Moor returned to the post under the Hime ministry. Without the restraining hands of Robinson and Escombe, he proved more amenable to farming pressure. Yet the legislation he proposed was never as draconian as that introduced by his successors. He was also prepared to turn a blind eye to the infringement of harsh laws, and many Africans regarded him as more sympathetic to their interests than Henrique Shepstone had been.[32]

This is more than can be said for his permanent under-secretary. Since 1893, S. O. Samuelson had done little to influence the ministries or to offer opinions of his own and, because of this, he was known among Africans as *Vumazonke*, 'assent to everything'.[33] Like his superiors, he insisted on absolute obedience from Africans while making no attempt to remain conversant with their predicament or to visit reserves. In 1900 he admitted to the Lands Commission: 'I have had no opportunity of travelling about the Colony . . . Since I have been in the Department, the country has been practically a closed book to me.'[34] Under his management, the Native Affairs Department proved incapable of meeting the demands brought about by changing conditions in the colony. 'It is worse than useless', wrote Umlaleli to the *Natal Witness*, 'everything is left to the magistrates who consider it is not their work, and therefore nothing is done.'[35]

The Hime government fell on 18 August 1903 and was replaced by a ministry headed by Sir George Sutton, which in turn was replaced by one under the premiership of Charles Smythe on 16 May 1905. Although the absence of party politics in Natal meant that frequent changes of government had little political significance, the advent of the Sutton ministry was to have profound repercussions on future race relations in the colony. Although Sir George shared few of the hardline attitudes towards Africans common to so many farmers, his appointment of George Leuchars as Secretary for Native Affairs was disastrous. Both Leuchars (1904–05) and his successor Henry Winter (1905–06) were stockfarmers who blatantly pandered to the prejudices of the farming community. Leuchars was described by J. Mapumulo in *Ilanga lase Natal* as a 'good for nothing Whiteman. He is harsh, cruel and remorseless.'[36] Winter was completely out of touch with African aspirations and grievances. He totally disregarded the views of chiefs and brooked no interference with his control over the African population.[37] Unfortunately, both men had the support of Sir Henry McCallum who succeeded Sir Walter Hely-Hutchinson as Governor in 1901. A soldier of autocratic temperament, McCallum was a dyed-in-the-wool white supremacist who believed that Africans had to be kept firmly in their place.[38]

During these post-war years, the colonial state abandoned the spirit of trusteeship which, however faintly, had been one of the forces that had motivated it in the nineteenth century. At the same time, while failing to acknowledge any sense of obligation for African welfare, the ministries actively intervened to consolidate settler dominance in Natal and to prevent African competition. The commercialization of settler agriculture was not yet sufficiently advanced for farmers to feel secure without official assistance. The ministries were sympathetic to their demands and so marked did the identification of the state with settler agricultural interests become during these years that a witness to the 1906–7 Native Affairs Commission, Sotobe, complained that there were now two kings in the country: 'There was the king on the one hand, and the European farmer, on the other.'[39] The government took vigorous steps to protect white farmers and to encourage them to stay on the land. These steps included providing them with services and credit, building branch railway-lines in previously neglected areas and constructing irrigation schemes. A Land Board was established to promote farming and the Natal Co-operative Mealie Growers' Union was formed to encourage mechanization and to offer marketing facilities.[40]

Government assistance was largely restricted to white farmers and could be directly detrimental to Africans as, for example, when Thuli *imizi* were moved from the Umnini reserve to make way for an experimental farm.[41] Legislation to protect settler interests was also rigorously enforced. Various stock-theft acts had been consolidated in 1898 and a new act was passed in 1905 which encouraged Africans to inform on each other by rewarding men for providing information, and by placing the onus of proof of innocence on *abanumzana* whose *imizi* were in the vicinity of a theft. Legislation such as this caused great bitterness among Africans, but its impact was less marked than those measures designed to meet farmers' demands for land and labour.

The requirement for land was partly met by closing Crown lands to African purchasers in 1903, and by releasing large areas of Zululand for settler occupation in 1904. The demand for labour was more difficult to meet, particularly as it was not confined to Natal but came from throughout southern Africa, giving rise in 1903 to the South African Native Affairs Commission. Although the main aim of the commission was to ensure a cheap, reliable labour supply for the gold-mines, in Natal the authorities bowed to settler demands that the needs of the mines should not interfere with the colony's own labour requirements.

In 1901, Moor introduced legislation prohibiting touting for the gold-mines. He also acceded to the farmers' demand for a general registration of all Africans to curtail desertion and to tighten their control over the sons of their labour tenants, men who, in the absence of written contracts, could not legally be forced to provide labour. This took the form of the 1901 Native Servants' Identification Act which established a system of registration for labourers in Natal and tried to protect employers against desertions by providing for a system of passes.[42] It unintentionally created a problem for farmers, however, for tenants could use the passes to seek work elsewhere. Accordingly, in 1903 the act was amended to allow an employer to endorse the back of a tenant's pass with the period he was allowed to be away from his place of employment. This placed the labour tenant in the absolute power of the farmer, who could refuse to allow a tenant to obtain a pass, or refuse to endorse one.[43]

The ministries also intensified the campaign against the *kholwa*. In terms of the then evolving segregationist ideology there was no place for a *kholwa* class which aspired to white cultural and socio-economic norms. A deliberate policy was followed to reduce the gradations of privilege between *kholwa* and other Africans and to make them equally subject to African law. This attitude was particularly obvious in relation to education and legal exemptions. The average grant per child to mission schools dropped from £1 2s. 8d. in 1893 to 13s. 3d. in 1903, and it became more difficult for some mission schools to obtain grants while others were closed on the pretext that their teachers were not qualified.[44] When John Langalibalele Dube, who had studied in the United States, established an industrial school at Ohlange, Inanda, in 1901, his application for a grant was rejected and he was told that none of his pupils would be accepted for the government examination.[45]

It also became far more difficult for *kholwa* to obtain exemption, and the undermining of the privileged status of exempted Africans, which had begun in 1893 was accelerated. Exempted Africans were specifically included in discriminatory legislation after 1898 while in 1905, Gallwey's 1880 ruling that exemption extended to the children of a succesful applicant was overturned by the Chief Justice, Sir Henry Bale, in the Supreme Court.[46] Although by now there were many *kholwa* who were qualified for the franchise, few who applied were successful. Stephen Mini told the 1906–7 Commission that his application had been rejected. The actual number of African voters is uncertain. In 1903 the South African Native Affairs Commission was told there were only two while in 1907 a figure of six was given.[47] By 1906 the status of exempted Africans had been so eroded that the consolidation of a prosperous *kholwa* middle class seemed increasingly improbable.

As far as the Native Affairs' Department was concerned, the integrity of the African hierarchy remained central to its African policy. The 1891 Code had underlined this and had attempted to ensure the position of chiefs, *izinduna* and *abanumzana*. Yet the actions of successive ministries undermined rather than bolstered the authority of African elders. In the reserves, the ministries used the management powers given to the Governor-in-Council under the 1896 Native Locations Act to issue numerous regulations and rules for the control of the reserves. These were often contradictory and confusing and, in the case of those which tightened beer-drinking restrictions, only served to anger people. Moreover, with the undermining of the position of chiefs and *izinduna*, and with an inadequate police force, the regulations usually remained ineffective.

The only common denominator in these rules and regulations was the increasing authority that they gave to officials. In 1902 magistrates were given widespread authority to control *imizi*. No *umuzi* could move into a reserve or within a reserve without a magistrate's permission while no new *umuzi* could be established with less than four huts.[48] These rules directly infringed on the remaining powers of chiefs and *izinduna*, who now found themselves prohibited from allotting land without a magistrate's permission. Government policy towards chiefs was becoming more self-defeating. Pressures on them to control their people were increasing; while the means to do so were steadily removed. At the same time, the administration exploited the growing territorial fragmentation of chiefdoms to undermine more powerful chiefs by formally dividing their chiefdoms. By 1906 there were 215 chiefs in Natal; since 1893, nineteen chiefdoms had been divided, the most significant being that of the Mphumuza chiefdom which was divided into three separate chiefdoms on Thetheleku's death in 1899.[49] In addition, the chief heir, Laduma, did not inherit the favoured position with the government that his father had enjoyed.

In 1901, the Native Code Amendment Act restored to the Supreme Chief the power to decide on personal inheritance as well as chiefly succession. Cases of disputed succession had encouraged faction fighting in the 1890s, and had led to considerable expenditures and anger within the affected chiefdoms. While the new act overwrote the immediate cause of friction, the Department of Native Affairs' ignorance of the chiefdoms led to unpopular decisions. Very little attempt was made to consult the elders within a disputed chiefdom; in the case of one of Thetheleku's appointed heirs, 100 of the 130 huts he was apportioned refused to pay hut tax under him.[50] The ministry also used the powers of the Supreme Chief to depose chiefs more frequently, at times for reasons as frivolous as daring to voice popular concern about new laws.[51]

The whole thrust of official policy was to stress the role of chiefs as government subordinates exercising authority at the government's pleasure rather than in their own right. This involved depreciating the prestige of hereditary chiefs and relying more heavily on the more amenable appointed chiefs and *izinduna*. Dividing hereditary chiefdoms was one way of achieving this end. It not only reduced each heir's following, but it also diluted the hereditary principle by giving that status to only one heir. In addition, in cases of disputed succession such as in the Qwabe chiefdom in Umvoti reserve in 1894, the appointed chief, Meseni, lost the hereditary status of his father.[52]

Despite the growing impoverishment of Africans, the government also looked to them to help balance the financial shortfall caused by the economic recession. Even after cutting back on normal spending, the Colonial Treasurer was finding it difficult to balance his annual budget. The Sutton and Smythe ministries looked for any means to increase revenue and, with Parliament determined to resist increased taxation on whites, they had little alternative but to tighten the screws on Africans. In 1903 the annual rent paid by squatters on Crown lands was increased from £1 to £2 a hut. The following year Leuchars used the Mission Reserves Act to levy a rent of £3 on every hut in these reserves, while in 1905 the Treasurer introduced a Native Tax Bill to provide for a tax of £1 on all adult African men. When the bill was rejected by the Legislative Council as discriminatory to Africans, it was replaced by a new bill which levied a poll tax of £1 on all unmarried adult males in the colony, irrespective of race.[53]

The ministries justified these taxes and rentals on the grounds that Africans paid less than their share of taxes, an argument which was as widely heard in early twentieth-century Natal as it had been in the first decades of colonial rule. That it remained equally invalid has been proved by Konczacki who points out that the income *per capita* accruing to whites in Natal was nearly twenty-four times higher than that earned by Africans and Indians, yet the latter people paid proportionately more of their earnings in taxes; 7 compared to 6 per cent. A comparison with the Cape also shows that although there were over 500 000 more Africans in that colony than in Natal, in 1903 they paid an estimated £266 925 in direct and indirect taxes compared to £268 182 paid by Natal Africans.[54]

By the early twentieth century, most of these taxes were paid in money earned by wage labour. As their ability to raise money through agriculture waned, so did the Africans' ability to dictate the length of time for which they worked. As James Stuart pointed out in 1904: 'At the outset the Native worked because he wanted to, now he works because the White men and the government want him to.'[55] Liege Hulett believed that each labourer worked on average eight months a year, thus spending two-thirds of his time away from his *umuzi*.[56] According to the census of 1904, 30 657 African men were employed in rural areas and a further 31 897 were employed in the towns. In the same year 32 878 men were given passes to leave Natal, 22 399 of whom were issued with passes to work in the Transvaal.[57] Thus, by 1904, at least 95 432 of a total male African population of 296 344, or 32,2 per cent of the total population, including children, were in full-time or part-time employment as agricultural or migrant labourers.

Yet, despite the wages they were earning, Africans were finding it difficult to meet their financial obligations. Not only were they having to find more money for rentals and taxes but, as more and more actions were criminalized, they were also having to find money for the payment of fines. Under responsible government no less than 48 laws applicable particularly to Africans were passed. In addition, many regulations were framed under these and previous laws. According to Maurice Evans:

These laws and regulations pressed upon the daily life of the Native on all sides, they imposed conditions and restrictions with which he had to comply before he could travel in the country, they put special disabilities upon him in respect of crime – cattle-stealing to wit, they increased the taxes he had to pay, they interfered with his social life. And though every year saw new edicts passed which he was bound to obey, there was no provision by which the uneducated Native could be told and made to clearly understand the obligations.[58]

By 1905, African fines and court fees were yielding a revenue of £41 337 with an average of 3 600 arrests every month for breaches of laws, regulations and municipal by-laws. A large proportion of convictions resulted; between 1903 and 1905, 129 722 people were charged of whom 99 678 or 76,8 per cent were convicted. In 1906, Joseph Baynes pointed out that the 'punishments inflicted in many cases constitute a greater crime than is the offence for which the punishment is inflicted' and warned that they were turning the Africans into a 'criminal, sullen, felonous [*sic*] and bitterly discontented people'.[59]

Magistrates were inflicting harsher sentences than in the past, and justified floggings and lengthy gaol sentences on the grounds that leniency encouraged crime and bred contempt for the white man.[60] The increase in the number of magisterial divisions had failed to improve the quality of legal administration. Most magistrates remained ignorant of African law and the Zulu language and their decisions continued to be overturned by higher courts with monotonous regularity. In his letter to the *Natal Witness* in 1901, Umlaleli attacked the calibre of recent appointments to the bench, while in 1902 the Native Suitors' Commission received numerous complaints from African witnesses about the inexperience of magistrates and conditions in their courts.[61] The 1906–7 Native Affairs Commission also pointed out that the fines imposed by magistrates were often excessive and commented that 'debts are also contracted in order to escape imprisonment, as the alternative of the non-payment of fines imposed by Magistrates'.[62]

The introduction of formal court rules and regulations during the 1890s, and the incompetence and legal ineptness of magistrates, meant that Africans were now having to retain lawyers in court cases. Shepstone had only allowed lawyers in cases where whites were involved, but by the early twentieth century their use had become widespread, reflecting the extent to which Africans had become enmeshed in the colonial political economy. As African commercial transactions became more common, the need for contracts, promissory notes, bonds and mortgages spread. A large proportion of a country solicitor's work was now taken up with African cases; between 1901 and 1905 lawyers appeared in 25 per cent of cases involving Africans.[63] Although the magistrates' records suggest that lawyers were usually retained only in more serious cases, there are examples of excessive use of them. For example, although a lawyer seldom charged a fee of less than £2 to £3, Boya in Upper Tugela retained G. Jackson when he sued Alexander Brothers for a mere 12s. in transport charges.[64] Yet many Africans would have agreed with the *kholwa* landowner, Qaijane, that 'if you go into court without a lawyer, what you have to say is not heard'.[65]

Lawyers' fees compounded African privations and hardship. Debts were incurred to pay costs, and these frequently led to further actions for recovery. In criminal cases, property was always confiscated by the Crown when a party was convicted of theft. Increasingly it was also being seized to pay judgement and costs in civil cases.[66] Invariably, confiscation involved not only cattle seizure, but also a low valuation of the cattle. The capital loss was the greater since cattle prices were high after the rinderpest epizootic, and the cost of replacing seized herds would have aggravated African indebtedness in the colony.

African landowners were also finding difficulty in avoiding sinking into debt. With land-purchase syndicates often ignorant of the liabilities and responsibilities of joint ownership of land, there were expensive internal legal disputes over property rights. Many of the poorer syndicate members found it impossible to pay their instalments and were either forced off the land or became indebted to wealthier shareholders, money lenders or lawyers.[67]

Indebtedness was becoming endemic in African society and clearly indicates the extent to which the famine-insurance mechanisms built into African society had been broken down. The erosion of homestead resources meant that few Africans remained capable of participating in the reciprocal relationships which underlay the *ukutekela* and *ukusisa* systems. As a result, needy people had little choice but to accept credit or loans and so fell into debt. In the reserves, Africans had become habituated to the trader as the supplier of their needs and it was an easy transition for them to become dependent on him for food when traditional methods of exchange and barter broke down.

This situation was compounded by the difficulties Africans experienced in obtaining credit or loans at prevailing colonial rates. Few Africans other than owners of land were able to offer collateral, and such people formed only a small minority. Although the prevailing rate was 6 per cent, excessive interest rates were not illegal in the colony. Consequently, African borrowers were required to pay high, usually usurious rates. Promissory notes had to be signed at magistrates' offices, but they seldom included the interest rate and money was fairly commonly advanced at 600 to 800 per cent, with the borrower having to surrender almost all his crop and much of his stock to pay the interest. In a particularly notorious case, three Africans in Stanger, Uhayi and Mboza kaGudu and Macala kaMlamula borrowed £7 10s. from Amod Mather, £20 to be repayed within the month, at an annual interest rate of 3200 per cent. Being unable to meet this schedule, they borrowed the required money from a second Stanger money lender, A. E. Jackson, and were required to pay him a further £8 interest.[68]

On white-owned land, indebtedness often assumed a more insidious form. In 1908 the South African Native Races Committee pointed out that labour tenants were generally underpaid and miserably housed and fed.[69] As they were often prevented from working off the farms, and were incapable of supporting themselves on the wages, gardens and grazing provided by the farmers, many tenants were obliged to borrow from their landlords. With little prospect of amassing cash to repay the loans they had to pay back in labour and so were tied into a cycle of indebtedness. As Charles Robinson, a member of the Legislative Assembly, commented in 1908, 'I think that in a great many cases these Natives for a long number of years remain practically slaves to their employers, and at the finish of their employment they have practically nothing.'[70] It is difficult to know how usurious this system was for few farmers kept records of such loans and even fewer drew up promissory notes. One exception was Henry Callaway Gold. Between 1898 and 1910 his diaries include references to loans to his tenants that were to be repaid in labour. Only two entries refer to loans to be repaid in cash; the first at a rate of 480 per cent and the second at 300 per cent per annum. White landowners were not alone in exploiting their tenants, however; Stephen Mini also charged usurious rates to his tenants.[71] In their attempts to protect themselves from their employers, farm labourers also began turning to lawyers although seldom with success. Yet, as Dhlozela told the Native Suitors' Commission, 'If we have no lawyer to assist us every white man on the farm will be his own lawyer.'[72]

For many *imizi*, indebtedness was the only way of surviving in an increasingly harsh world. It provided a short-term respite from poverty in the hope that wages from migrant labour would eventually enable *abanumzana* to pay off their debts. Indeed, in the years before the closing of the Natal Agency in Johannesburg in 1899, as much as one-third of the money remitted to Natal was designated for debt repayment.[73] Indebtedness was, therefore, often a mechanism for survival, a mechanism, however, denied to smaller *imizi* which lacked the means of supplying migrant labourers. Yet, even those *imizi* with men to spare did not derive as much benefit from migrant labour as they might have done, or entirely escape the debt trap.

This was largely the result of the touting system. The prohibitions against touting in Natal were widely ignored – about two thousand men were being sent to the gold mines every month by touts. The touts, often traders, offered large advances, frequently of as much as £15 or £20, to encourage Africans to go to the Transvaal. This amount was often given in the form of stock and usually the worker was made to repay about double the value of all cattle advanced. The result was that he received hardly any monthly pay and sank further into debt.[74] The 1906–7 Native Affairs Commission was told that nine out of ten African labourers were working off advances, while a *kholwa* witness, Kambule, complained to the South African Native Affairs Commission that because of this, many Africans felt that it was pointless to look for work.[75]

By 1906, African indebtedness was widespread throughout Natal. At one level, it can be argued that it had become a mechanism which could be used to ensure the survival of those *imizi* which were in the process of losing access to cattle and which were incapable of feeding themselves. The disruption of the pre-colonial support system meant that without loans, many *imizi* might have been unable to survive. In general, however, indebtedness and the growing impoverishment of African society were combining to hasten the process of African proletarianization. Together with anger and despair, they were also creating a climate conducive to revolt.

Notes

1. V. Woodley, *On the high flats of Natal: earliest pioneers of the Highflats/Ixopo area of southern Natal*, Highflats, 1984, p. 72.
2. Warwick, *Black people*, pp. 132–3; see also B. Nasson, *Abraham Esau's war: a black South African war in the Cape, 1899–1902*, Cambridge, 1991, p. 75.
3. See CSO, 2917–1919, Invasion Losses Enquiry Commission, Native claims.
4. Klip River Magistracy, Minute papers, 3/3/14, 5 June 1900; 3/3/15, 25 February 1902.
5. Warwick, *Black people*, p. 76.
6. Ibid., pp. 87f.
7. Klip River Magistracy, Minute papers, 3/3/16, 1903–1905.
8. Natal, *Report . . . Native population*, 1901, pp. B1, 17, 55.
9. Ibid., p. A53; 1902, p. B52.
10. Natal, Department of Native Affairs, *Annual report*, 1905, pp. 129f. These and all other figures in this chapter do not include Zululand and the new territories.
11. NL&C, 273, no. 78, Smith to General Manager, Durban, 5 December 1904.
12. Natal, Department of Native Affairs, *Annual report*, 1906, pp. 49f; *SANAC*, 1, p. 28.
13. *SANAC*, 3, H. C. Shepstone, p. 88, Ndunge, p. 948.
14. See, for example, Henry Callaway Gold Papers, Diaries, *passim*; Evans, *Problem of production*, pp. 7–8.
15. *NSYB*, 1902–1904.
16. Natal, *Report . . . Native population*, 1902–1904.
17. *SANAC*, 3, Hulett, p. 165, Mason, p. 435, McKenzie, p. 559.
18. See for example *SANAC*, 3, Mahashi, p. 896.
19. Z. A. Konczacki, *Public finance and economic development of Natal, 1893–1910*, Durham, N.C., 1967, p. 186.
20. Natal, *Report . . . Native population*, 1901, p. B35; 1902, p. A6, 27; 1903, pp. A11, 21, 25; *SANAC*, 3, R. C. Samuelson, p. 505.
21. Natal, Department of Native Affairs, *Annual report*, 1905, p. 10.
22. Natal, *Report . . . Native population*, 1903, pp. A52, 69; Natal, Department of Native Affairs, *Annual report*, 1905, p. 58; see also Booth, 'Homestead, state and migrant labour', p. 16.
23. Interview with R. T. Mazibuko, Edendale, 8 August 1979; *SANAC*, 3, Plant, p. 254, Rudolph, p. 309; Natal, Department of Native Affairs, *Annual report*, 1905, p. 42.
24. *NSYB*, 1895–1903.
25. *LA Hansard*, XXVIII, Bainbridge, 20 June 1899, p. 260.
26. AGR, 9, 243/1905, President, Bergville Farmers' Association to Minister of Agriculture, 19 January 1905; SNA, 1/1/324, 1892/1905, District Officer, Natal Police to Magistrate, Newcastle, 7 August 1905.
27. Natal, Department of Native Affairs, *Annual report*, 1905.
28. *SANAC*, 3, Kumalo, p. 456, Kambule, p. 459, Gule, p. 495, Lutuli, p. 872; Sir Matthew Nathan Papers, 363, p. 10.
29. Natal, *Evidence . . . Lands Commission (1900–01–02)*, Acutt, p. 268; *SANAC*, 3, H. C. Shepstone, p. 76, Hulett, pp. 154, 166–168, 186; Mini, p. 964; Natal, *Native Affairs Commission, 1906–7, Evidence*, Mini, p. 910, Kunene, p. 916.
30. Natal, Department of Native Affairs, *Annual report*, 1906, pp. 49f.

31. Natal, *Evidence . . . Lands Commission (1900–01–02)*, Mgoduka, p.78; Interviews with Miss B. Mkize, Inanda, 4 August 1979, Mr Mnguni and Mr R. Magwaza, Inanda, 6 August 1979.
32. Marks, *Reluctant rebellion*, p.22.
33. Baynes, *Letters addressed to His Excellency the Governor of Natal and His Majesty's Secretary of State for the Colonies regarding the absence of consideration in our present form of government for our coloured population*, Pietermaritzburg, 1906, p.16; CO 179, 244, Minute by Lambert, 26 February 1908, p.157.
34. Natal, *Evidence . . . Lands Commission (1900–01–02)*, p.20.
35. *Natal Witness*, 18 January 1901.
36. Translation of 12 October 1906 in SNA, 1/1/353, 3478/1906.
37. SNA, 1/1/354, 3631/1906, SNA to Prime Minister, 1 November 1906; 1/1/356, 3882/1906, SNA to USNA, 28 November 1906; See also Marks, *Reluctant rebellion*, p.23.
38. Sir Matthew Nathan Papers, 401, Memo on Native affairs from McCallum, n.d., p.225.
39. Natal, *Native Affairs Commission, 1906–7, Evidence*, p.827.
40. *Natal Agricultural Journal*, XIV, no.5, 27 May 1910, pp.477–80; Natal, Department of Agriculture, *Agricultural industries and land settlement of Natal*, n.p., 1907, pp.7–8.
41. *Natal Mercury*, 14 December 1903.
42. *LA Hansard*, XXX, 27 June 1901, SNA, pp.459–60.
43. *LA Hansard*, XXXIII, 1 June 1903, pp.367f; XXXIV, 2 July 1903, pp.46f; Natal, *Report . . . Native population*, 1903, p.A65.
44. *SANAC*, 3, Superintendent of Education, pp.235, 237.
45. *Natal Mercury*, 12 December 1903.
46. Ibid., 3 May 1905.
47. Natal, *Native Affairs Commission, 1906–7, Evidence*, Mini, p.909; A. Odendaal, *Vukani Bantu! The beginnings of black protest politics in South Africa to 1912*, Cape Town, 1984, p.17; L.M. Thompson, *The unification of South Africa, 1902–1910*, Oxford, 1960, p.111.
48. Natal, *Report . . . Native population*, 1902, p.B57.
49. Ibid, 1895–1901.
50. *LA Hansard*, XXXIX, 11 June 1900, Baynes, p.187.
51. Marks, *Reluctant rebellion*, p.146.
52. SNA, 1/1/216, 238/96, USNA to SNA, 18 February 1896.
53. Act 48, 1903, *To amend the Squatters' Rent Law of 1884*; Natal, *Report . . . Native population*, 1904, p. vii; *LA Hansard*, XXXIX, 13 July 1905, Treasurer, p.661; Act 38, 1905, *To impose a poll tax*.
54. Konczacki, *Public finance*, pp.154, 175; *SANAC*, 1, pp.29, 69.
55. Stuart Papers, 2, 'What then is to be done?', p.3.
56. *SANAC*, 3, Hulett, p.164.
57. Natal, *Report . . . Native population*, 1904, pp.117, 174.
58. Evans, *Black and white*, p.187.
59. Baynes, *Letters addressed*, pp.10, 22; see also Natal, Department of Native Affairs, *Annual report*, 1903–1905.
60. *NBB Departmental reports*, 1899, p.B33; *Ilanga Lase Natal*, 19 February 1904 (speech by Magistrate Cross).
61. *Natal Witness*, 18 January 1901; CSO, 2811, Native Suitors' Commission Evidence, Matiwane, pp.912–13, Lutuli, pp.1017–19, Mlolshwa, p.653; See also Natal, *Native Suitors' Commission, 1902, Report*, USNA minority report, p.27.
62. Natal, *Report of the Native Affairs Commission, 1906–7*, p.31.
63. CSO, 2811, Native Suitors' Commission Evidence, Waller, p.575, G. Hulett, p.810, Matiwane, p.917; Natal, *Native Suitors' Commission, 1902, Report*, p.24; Natal, Department of Native Affairs, *Annual report*, 1905, p.170.
64. Upper Tugela Magistracy, 2/1/1/1/1, 16/92.
65. CSO, 2810, Native Suitors' Commission Evidence, p.265.
66. See Upper Tugela Magistracy, 2/1/1/1/3, Civil records.
67. See Lambert, 'The impoverishment of the Natal peasantry, 1893–1910', in Guest and Sellers, eds, *Enterprise and exploitation*, pp.301–2.
68. SNA, 1/1/349, 2823/1906, Replies to circular 126/1905.

69. South African Natives Races Committee, *The South African Natives, their progress and present condition*, London, 1908, p. 13.
70. *LA Hansard*, XLIV, 2 July 1908, p. 248.
71. S. M. Meintjes, 'The ambiguities of ideological change: the impact of settler hegemony on the *amaKholwa* in the 1880s and the 1890s', Conference on the history of Natal and Zululand, University of Natal, 1985, p. 23.
72. CSO, 2810, Native Suitors' Commission Evidence, Waller, p. 575.
73. Natal, *Report . . . Native population*, 1898, p. A55.
74. SNA, 1/1/446, 3283/1909, Minutes on the Touts Act, n.d.
75. Natal, *Native Affairs' Commission, 1906–7, Evidence*, Chairman, p. 767; *SANAC*, 3, Kambule, p. 463.

CHAPTER ELEVEN

'Happy Are Those Who Are Dead'

In May 1905, less than a year before the outbreak of the Bhambatha rebellion, Madikane kaMlomowetole confided to James Stuart the fears of many Natal Africans: 'There is a restlessness in the heart of all the people. What is now clear is that we shall be done harm, we shall die, we shall be done harm by the government.'[1] His fears would have found a response in many *imizi* and forcefully express the African condition after sixty years of colonial rule. Hard hit by misgovernment, stock losses and all too frequent crop failures, homestead life was a far cry from what it had been in the early decades of the British settlement.

Although most Africans in Natal would have retained some access to land and, through this access, to at least some of the resources controlled by kinship groups, few would have lived in *imizi* with sufficient land to provide for any but their most basic needs. In many *imizi* the orderly pattern of a cattle kraal within a circle of huts had disappeared,[2] reflecting the breakdown of control within them. Other *imizi* had broken up completely, either through the ravages of rinderpest or as a result of evictions from private lands. Their inhabitants had either sought refuge with relatives or had drifted to the towns. Even for those Africans who were able to recreate a semblance of homestead life on new land, the impact of their removal from land intimately associated with their past and with ancestral spirits would have involved a traumatic change in lifestyle, one to which it would have been difficult to adapt. James Stuart himself was only too aware of the deterioration and described the average African *umuzi* as 'a mere shelter from the sun, rain and wind and cold . . . filled with nothing else but distressed and careworn creatures whose constant solicitude are [*sic*] the next years [*sic*] taxes or rent'.[3]

Although the declining ability of *abanumzana* to enforce their authority over their subordinates must not be exaggerated, their restricted access to land and cattle had weakened their position. The days of the large *umuzi* were virtually over. Only 20 per cent of married Africans in Natal remained polygamists, compared to 25 per cent in the Cape.[4] The drop in the number of polygamous marriages and the declining position of *abanumzana* had much to do with their rinderpest losses. So much of their authority rested on their ability to distribute cattle as *lobola* for the men within their *imizi* that, deprived of this resource, the hold of the *abanumzana* over their subordinates was seriously threatened. They were finding it difficult to provide *lobola* for their sons and the prospect of receiving cattle for their daughters was likewise reduced.

And yet, despite their declining authority, many *abanumzana* would have been destitute without the earnings of their sons. 'We were saved by our sons', Africans in Umlazi admitted. 'They became the wagons which carried us, the gardens that fed us.'⁵ Migrant labour had now become as essential as agriculture to the survival of the *umuzi*. Although it enabled Africans to raise some of the money they needed, its impact on the social and economic life of the *umuzi* was far reaching. In 1908 the South African Native Races Committee referred to this impact as no less than a social revolution:

> Natives cannot come into contact with the freedom of civilized life, enter into individual contracts and secure earnings hitherto undreamt of, and yet retain their old communal ideas and submit to the caprice and exactions of their tribal superiors. Slowly but surely the economic changes must undermine the tribal societies, already weakened by the spread of education and by the growing influence of the White magistrate.⁶

The most damaging blow to homestead life came when men and women moved permanently to urban areas. Very few had yet done so, however; in 1904, only 4 per cent of the colony's African population was urbanized. Yet for the great majority who remained migrant labourers, the conditions experienced in the towns or mining and harbour compounds filtered back into their *imizi*. Neither the colonial nor the various municipal authorities had made any real attempt to meet the needs of African workers. Barracks had been established for togt labourers in Durban but were seldom used, despite being made compulsory in 1902. In 1904, a Native Locations Act was passed, but no urban locations were laid out for Africans until after 1910. In the towns both men and women had to make do with whatever accommodation they could find. This included over-crowded and insanitary outbuildings and stables on the premises of their employers.⁷

Because of the close proximity of Africans to settlers in the towns, mechanisms to control them were far more stringent than in rural areas. There was a steadily augmented host of laws and rules regulating and circumscribing their lives. As in the country, it became virtually impossible to avoid contravening these regulations. Of an urban population in Durban of approximately 20 000 Africans, an average of 8 000 were arrested each year.⁸ Aggravation and resentment at the restrictions and controls encouraged opposition to colonial authorities that spilled over into rural life. By the early twentieth century, an African proletariat was emerging and this process was already having profound repercussions on rural relations. The effects of this proletarianization were given expression in increased incidents of assault on white inhabitants in the towns and of violent resistance by workers to the police. And, as the number of young men in the towns increased, so the potential for conflict grew. Gangs of youths known as *amalaita* were being formed, their origin often going back to the secret societies of robbers which had flourished on the Rand in the 1890s. With the outbreak of the South African War, members of societies such as the Ninevites or Isigebengu moved to colonial towns where they became responsible for much of the crime.[9]

Although it is usually argued that migrant labour was destructive of attitudes of communal feeling and responsibility, many urban workers tended to gravitate towards members of their lineages or wider kinship groups. Wherever possible, they also carried on homestead traditions such as the taking of meals together and the provision of hospitality to newcomers.[10] The *amalaita* gangs, themselves, often reflected rural or age-group identities that both reinforced rural enmities and carried the potential for further reinforcing these when the labourers returned to their homes. In 1906, alienated by the treatment they were receiving from the authorities, large numbers of these labourers obeyed the call by their chiefs or *abanumzana* to return to their *imizi* to participate in the rebellion.[11]

The SNA files and the Natal *Reports on the condition of the Native population* reveal the extent of the rural changes brought about by migrant labour. Despite migrants' attempts to retain traditional observances, values such as hospitality, communal responsibilities and respect for their elders were diminished. As the financial demands of the state and the settlers increased, the young men on whom the burden of payment fell became alienated and often refused to fulfil their homestead obligations. In addition, few migrant labourers were prepared to use their acquired skills to improve conditions within their *imizi* when they returned home. And, by divorcing themselves from the day-to-day work of the homestead, they lost their fathers' expertise in agriculture. They steadily became a reservoir of unskilled labour supplying the needs of farmers, urban employers and industrialists.[12]

African elders complained bitterly to the various commissions of the early twentieth century about the effects of urban and compound conditions. Their evidence reveals two main grievances. Migrant labour was, they insisted, responsible firstly for an increase in disease and immorality; and secondly for the breakdown of respect for elders.

There was considerable truth in their complaints: the incidence of smallpox and tuberculosis increased as labour migrancy grew, while the growing frequency of syphilis adds weight to the complaints of immorality. Although these latter complaints went hand in hand with the breakdown of the *lobola* custom consequent on rinderpest, they should also be seen in the context of the growing freedom enjoyed by young men and women.

As the financial demands on *imizi* increased so the need grew to send out ever younger people to work. Not only youths but also boys as young as ten years old, no longer needed for cattle herding, were being sent to the towns; in Durban alone, as many as 6 000 were employed as kitchen umfaans.[13] At so young an age, few would have been exposed to much homestead discipline. The independence youths and young men and women enjoyed in the towns reinforced the lack of discipline and there were many complaints about their insubordination when they returned home. 'The behaviour of today is beyond me. Your own child can abuse you even as he helps himself to your food',[14] lamented the *kholwa* landowner, John Gama. This was particularly the case in divisions such as Umgeni and Inanda which were close to urban areas and where *amalaita* gangs were carrying their gang warfare and crimes over into rural environments.[15]

The absence of youths and young men from an *umuzi* upset the economic and social patterns within it and increased the burdens placed on women. Antagonism between homestead men and women was becoming more widespread, and the number of women refusing to accept the roles assigned to them was growing. As their labour was essential for the survival of the *umuzi*, their attitude caused alarm to the state as well as to *abanumzana* and was met by a tightening of the 1891 Code's provisions for the control of women. Yet, as Chief Mketengu complained to the 1906–7 Native Affairs Commission, 'even when a woman was ordered by the magistrate to return to her home, she point-blank refused, and too frequently broke loose entirely, went to the towns, and helped to swell the already large numbers of prostitutes to be found there'.[16] Some women were also breaking free from homestead restraints through the need to earn a living. In *imizi* where male migrants had moved away permanently or where there were no sons to be sent out to earn money, women were becoming migrants and seeking employment both in towns and on farms.[17]

To many *abanumzana*, faced with insubordination from within their *imizi* and yet increasingly dependent on their sons, the imposition of the poll tax was the last straw. Having become responsible for a personal tax, many young men no longer felt obliged to provide money for the communal hut tax. As the *induna*, Mjapansi, complained in 1906, the tax had 'the effect of separating their children from them'.[18] A constant refrain in the evidence given to the 1906–7 Native Affairs Commission was that of the loss of the *abanumzana*'s authority and the insubordination of children and of the realization of the way in which the colonial state had made this insubordination possible. Many leading rebels in 1906 were *abanumzana* who rose in an attempt to escape the consequences of these changes, an attempt to restore older social relationships and patriarchal authority. And in doing so, they were often successful, for, as mentioned above, many young men rebelled when their fathers called upon them to do so.[19]

The breakdown in the *abanumzana*'s authority was particularly serious on labour-tenancy farms where the refusal of a young man to perform allotted tasks or to return home could bring down the wrath of the farmer on his *umuzi*. The 1906–7 commission received numerous reports of homestead inhabitants being beaten and otherwise ill-treated because of this refusal, and also of *imizi* being evicted.

Evictions of recalcitrant tenants were as widespread throughout the colony, causing bitterness and anger. In northern Natal, Africans greatly resented the return of their farms to rebel Afrikaner farmers and the government's failure to prevent those farmers from demanding rentals for the wartime years or evicting tenants who had sided with the British.[20] Fears of eviction could also have played a role in the rebellion in south-western Natal. The close juxtaposition of farms and reserves in the area was causing great tension between Africans and settlers. Farmers frequently trespassed on reserve lands, while the growing commercialization of agriculture, particularly in the Upper Umkomazi and Ixopo divisions, was accompanied by large-scale evictions.[21] In these divisions, the African peasantry, which had been among the wealthiest in the colony, had been seriously impoverished by 1906.

Frustration and anger were also widespread among the colony's chiefs. In their evidence to the Native Suitors' Commission in 1902 and to the 1906–7 Native Affairs Commission they revealed the full extent to which their position had been undermined by the time of the rebellion. The transferral to magistrates of their jurisdiction over their people on white-owned land in 1896 had seriously weakened the binding force of kinship within chiefdoms. As the farmers' control over labour tenants increased, so it became less easy for these to attend kinship gatherings such as the now infrequently held *umkhosi* ceremonies. The situation which was to become common in the twentieth century, that of a community spirit involving neighbours, rather than kin, would have been strengthened by this development. As Ntando, a Chunu *induna* complained to the 1906–7 commission, Africans no longer 'know one another and to whom they belonged'.[22]

Kinship was also undermined by the difficulty experienced by many chiefs in building up patronage networks through the distribution of resources. Few were able to enforce the powers over reserve *imizi* confirmed by the 1891 Code,[23] owing mainly to the shortage of land and the restrictions placed on their powers of allocation. Furthermore, since the rinderpest very few remained able to continue to *sisa* cattle. Deprived of the benefits associated with the chiefly system, few of their followers were prepared to continue supplying their customary services. Chiefdoms which continued to recruit *amabutho* were seldom in a position to call them together. Of the great chiefs, Silwana of the Chunu no longer retained *amabutho* while Thetheleku's main heir, Laduma, called together far fewer of the Mphumuza than his father had done. Only Ncwadi of the Ngwane appears to have been able to continue enforcing attendance at the *umkhosi* celebrations.[24]

But, despite the chiefs' inability to exercise the same control over their people as they had in earlier years, the government's demands continued to grow. This was particularly true of its demand for *isibhalo* labour. Yet, as migrant labour spread, so the number of men available in the reserves for the chiefs to call up dwindled. In 1904, a further source of *isibhalo* labour was closed when the Mission Reserves Regulations prohibited chiefs from calling up men on these reserves. Despite this, the government's continuing need for forced labour meant that it increased its demands for *isibhalo* labourers, while seldom revising the number of men required from each chief.[25]

Unable to comply, many chiefs attempted to evade their obligations, or tried to enforce their rights by calling out men from private farms or from the same *umuzi* each year. This naturally increased their people's resentment. Yet the pressure of land and the restrictions imposed by the government on movement within reserves, made it difficult for *abanumzana* to find alternative chiefs.[26]

Chiefs also tried to recoup their fortunes by making excessive demands on their people and fining, often illegally, those who refused to comply. In 1901, the magistrate of Mapumulo accused some of the Umvoti reserve chiefs of resorting to every conceivable device to impose fines on their people.[27] Evidence given to the Native Suitors' Commission also reveals that people were seeking legal advice to prevent harassment from their chiefs. Dhlozela's words sum up much of the evidence given: 'Lawyers are the pillars that support the world, and from whom we get our salvation because they assist the person who is being skinned by the very chiefs.'[28] Yet many Africans were afraid to oppose their chiefs because they knew that to do so could invite retaliation possibly in the form of being ordered out for *isibhalo* services.[29]

The deteriorating relations between chiefs and their followers, combined with the fact that few chiefs could any longer provide benefits to their people, caused a large number of the latter to distance themselves from their chiefs and refuse to acknowledge their commands. The inability of many chiefs to control their followers was particularly evident during 1906 when large numbers ignored their chiefs' instructions. The men of the Nadi chiefdom, whose actions precipitated the rebellion in February, had refused to accept Chief Mveli's orders that they pay their poll tax, while other chiefs who stayed loyal during the rebellion found it difficult to persuade their men to fight against the rebels. In south-western Natal with its tiny reserves and small, jostling chiefdoms, it proved difficult for chiefs to maintain control. In northern Natal, where most Chunu and Thembu *imizi* were on private lands, neither Silwana nor the acting chief of the Thembu, Ngqamuzana, was able to secure the support of all his people. Of the 1 000 men called out by each of the two chiefs, only 400 Chunu and 200 Thembu responded.[30] James Stuart believed that had the colonial troops met with initial reverses, many more Africans might have ignored their chiefs' orders and joined the rebels.[31]

Disaffection was equally widespread amongst the *kholwa*. The government's policy of placing *kholwa izinduna* on the same level as appointed chiefs had created tensions within the communities they administered. A man such as Stephen Mini was very conscious of his chiefly status, and his attempts to enforce obligations on his fellow *kholwa* at Edendale caused widespread resentment.[32] On lands under *kholwa* chiefs, distinct chiefdoms were emerging consisting not only of unexempted Christians, but also of those inhabitants who had previously owed allegiance to their own chiefs. This gave impetus to the development of the territorial nature of chiefship. It also stressed the similarities between *kholwa* and traditionalist chiefs, and caused the same attitude of resentment amongst their peoples.

Frustrated and embittered by the rebuffs they were receiving and by the steady erosion of their privileges, the *kholwa* were forming vigilance and welfare societies to protect their interests and turned to the political arena to gain redress for their grievances. In 1900 the leaders of the Funemalungelo Society founded the Natal Native Congress. The defunct newspaper, *Inkanyiso Yase Natal*, was replaced by the short-lived *Ipepa lo Hlange*, and then by *Ilanga lase Natal* under the editorship of John Langalibalele Dube. The demand for land dominated Congress meetings and the columns of *Ilanga*, but the need for better education and the question of franchise rights were also stressed. *Kholwa* demands were, on the whole, remarkably moderate. For example, they sought white rather than African representation in Parliament. Despite this, the government was deeply suspicious of Dube, and of Congress in general, and took every opportunity to snub its members.[33]

Kholwa who had supported the war effort were bitterly disappointed by the official lack of recognition for their services once hostilities had ended. Many had believed strongly that after the war a new dispensation would arise in Natal, as well as in the old republics and their disillusionment was correspondingly great. Not only were promises to the Native Scouts ignored, but the government refused to allow the War Office to award them silver campaign medals, insisting that inferior bronze medals be cast for them. This led to considerable disenchantment, and to a refusal to accept the medals.[34]

Their rejection by Natal's white population alienated many *kholwa*. Most were torn between a continuing desire for acceptance and a recognition that neither the settlers nor the government would accommodate it. This recognition was forcefully brought home by the Natal government's rejection of the South African Native Affairs Commission's recommendations on the franchise, education and individual land tenure. The career of John Dube provides an example of a member of the Christian petty bourgeois elite who tried to reconcile the *kholwa* desire for acceptance with the reality of white rejection. Through his membership of Congress he strove to gain white acceptance of an African middle class, while at the same time he worked for a reconciliation between the *kholwa* and the traditional chiefly ruling class. More than any other man in Natal, he worked towards an acceptance by Africans in the colony of the Usuthu chief, Dinuzulu kaCetshwayo, as the symbol of African unity.[35]

Ironically, Christianity in a more popular and militant form was itself beginning to provide a bridge between *kholwa* and other Africans in Natal. Growing disillusionment seriously undermined *kholwa* confidence in the established churches. This was particularly true of young *kholwa* whose resentment at their own impotence encouraged them to turn to new forms of Christian authority usually, if erroneously, classified together as Ethiopian. Although Ethiopianism arose primarily out of an awareness that the missionaries were failing to promote the interests of their converts, its main impetus in Natal came from the 1896 visit of the American missionary, Joseph Booth, to establish an African Christian Union in South Africa.

Although *kholwa* leaders rejected his call, his message was taken up by those

Christians who were disillusioned with the missionaries' moderate, evolutionary policies. In 1896, Simungu Shibe seceded from the American Board Mission to form the Zulu Congregational Church. Similar secessions occurred in other churches, particularly in poverty-stricken areas such as the Thukela reserves where Ethiopianism became a rallying point for both religiously and politically disaffected Africans. Realizing the political implications inherent in Ethiopianism, the government moved swiftly to stifle it. Churches without resident white ministers were demolished, school grants withdrawn and steps were taken to stem all forms of 'seditious' religion.[36]

Despite government accusations that *kholwa* generally, and Ethiopians in particular, were in the forefront of seditious movements and that they played a prominent role in the 1906 disturbances, remarkably few sided with the rebels. Only 5,3 per cent of the Africans taken prisoner were *kholwa* and of the 214 Christians convicted of rebellion, few belonged to a recognized church.[37] Where *kholwa* did rise in revolt, religious motives were often part of a wider discontent. Chief Mveli had rigorously opposed the spread of Christianity within his chiefdom, and the rebels who refused to accept his command to pay their poll tax were members of the Presbyterian Church of Africa.[38] In general, Ethiopianism provided a safety valve for discontented Christians and was not a catalyst for revolt.

But to ministries which were unable to appreciate the damage caused by their own policies, Ethiopianism provided a ready explanation for African discontent and was believed to be behind the rumours of unrest that were sweeping through the colony in the early twentieth century. Yet the government's decision to include an enumeration of the African population in the 1904 census was itself largely responsible for these rumours. The arrival of census officials in the reserves was greeted with anger and alarm which was confirmed by the use of the Zulu word, *ukubalwa*, meaning to be counted out. The word was usually used when men were turned out for *isibhalo* service and, according to Harriette Colenso, many Africans thought that the counting of their cattle meant that they were being counted out to become government property.[39]

The imposition of the poll tax, coming as it did on the heels of the census, confirmed Africans in their suspicions of official intentions. Many of the descriptions used by Africans in these years to describe the government conjure up the image of an avaricious and ever hungry monster devouring everything in its path. As Mbovu kaMtshumayeli told James Stuart: 'Government is expanding every few years. The Government resembles Tshaka, for he never got tired. Its army is money.'[40] Similarly, John Mpetwana told the 1906–7 commission that the ministers 'did not like to see people eating, because, when they saw them chewing anything, they seem to put their fingers into their very mouths and scoop the food out to eat themselves'.[41]

Both McCallum and the 1906–7 commission identified the government's financial demands as a major cause of disaffection. By 1906 these demands had become intolerable and the falling due of the poll tax in January of that year was more than many were prepared to bear. A correspondent to *Ilanga lase Natal* lamented that 'the strings of one's money bags will remain loose now and be ever ready to shake out all that is in it for taxation'.[42] Bhambatha himself was heavily in debt,[43] and the lament of Jobongo, a witness to the Native Affairs Commission, that because of the tax burden, 'happy are those who are dead'[44] would have struck a responsive chord in many an African.

Although ministerial decisions created many of their difficulties, most Africans were more directly confronted by local government officials. They felt constantly humiliated by the treatment they received from these officials, a humiliation which was not lessened by the contempt they felt for many of them. An instance of their contempt for magistrates occurred during the visit of the Duke and Duchess of Cornwall and York to Natal in 1901. Chiefs who were summonsed to Pietermaritz-burg to greet the couple were reluctant to do so with the customary royal *Bayete* as they felt it had become debased through its use for magistrates. 'It has been so much dragged in the mud, so degraded, that to offer it to these, whom we would delight to honour, would be nothing less than a gross insult, from which we shrink in horror. To greet these with *Bayete* would be but to bracket them with a lot of empty headed boys, dogs in comparison.'[45]

African contempt and resentment were directed particularly against the police. The police force's reorganization in 1894 had been intended to secure greater government control of the reserves. The rural force had been removed from magisterial control and placed directly under a central command. Recruitment had been stepped up and by 1897 there were 832 white, African and Indian policemen serving in the country districts. On average there were 22 white and 32 African policemen in each division compared to four Africans in the 1880s.[46] As their presence impinged directly on the functions of chiefs, *izinduna* and *abanumzana*, the policemen were regarded with thinly veiled hostility. Madikane, a *kholwa* from Inanda, complained to Stuart in 1905 that there 'are now policemen in the land who go around looking for crime that in former times was not there. In former times it was the chiefs who were the policemen.'[47]

In general African policemen were poorly paid and dissatisfied with their treatment, tending to take out their frustrations on their fellow Africans. There was much antagonism between the African members of the force and the homestead inhabitants, particularly over the requirement that a policeman attend beer-drinking ceremonies. There were also frequent clashes between African policemen and labourers in the towns, and the repercussions of these tended to spill over into rural disputes. But the position of the African police was ambiguous, and many found the strain of being part of a system maintaining white dominance intolerable. Some of the rural policemen rebelled in 1906. The Durban municipal police force was drawn mainly from the Umvoti reserve and at least a quarter of its members deserted to join the uprising of their kinsmen.[48]

African relations with the mounted white members of the force were particularly strained. Many had been recruited in Britain and were unable to communicate effectively with Africans. Yet they were notorious for their arrogance. Witnesses to the 1906–7 commission complained bitterly about this: 'You cannot walk along the road without being knocked about by the police for not giving them the royal salute',[49] John Hlonono complained, while the habit of handcuffing even the elderly when arresting them caused humiliation and resentment.[50] The most common cause of anger was the increasing incidence of police rapes of African women. There was a growing concern at the number of half-caste children sired by policemen, while fathers resented the fact that should their daughters be made pregnant by a white man, they were unable to claim compensation.[51] Sub-Inspector Sidney Hunt was typical of many of the British-recruited policemen. On his arrival in the colony in the 1890s he had confidently written home of his intentions of 'licking the niggers into shape' and of 'knocking hell out of them'. By 1906 he had not yet mastered the Zulu language and his immediate reaction to the troubles near Richmond was that they marked the start of an uprising.[52]

Officials' attitudes towards Africans were symptomatic of serious defects in the administrative system, defects which McCallum believed to be a cause of the rebellion. Maurice Evans agreed and further singled out the systematic way in which officials prevented Africans from expressing their grievances.[53] Magistrates were usually too busy to attend to them, their access to the Governor had been removed, and it was seldom possible to see the officials of the Native Affairs Department. The comments of chiefs who gave evidence before the 1906–7 commission, and at a meeting with McCallum before his departure from the colony in 1907, bear out Evans's view.[54] This alienation, particularly of chiefs, from the centres of power had serious consequences. Before 1893 they had been a source of information. Now, resenting the restrictions placed on their access to officials, they stayed away from Pietermaritzburg and one of the few ways the government had of obtaining accurate knowledge of what was happening in the reserves was lost. In 1906, H.C.M. Lambert in the Colonial Office commented that the 'Natal authorities are a good deal in the dark about Native affairs'.[55]

This ignorance created a strange dichotomy in official attitudes. On the one hand, government policy towards Africans was marked by complacency. Officials firmly believed that they understood the 'Native problem' and knew what was best for Africans.[56] On the other hand, there was a growing obsession with, and fear of, African sedition. Rumours of discontent and unrest predated the census and had in fact begun circulating even before the South African War.[57] The government had responded by employing spies and informers whose reports had caused sufficient alarm by 1904 for questions to be asked in Parliament.[58] Yet so much of their information was inaccurate that by late 1905, when they had something concrete to report, they tended to be ignored. One month before the first manifestations of the rebellion, the magistrate of New Hanover confidently asserted that 'nothing is more remote than any probability of trouble with the natives'.[59]

Other magistrates were more perceptive. In the same year the magistrates of

Impendhle and Alexandra both drew attention to a tendency for Africans in their divisions to look to Zululand and particularly to Cetshwayo's son and heir, Dinuzulu, for guidance.[60] This was a new and in many ways radical departure for Africans who in earlier years had seen the colonial presence as a protection against the Zulu. Impoverished and embittered by settler exactions and neglect, and with little prospect of any improvement, many Africans felt they had little alternative but to look north of the Thukela for salvation. 'If our rule had been more fatherly and personal', Maurice Evans later pointed out; 'if our officials had been men in whom our natives had full confidence, they would never have looked to the Black House as they did.'[61] James Stuart concurred, pointing out that

> when once a people begins to feel that it is accorded no particularly definite status in the country, that its welfare is of no special concern to the rulers, except as a means to the latter's material advancement, that its members, in short, are pariahs in what a few years before was their own country, then the time is not far distant when they may be expected to make a bid for liberty . . .[62]

Largely as a result of the alienation of Africans in Natal, a Zulu royalist sentiment was emerging that focused on Dinuzulu and was beginning to transcend the old divisions between those who lived north and those who lived south of the Thukela. In Natal itself, subjected to a rigid colonial authority, *amantungwa* and *amalala* chiefs alike were being drawn together by a common sense of identity that was beginning to blur the historic distinctions between them.

When the British had annexed the remnants of the Zulu kingdom in 1887, they had exiled Dinuzulu to St Helena. He had been returned to Zululand in 1897, when the colony was annexed to Natal, but to play down his special position among the Zulu as the heir to the monarchy and symbol of past independence and greatness, he had been given a minor position as the Usuthu chief. The colonial officials had not been able to prevent him from becoming a focus of opposition to white rule in Zululand, and the reverence in which he was held filtered through into Natal. During the 1906 uprising, the rebels used royal symbols including the Usuthu badge, the *uboshokobezi*, a strip of white cowhide worn on the headdress. In addition, Cetshwayo's grave became a rallying point.[63]

Dinuzulu's attitude during the rebellion and his long-term ambitions remain matters of controversy. It is debatable whether he either hoped to restore the kingship, or had ambitions south of the Thukela, and during the rebellion he made no attempt to take an active part in the fighting. Yet, regardless of his own view of his position, many Africans in Natal, most noticeably Bhambatha, viewed him as the rallying point of the rebellion. The contradictions inherent in Dinuzulu's position were evident throughout African society. The arguments for and against participation in the rebellion were many and varied, and decisions were dictated by factors such as the strength of a chief's position in his chiefdom, his relations with his neighbours, and the possibility of gaining advantages from collaboration or from resistance.

Bearing in mind the treatment they had been receiving, it is remarkable how many chiefs remained loyal to the government. Ncwadi, for example, proved as conspicuously loyal as he had been during the South African War when he had provided 200 men for scouting and constable duties and contributed £366 towards the care of wounded soldiers.[64] Of the great chiefs he, Ngqamuzana of the Thembu, and, despite the rebuffs they constantly received from officials, Laduma and Silwana acceded to the government demand for troops. In addition to supplying levies, both Laduma and Silwana and their sons enlisted to fight in the Natal Native Horse.[65] It is possible that these chiefs identified with the government in order to retain (or even to regain) the position they held within the colonial state. Other loyal chiefs had other motives: for example, Mveli's motive for loyalty could have been his desire to avenge himself on those Ethiopian followers who denied his authority over the Nadi chiefdom; he was responsible for capturing at least some of the twenty-seven rebels who had murdered Hunt.

Frustration was growing amongst loyal chiefs, however, even amongst those who responded to the call for troops. Silwana obeyed the government's orders reluctantly, while increasing disenchantment caused even as loyal a chief as Mqawe to flirt with the idea of rebellion.[66]

Chiefs who rebelled in 1906 were usually those whose position had been most undermined by official actions and the settler presence, and who hoped to find in popular resistance a restoration of their position. Most of them were joined by their followers in their revolt. Chief Msikofeli presided over the largest chiefdom in south-western Natal, the Khuse. The sale of Crown lands in the region had scattered his people on private farms and deprived the chiefdom of its unity. In the Thukela valley, Meseni of the Qwabe, who had been deprived of his father's property and hereditary rank in the disputed inheritance case of 1894, was one of the first chiefs to show disaffection in 1906. The densely populated and arid Umvoti reserve provided a fertile soil for the rebellion. Angered by years of official attempts to diminish their position, the Mthethwa chief, Matshwili and Zulu chief, Ndlovu, joined Meseni and rose in revolt. Further north, Kula, chief of the old 'government tribe', the Qamu, also rebelled against the treatment his chiefdom had received since Ngoza's death had deprived it of its favoured position.[67]

It was inevitable that the Zondi chief, Bhambatha, should rebel. Since his installation as chief in 1890, he had been involved in constant conflict with the government and in 1895 had been suspended for four months for insubordination. In August 1905 he was fined for faction fighting in his chiefdom, and at the time the rebellion began the government was considering deposing him from his chiefship.[68] By 1906 he was prepared to go to 'extremes simply because he was tied hand and foot by the network of troubles in which he found himself . . . He was very much like a beast which, on being stabbed, rushes about in despair.'[69]

Whether the grievances of the Africans would have erupted into rebellion without the catalyst of the poll tax remains controversial. In the years before 1906 there were many outlets for pent-up anger. Individual acts of resistance to settler farmers such as cutting fences, stabbing cattle or setting fire to grass remained as common as in the 1880s and 1890s and acted as a safety valve for repressed grievances. Passive resistance to the state was also common and usually found expression in non-co-operation with officials. It was often impossible for the police or magistrates to obtain evidence after a crime. Resistance could also take on a millennial form, often involving the killing of white animals or the destruction of European-made implements, a form of transferred aggression which, while extremely frightening for the settlers, would not bring the retribution which attacks on their persons would have done. The upsurge in millennial feeling was closely tied to the tendency to see Dinuzulu as a potential saviour. He alone of all the chiefs in Natal and Zululand could be seen to possess supernatural qualities of a kind capable of being used to drive the settlers out of the region.[70]

Ultimately, it would appear that most Africans who rose against white domination in 1906 were driven to rebel by a sense of desperation and frustration. Faced with discriminatory legislation, overcrowding, insecurity of tenure on private lands, poor wages, debts, and with increasing demands for taxes and rents, many Africans in reserves and on private lands alike were driven into rebellion in a desperate attempt to save themselves.

In 1902, one of James Stuart's informants, Mkando kaDhlova, had given voice to the despair and frustration felt by Africans. The words expressing alienation from white rule and the feeling of betrayed trust brought about by decades of neglect and oppression ring as clear today as when they were written down:

> You make a law; we obey it. Again you make a law and we accept and obey it. Over and over again you promulgate fresh laws and we abide by them cheerfully, and this sort of thing has continued until we have become old and greyheaded, and not even now, advanced in years as we are, do we know the meaning of your policy. We cut away the wild forests for sugar plantations and towns; we dig your roads. When will this digging of roads cease? We are made to live on farms and pay rent, and are imprisoned if we cannot pay. You chase our wives out of our homes by facilitating divorce. How is it you come to treat us thus, seeing we are your people? Where is that government or king that owns no land? Why are individuals able to oust government subjects from the soil? Why are we put to trouble in respect to farms, with the numerous regulations in connection therewith . . . We have to go out leaving no one in charge of our homes and children behind. Where shall we run to? When you went to fight Cetshwayo, you called us to help; we did so, and marched off to fight with you as allies. Had you called on us in the last war to fight we would readily have done so, but no demand was made for our services. How can you tell that we do not belong to you? What is it we do that bars and negatives our belonging to you?[71]

Notes

1. Webb and Wright, eds, *James Stuart archive*, 2, 27 May 1905, p.54.
2. Natal, Department of Native Affairs, *Annual Report*, 1905, p.48.
3. Stuart Papers, 2, 'What then is to be done?', p.3.
4. *SANAC*, 1, p.28.
5. SNA, 1/1/328, 2678/05, Minute, 9 October 1905.
6. South African Native Races Committee, *The South African Natives: their progress and present condition*, p.4.
7. M.W. Swanson, '"The Durban system": roots of urban apartheid in colonial Natal', *African Studies*, 35, no.3–4, 1976, pp.159–76.
8. P. la Hausse, 'The struggle for the city: alcohol, the Ematsheni and popular culture in Durban, 1902–1936', MA thesis, University of Cape Town, 1984, p.27.
9. Ibid., pp.35f; *Natal Witness*, 7 December 1901.
10. For an examination of the maintenance of communal and kinship traditions in the towns, see K.E. Atkins, 'The cultural origins of an African work ethic and practices, Natal, South Africa, 1843–1875', Ph.D. thesis, University of Wisconsin-Madison, 1986.
11. Marks, *Reluctant rebellion*, p.310.
12. Interview with R.T. Mazibuko, Edendale, 8 August 1979; see also D. Denoon, *Southern Africa since 1800*, London, 1972, pp.74–5; J.M. Davis, *Modern industry and the African*, London, 1933, pp.123–6.
13. P. la Hausse, '"The cows of Nongoloza": youth, crime and amalaita gangs in Durban, 1900–1936', *Journal of Southern African Studies*, 16, no.1, March 1990, p.86.
14. Webb and Wright, eds, *James Stuart archive*, 1, 18 December 1898, p.137.
15. Natal, Department of Native Affairs, *Annual Report*, 1905, p.9; *LA Hansard*, XIII, Jameson, 31 May 1904, p.46.
16. Natal, *Native Affairs Commission, 1906–7, Evidence*, p.769.
17. Choles, 'Effects of rinderpest', p.1238.
18. Natal, *Native Affairs Commission, 1906–7, Evidence*, p.838.
19. Marks, *Reluctant rebellion*, p.309.
20. Natal, Department of Native Affairs, *Annual report*, 1905, p.B51.
21. Ibid., p.1
22. Natal, *Native Affairs Commission, 1906–7, Evidence*, p.719; see also L. Mair, *African marriage and social change*, London, 1969, p.27.
23. *SANAC*, 3, H.C. Shepstone, p.87.
24. Natal, *Native Affairs Commission, 1906–7, Evidence*, Ntando, p.721; Umgeni Magistracy, Add 3/3/2/4, Magistrate to USNA, 29 December 1902; Webb and Wright, eds, *James Stuart archive*, 1, John Kumalo, 22 November 1900, p.224.
25. See Ipolela Magistracy, 4/1/4, 19/98, Magistrate to SNA, 13 January 1898.
26. Marks, *Reluctant rebellion*, p.42.
27. Natal, *Report . . . Native population*, 1901, p.B10; See also 1903, p.A50.
28. CSO, 2810, Native Suitors' Commission, Evidence, p.255.
29. Natal, *Report . . . Native population*, 1904, p.37.
30. Marks, *Reluctant rebellion*, pp.317–8.
31. J. Stuart, *A history of the Zulu rebellion, 1906 and of Dinuzulu's arrest, trial and expatriation*, London, 1913, p.90.
32. Meintjes, 'Ambiguities of ideological change', p.23; *Ilanga lase Natal*, 4 March 1904.
33. GH, 1085, no number, Minutes, December 1901, pp.77, 86; Marks, *Reluctant rebellion*, pp.69f.
34. Natal, *Native Affairs' Commission, 1906–7, Evidence, passim*, see particularly Mini, pp.909, 910, Mdolomba, p.913; R.C.A. Samuelson, *Long, long ago*, Durban, 1929, p.149.
35. S. Marks, *The ambiguities of dependence in South Africa: class, nationalism and the state in twentieth-century Natal*, Johannesburg, 1986, pp.42–73.
36. Marks, *Reluctant rebellion*, pp.59f.
37. Stuart, *History of the Zulu rebellion*, p.421.
38. Marks, *Reluctant rebellion*, p.178.
39. *Natal Mercury*, 21 May 1904.

40. Webb and Wright, eds, *James Stuart archive*, 3, 8 February 1904, p.29.
41. Natal, *Native Affairs Commission, 1906–7, Evidence*, p.716.
42. SNA, 1/1/329, 2966/05, Translation, 3 November 1905.
43. C.T. Binns, *Dinuzulu: the death of the House of Shaka*, London, 1968, p.189.
44. Natal, *Native Affairs Commission, 1906–7, Evidence*, p.712.
45. Plant, *Zulu in three tenses*, pp.70–1.
46. *NGG*, XLIX, no.2859, 16 March 1897, GN 146, 1897, p.264.
47. Webb and Wright, eds, *James Stuart archive*, 2, 27 May 1905, p.54.
48. Marks, *Reluctant rebellion*, p.181; La Hausse, 'Struggle for the city', p.50.
49. Natal, *Native Affairs Commission, 1906–7, Evidence*, p.850.
50. Ibid., Mvinjwa, p.713.
51. Ibid., Mpetwana, p.716, Sibindi, p.844, Hlonono, pp.849–50, Nyongwana, p.915, Lutuli, p.974.
52. Marks, *Reluctant rebellion*, p.177.
53. GH, 1303, Confidential, Governor to Secretary of State, 21 June 1906, p.193; Evans, *Black and white*, p.188.
54. GH, 1532, Interview between Governor and chiefs, 3 June 1907; pp.63f; Natal, *Native Affairs Commission, 1906–7, Evidence*, Mavandhla, p.698, Njome, p.715, Tshika, p.771, Bope, p.826.
55. CO, 179, 236, Confidential, Governor to Secretary of State, Minute, 30 August 1906, p.188; See also Colenso, *Problem of the races*, p.18.
56. Marks, *Reluctant rebellion*, p.149.
57. CSO, 2574, c95/96, Reports from Dundee, Newcastle and Umsinga; 2576, c13/98, Report by Magistate, Ixopo, 20 January 1898; Colonel Clarke diaries, [Talana Museum, Dundee], 3 October 1899.
58. GH, 303, Confidential, Secretary of State to Administrator, 3 September 1904, enclosure; *LA Hansard*, XXXVII, 20 July 1904, Prime Minister, p.691; C.J. Smythe Papers, 12, Diary, 31 December 1905.
59. Natal, Department of Native Affairs, *Annual report*, 1905, p.55.
60. Ibid., pp.12, 62.
61. Evans, *Black and white*, p.189.
62. Stuart, *History of the Zulu rebellion*, p.515.
63. Ibid., p.202; Marks, *Reluctant rebellion*, p.252.
64. Natal, *Report . . . Native population*, 1901, p.A81; Warwick, *Black people*, p.76.
65. Stuart, *History of the Zulu rebellion*, p.90.
66. Marks, *Reluctant rebellion*, p.334.
67. Ibid., *passim*.
68. Umvoti Magistracy, 3/2/6, Magistrate to Auditor General, 3 July 1895; Binns, *Dinuzulu*, p.189.
69. Natal, *Native Affairs Commission, 1906–7, Evidence*, Mvinjwa, p.713.
70. Marks, *Reluctant rebellion*, pp.165–8.
71. Webb and Wright, eds, *James Stuart archive*, 3, 29 July 1902, p.155.

Select Bibliography

MANUSCRIPT SOURCES

Natal Archives, Pietermaritzburg

Official papers

Agriculture (AGR)
  Minutes, 1–22, 1898–1905; 153–4, 1899–1906
Colonial Secretary's Office (CSO)
  Rinderpest papers, 1942, 1896
  Minutes, 2552–2607, 1877–1906; 2624, 1897–1904
  Crown Lands Commission, 2773, 1885
  Immigration and Crown Lands Commission, 2774–6, 1891
  Native Suitors' Commission, 2810–1, 1902
  Lands Commission, Minutes, 2839, 1900–2
  Invasion Losses Enquiry Commission, 2917–9, 1899–1905
Dundee Magistracy
  Criminal record book, 1/2/1/1/1–5, 1899–1904
  Native criminal record book, 1/2/1/2/1–2,4, 1899–1900, 1903–4
  Native hut tax evasions criminal notebook, 1/5/1/1, 1893–5
  Civil record book, 2/2/1/1/1–2, 1900–6
  Register of civil cases tried by Native chiefs, 2/2/1/3/1, 1902–20
Government House (GH)
  Despatches from the Secretary of State for the Colonies, 96–272, 1880–1910; 275–9, 1877–1910; 285–313, 1880-1910
  Minutes from the Prime Minister, Natal, 1032–9, 1893–1910; 1039–40, 1895–1909; 1040–3, 1894–1910
  Letters from private individuals, 1055–1133, 1880–1910
  Despatches to the Secretary of State for the Colonies, 1221–36, 1879–1910; 1256–81, 1902–10; 1282–4, 1893–1910; 1300–3, 1871–1910
  Minutes to the Prime Minister, Natal, 1382–3, 1893–1910
  General memoranda on Native affairs, 1545–52, 1881–1910; 1552–4, 1878–1907; 1555–6, 1878–1909
Impendhle Administrator of Native Law
  Civil cases, 1, 1892–4
  Minutes and letters, 2, 1893–4; 3, 1889–90
Impendhle Magistracy
  Criminal record books, 1/2/1/1/1/1, 1888–1900; 1/2/1/1/2/1, 1900–12
  Native cases, 1/2/2/1, 1894–1900
  Civil cases, 2/2/1/2/1, 1888–1900
  Minutes and letters, 3/1/1, 1894–1901; 3/2/1, 1894–1903

Ipolela Administrator of Native Law
  Minutes and letters, 7, 1882–5; 9–10, 1875–85
  Crown lands sales, 11, 1884–8.
Ipolela Magistracy
  Civil records' annexures, 2/1/1/1/1, 1889–1902
  Minutes and letters, 4/1/1–6, 1889–1906; 4/2/1–2, 1885–1900
Ixopo Magistracy
  Native criminal record book, 1/2/2/1, 1888–95
  Native civil cases, 2/2/2/1–7, 1880–1902
Klip River Magistracy
  Native civil divorces, 2/5/1/1, 1871–6
  Minutes, 3/3/1–18, 1850–1906
Natal, Native Education Department, 4/1/1
Natal Parliamentary Papers (NPP), 85–220, 1856–1906;
    643–667, 1884-1906
Native High Court
  Cattle stealing cases, II/4/20–32, 1877–95
Newcastle Magistracy
  Evasion of Native hut tax notebook, 1/4/2, 1884–98
  Native civil cases, 2/2/2/1, 1900–12
  Minutes, 3/1/1/1–10, 1885–1903
Pietermaritzburg Corporation
  Market committee minute book, 7/4/1–2, 1866–1893
Secretary for Native Affairs (SNA)
  Minutes, 1/1/1–468, 1848–1910
  Letters from magistrates, 1/3/1–30, 1850–78
  Confidential papers, 1/4/1–22, 1876–1910
  Reports on border disturbances, locations, etc., 1/6/6, 1865–76
  Exemption of Natives from Native law, 1/6/10, 1877–87
  Papers *re* Zibula and Alexandra division, 1/6/19–20, 1885–94
  Confidential letters, 1/8/10a, 1885–1911
Surveyor-General's Office (SGO)
  Minutes, III/1/46–156, 1880–1906
Umgeni Magistracy
  Minutes, Add 3/3/2/1–6
Umsinga Magistracy
  Criminal cases, 1, 1901–9
  Civil note book, 18, 1897–9
  Minutes, 28–31, 1899–1904
  Land sales ledger, 39, 1890–1909
Umvoti Magistracy
  Minutes, 3/2/1–9, 1877–1903
Upper Tugela Administrator of Native Law
  Civil records, 1, 1880–1; 2, 1891–3
  Letters, 4, 1880–91
Upper Tugela Magistracy
  Native criminal cases, 1/2/2/1, 1882–99; 1/2/1/1/2/1, 1899–1908
  Civil records, 2/1/1/1/2–6, 1882–1903; 2/1/2/1, 1894–96; 2/1/1/2/1–3, 1897–1904
  Minutes, 4/1/1–3, 1898–1902
Upper Umkomazi Magistracy
  Native criminal cases, 1/2/3/1, 1896–9

Native civil cases, 2/2/2/1, 1896–8; 2/2/1/2/1, 1901–14
Minutes, 3/2/1–3, 1873–1904
Letters, 3/1/2/2, 1887–90

Private papers

American Board Mission (ABM)
  Minutes, A/1/1–2, 1846–1900
  Letters received, A/2/10, 1835–1900
  Letters from government officials, A/2/22, 1838–1900
  Letters despatched, A/3/34, 1880–1900
  Letters to Boston, A/3/39, 1880–91
  Annual reports, A/3/41, 1890–7
  Letters to the Natal Government, A/3/49, 1880–1900
  Native churches, general, A/4/53, 1883–1903
  Church records, A/4/55, 1880–1905
  Historical and biographical, A/4/58–60
Colenso Collection
  Bishop Colenso, 1–3, 1880–3
  H.E. Colenso, 22–49, 72–5, 1880–1910
Escombe Collection
Forsythe Accession
H.C. Shepstone Papers, 10–11, 1879–92
J.W. Shepstone Papers, 1–4, 1848–95
Natal Land and Colonisation Company (NL&C)
  1–283, 1861–1906
Natal Wesleyan Mission (NWM)
  Minutes, 1/1/5–6, 1881–95
  Correspondence, 2/3/1–6, 1880–84
P.H. Zietsman Papers
Parkinson Accession, 1, 1880–95
Sir Evelyn Wood Collection
Sir John Robinson Collection
Sir Theophilus Shepstone Papers, 13–63, 70–5, 1835–95
Sutton Collection
  Diaries, 1–4, 1874–98
  Letters, 6–11, 1874–98

Killie Campbell Africana Library, University of Natal, Durban.

C.J. Smythe Papers
  Diaries, 8–12, 1882–1906
  Correspondence, 18,53, 1882–1906
Dr J.C.A.L. Colenbrander Papers
  Tugela Division Planters' Association, Minute book, 1875–86
Henry Callaway Gold Papers
  Diaries, 1898–1910
Inanda Seminary Papers, 1a, 1885–93
John Bird Papers, 2, 1884–95
Marshall Campbell Collection, 1–2, 1854–1934
Mooi River Farmers' Association, 1, 1893–1905.

Natal Agricultural Union, 6–8, 1891–1905
Richmond Agricultural Society, 1, 1885–9
Shepstone Papers
  H.C. Shepstone, 3–11
Sir H. Evelyn Wood Papers, 7, 1878–1900
Stuart Papers
  Lectures and notes, 2
  Papers and articles, 9,30

Talana Museum, Dundee.

Anglo-Boer War Archives, Dundee, 1898–1903
Colonel Clarke diaries, 1888–1902

William Cullen Library, University of the Witwatersrand

S.O. Samuelson Diary
Sir John Robinson Letterbook, 1895–96

Public Record Office, Kew

Carnarvon Papers, PRO 30/6, 38, 1874–8
Colonial Office
  Despatches from the Governor of Natal to the Secretary of State, CO 179, 1–254, 1845–1909
War Office
  Buller Papers, WO 132/2, 1899–1900

British Library, London

Carnarvon Papers, 60792–8, 1874–8
Ripon Papers, 43563, 1893–5

Bodleian Library, Oxford

Sir Matthew Nathan Papers
  Diaries, 42–4, 1907–9
  Letters to his mother, 119–20, 1907–9

Rhodes House Library, Oxford

Sir Matthew Nathan Papers
  Notebooks, 359–367, 1907–10
  Letters, 368–78, 1907–9
  Papers relating to Native Affairs, 401
Society for the Propagation of the Gospel (SPG)
  CLR 137–9, D8, 1858-1928

Gloucestershire Record Office, Gloucester

Sir Michael Hicks-Beach Papers
  PCC/1–2, Frere to Hicks Beach, 1878–9
  PCC/6, Wolseley to Hicks-Beach, 1879–80

Lincolnshire Archives Office, Lincoln

G.W. Johnson deposit, Logbook and diary, 1865–9

University of London, King's College, Liddell Hart Centre for Military Archives
Lyttelton Papers
1st Accession, Miscellaneous letters, 1899–1901
Copies of letters from General Sir Neville Lyttelton to his family, NGL/Fam/388–426, 1899–1904
Copies of letters from General Sir Neville Lyttelton to his wife, NGL/KL/543–653, 1899–1904

University of London, School of Oriental and African Studies
Wesleyan Methodist Missionary Society (London) Archive (WMMS), Natal, 16–9, 1858–85

PUBLISHED SOURCES

Natal
Legislative Assembly (LA) Hansard, XXI-IL, 1893–1910
Legislative Assembly (LA) Sessional Papers, 1893–1910
Legislative Council (LC) Hansard, I-XX, 1879–93; I-VII, 1893–9
Legislative Council (LC) *Selected Documents Presented, 1857–74*, Pietermaritzburg, 1901
Legislative Council (LC) Sessional Papers, 1873–93
Natal, *Auditor's report on the public accounts*, 1871–92
Natal, *Auditor-General's report*, 1893–1902
Natal, *Census of 1891: report with tables and appendices*, Pietermaritzburg, 1891
Natal, *Census of the Colony of Natal, 17th April 1904 . . .*, Pietermaritzburg, 1904
Natal, *Code of Native law as at present (1876–8) administered*, Pietermaritzburg, 1878
Natal, *Commission appointed to enquire into and report upon the extent and condition of forest lands in the colony*, Pietermaritzburg, 1880
Natal, *Correspondence between Her Majesty's Secretary of State for the Colonies and the Lieutenant-Governor of Natal in reference to the sum of £5,000 reserved by the Royal Charter, out of the annual revenue of the Colony of Natal for 'Native purposes'*, Pietermaritzburg, 1859
Natal, *Correspondence on the subject of increased drunkenness and use of intoxicating liquors, among the native population, especially in the coast districts*, Pietermaritzburg, 1877
Natal, *Correspondence relative to the eviction of Native occupants from Crown lands . . .*, Pietermaritzburg, 1883
Natal, *Crown Lands Commission*, Pietermaritzburg, 1886
Natal, *Despatch with enclosures from Lieut-Governor Scott to His Grace the Duke of Newcastle, no. 34, 1864*, n.p., 1864
Natal, *Evidence given before the Lands Commission (1900–01–02)*, Pietermaritzburg, 1903
Natal, *Evidence taken before the Natal Native Commission, 1881*, Pietermaritzburg, 1882
Natal, *Native Affairs Commission, 1906–7, Evidence*, Pietermaritzburg, 1907
Natal, *Native Suitors' Commission, 1902, report, annexures and correspondence*, Pietermaritzburg, 1903
Natal, *Payments to Native chiefs under Law no. 13, 1875*, Pietermaritzburg, 1886
Natal, *Proceedings of the commission appointed to inquire into the past and present state of the Kafirs in the district of Natal, and to report upon their future government . . .*, I-VII, Pietermaritzburg, 1852

Natal, *Report of the commission appointed . . . to inquire into and report upon the sufficiency or otherwise of the magisterial divisions of the colony, 1890–91,* Pietermaritzburg, 1891

Natal, *Report of the commission appointed to inquire into the past and present state of the Kafirs in the district of Natal, and to report upon their future government . . .,* n.p., 1852–3

Natal, *Report of the commission . . . to inquire into and report upon the best means to be adopted by the government with the view of improving the breed of cattle and horses in Natal, 1889–1890,* Pietermaritzburg, 1890

Natal, *Report of the Lands Commission, February 1902, report and appendix with digest,* Pietermaritzburg, 1902

Natal, *Report of the Natal Native Commission, 1881–2,* Pietermaritzburg, 1882

Natal, *Report of the Native Affairs Commission, 1906–7,* London, 1908

Natal, *Report of the Secretary for Native Affairs for the years 1899–1900,* Pietermaritzburg, 1901

Natal, *Report of the Surveyor-General for the year ended 31st December 1903,* Pietermaritzburg, 1904

Natal, *Report on the condition of the Native population,* 1879–82, 1884, 1885, 1894–98, 1901–4

Natal, *Report on the Natal forests,* Pietermaritzburg, 1889

Natal, *Report on the Native mission reserves,* Pietermaritzburg, 1886

Natal, *Report on the Wilge Fontein settlement, May 1885,* Pietermaritzburg, 1885

Natal, *Report upon the coalfields of Klip River, Weenen, Umvoti and Victoria counties . . .., by Frederick North,* London, 1881

Natal, *Votes and proceedings of the Legislative Assembly,* IL-LXIV, 1893–1906

Natal, *Votes and proceedings of the Legislative Council,* XXX-XLVIII, 1880–93; I-VII, 1893–9

Natal, Department of Native Affairs, *Annual reports,* 1905–9

Natal, Native Education Department, *Annual report of the Inspector of Native Schools for 1893–94,* Pietermaritzburg, 1894

Natal Blue Books, 1850–1892/3

Natal Blue Books Departmental reports, 1884–1900

Natal Government Gazette, XXXII-LVI, 1880–1905

Natal Statistical Year Book, 1893/4–1909

South African Archival Records, Natal no. 3–5, Records of the Natal Executive Council, 1849–59, Cape Town, 1962–4

Cape

Cape, *Report and proceedings with appendices of the government commission on Native laws and customs,* Cape Town, 1883

Cape, *Statistical Register,* 1892–9

Southern African

South African Native Affairs Commission, 1903–1905; 5 volumes, Cape Town, 1905

JOURNALS AND NEWSPAPERS

The Aborigines Friend, 1893–1910

The Colonist, 1903–05

Dundee Commercial Advertiser, July-October 1901

Dundee and District Advertiser, 1901–03

Ilanga lase Natal, 1903–06
Inkanyiso Yase Natal, 1889–95
Ipepa lo Hlange, 1903–04
Natal Advertiser, 1878–99
Natal Agricultural Journal and Mining Record, I-XIV, 1898–1910
Natal Almanac, Directory and Register, 1863–1906
Natal Farmers' Magazine, 1893
Natal Mercury, 1854–1906
Natal Witness, 1864–1906

INTERVIEWS

Conco, Mr W. M., Ncalu, 7 August 1979
Kubone, Mrs R., Umlazi, 5 March 1979
Makhanya, Mr H. M. S., Umbumbulu, 6 March 1979
Mazibuko, Mr R. T., Edendale, 8 August 1979
Mkize, Miss B., Inanda, 4 August 1979
Mnguni, Mr, Inanda, 6 August 1979
Ndhlovu, Mrs; Magwaza, Mr R; and Magubane, Mr A, Inanda, 6 August 1979
Nduna, Mrs M., Inanda, 5 March 1979

BOOKS, ARTICLES AND PAMPHLETS

Allan, W., *The African husbandman*. Westport: Greenwood Press, 1965.
Ballard, C., '"A year of scarcity": the 1896 locust plague in Natal and Zululand', *South African Historical Journal*, 15, 1983, pp. 34–52.
Barker, Lady, *Life in South Africa*. Reprint edition. New York: Negro Universities Press, 1969.
Baynes, J., *Letters addressed to His Excellency the Governor of Natal and His Majesty's Secretary of State for the Colonies regarding the absence of consideration in our present form of government for our coloured population*. Pietermaritzburg: Joseph Baynes, 1906.
Beinart, W., *Political economy of Pondoland, 1860–1930*. Cambridge: Cambridge University Press, 1982.
Beinart, W. and Bundy, C., eds, *Hidden struggles in rural South Africa: politics and popular movements in the Transkei and eastern Cape, 1890–1930*. Johannesburg: Ravan Press, 1987.
Beinart, W., Delius, P. and Trapido, S., eds, *Putting a plough to the ground: accumulation and dispossession in rural South Africa, 1850–1930*. Johannesburg: Ravan Press, 1986.
Binns, C. T., *Dinuzulu: the death of the House of Shaka*. London: Longmans, 1968.
Bird, J., *The annals of Natal, 1495 to 1845*, 2 vols. Facsimile reprint. Cape Town: Maskew Miller, n.d.
Bleek, W. H. I., *The Natal diaries of Dr W. H. I. Bleek, 1855–1856*, translated by O. M. Spohr. Cape Town: Balkema, 1965.
Booth, A., 'Homestead, state and migrant labour in colonial Swaziland', *African Economic History*, 14, 1985, pp. 107–45.
Bosch, D. W., 'The Wilgefontein settlement, 1880', *Archives Year Book for South African History*, part 1, 1964.
Bosman, W., *The Natal rebellion of 1906*. London: Longmans, Green, 1907.
Bozzoli, B., *The political nature of a ruling class: capital and ideology in South Africa, 1890–1933*. London: Routledge and Kegan Paul, 1981.

—— ed., *Town and countryside in the Transvaal: capitalist penetration and popular response*. Johannesburg: Ravan Press, 1983.

—— ed., *Class, community and conflict: South African perspectives*. Johannesburg: Ravan Press, 1987.

Bradford, H., 'Highways, byways and cul-de-sacs: the transition to agrarian capitalism in revisionist South African history', *Radical History Review*, 46/7, 1990, pp. 59–88.

Brookes, E. H. and Hurwitz, N., *The native reserves of Natal*, Natal Regional Survey, vol. 7. Cape Town: Oxford University Press, 1957.

Brookes, E. H. and Webb, C. de B., *A history of Natal*. Pietermaritzburg: University of Natal Press, 1965.

Bryant, A. T., *Description of native foodstuffs and their preparation*. Pietermaritzburg: Times Printing and Publishing Co., 1907.

—— *Olden times in Zululand and Natal: containing earlier political history of the Eastern-Nguni clans*. London: Longmans, Green, 1929.

—— *The Zulu people as they were before the white man came*, 2nd edition. Pietermaritzburg: Shuter and Shooter, 1967.

Bundy, C., *The rise and fall of the South African peasantry*. London: Heinemann, 1979.

Burke, P. ed., *The new Cambridge modern history*, vol. 13, companion volume. Cambridge: Cambridge University Press, 1979.

Chanock, M., *Law, custom and social order: the colonial experience in Malawi and Zambia*. Cambridge: Cambridge University Press, 1985.

Chigwedere, A. S., 'The 1896 rinderpest disease and its consequences', *Heritage*, 2, 1982, pp. 29–34.

Clark, J., *Natal settler-agent: the career of John Moreland, agent for the Byrne emigration scheme of 1849–51*. Cape Town: Balkema, 1972.

Colenso, H. E., *The principles of Native government in Natal: an address . . . delivered before the Pietermaritzburg Parliamentary Debating Society on Tuesday 14th April 1908*. N.p., n.d.

Colenso, J. W., *Bringing forth light: five tracts on Bishop Colenso's Zulu mission*, edited by R. Edgecombe. Pietermaritzburg: University of Natal Press, 1982.

Crush, J. and Ambler, C., eds, *Liquor and labour in southern Africa*. Pietermaritzburg and Athens, Ohio: University of Natal Press and Ohio University Press, 1992.

Cutrufelli, M. R., *Women of Africa: roots of oppression*. London: Zed, 1983.

Dahl, G. and Hjort, A., *Having herds: pastoral herd growth and household economy*. Stockholm: University of Stockholm, Department of Social Anthropology, 1976.

Dalby, D. et al. eds, *Drought in Africa*. London: International African Institute, 1977.

Davies, J. N. P., *Pestilence and disease in the history of Africa*. Johannesburg: Witwatersrand University Press, 1979.

Davis, A., *The Native problem in South Africa*. London: Chapman and Hall, 1903.

Davis, J. M., *Modern industry and the African*. London: Macmillan, 1933.

De Kiewiet, C. W., *The imperial factor in South Africa: a study in politics and economics*. Cambridge: Cambridge University Press, 1937.

—— *A history of South Africa: social and economic*. Oxford: Oxford University Press, 1941.

Denoon, D., *Southern Africa since 1800*. London: Longmans, 1972.

—— *Settler capitalism: the dynamics of dependent development in the southern hemisphere*. Oxford: Clarendon Press, 1983.

Dhupelia, U. S., 'African labour in Natal: attempts at coercion and control, 1893–1903', *Journal of Natal and Zulu History*, 5, 1982, pp. 36–48.

Dobie, J. S., *South African journal, 1862–6*, edited by A. F. Hattersley. Cape Town: Van Riebeeck Society, 1945.

Dube, J.L., *The Zulu's appeal for light and England's duty*. N.p., 1909.

Dubow, S., *Land, labour and merchant capital in the pre-industrial rural economy of the Cape: the experience of the Graaff-Reinet district (1852–1872)*. Communication 6. Cape Town: University of Cape Town, Centre for African Studies, 1982.

Duff, T., 'First impressions of Natal by a Perthshire ploughman', *Natalia*, 7, December 1977, pp. 8–23.

Duminy, A. and Guest, B., eds, *Natal and Zululand from earliest times to 1910: a new history*. Pietermaritzburg: University of Natal Press and Shuter and Shooter, 1989.

Eldridge, E.A., 'Drought, famine and disease in nineteenth-century Lesotho', *African Economic History*, 16, 1987, pp. 61–93.

Etherington, N., *Preachers, peasants and politics in southeast Africa, 1835–1880: African Christian communities in Natal, Pondoland and Zululand*. London: Royal Historical Society, 1978.

—— 'Natal's black rape scare of the 1870s', *Journal of Southern African Studies*, 15, 1, October 1988, pp. 36–53.

Evans, M.S., *The problem of production in Natal*. Durban: P. Davis and Sons, 1905.

—— *The Native problem in Natal*. Durban: P. Davis and Sons, 1906.

—— *Black and white in south-east Africa: a study in sociology*, 2nd edition. London: Longmans, Green, 1916.

Feilden, E.W., *My African home: or, Bush life in Natal when a young colony [1852–7]*. London: Sampson Low, Marston, Searle and Rivington, 1887.

Fisher, J., 'Farming in Natal – past and future', *South African Journal of Science*, 35, December 1938, pp. 52–68.

Fox Bourne, H.R., *Blacks and whites in South Africa: an account of the past treatment and present condition of South African Natives under British and Boer control*. London: P.S. King, 1900.

Fuze, M.M. *The black people and whence they came: a Zulu view*, translated by H.C. Lugg, edited by A.T. Cope. Pietermaritzburg: University of Natal Press, 1979.

Giblin, J., 'Famine and social change during the transition to colonial rule in northeastern Tanzania, 1880–1896', *African Economic History*, 15, 1986, pp. 85–105.

Glantz, M.H. ed., *Drought and hunger in Africa: denying famine a future*. Cambridge: Cambridge University Press, 1987.

Goodman, D. and Redclift, M., *From peasant to proletarian: capitalist development and agrarian transition*. Oxford: Blackwell, 1981.

Gordon, R.E., *Dear Louisa: history of a pioneer family in Natal 1850–1888*. Cape Town: Balkema, 1970.

Grout, L., *Zulu-land; or, life among the Zulu-kafirs of Natal and Zululand*. London: Trüber and Co., 1863.

Guest, W.R., *Langalibalele: the crisis in Natal, 1873–1875*. Durban: University of Natal, Department of History and Political Science, 1976.

Guest, B. and Sellers, J.M., eds, *Enterprise and exploitation in a Victorian colony: aspects of the economic and social history of colonial Natal*. Pietermaritzburg: University of Natal Press, 1985.

Guy, J., *The destruction of the Zulu kingdom*. London: Longman, 1979.

Hamilton, C. and Wright, J., 'The making of the amalala: ethnicity, ideology and relations of subordination in a precolonial context', *South African Historical Journal*, 22, 1990, pp. 3–23.

Hammond-Tooke, W.D. 'In search of the lineage: the Cape Nguni case', *MAN*, 19, 1, March 1984, pp. 77–93.

—— ed., *The Bantu-speaking peoples of southern Africa*; 2nd edition. London: Routledge and Kegan Paul, 1974.

Harries, P., 'Plantations, passes and proletarians: labour and the colonial state in nineteenth century Natal', *Journal of Southern African Studies*, 13, 3, April 1987, pp. 373–99.

Hattersley, A. F., *More annals of Natal*. Pietermaritzburg: Shuter and Shooter, 1936.

—— *Later annals of Natal*. London: Longmans, Green, 1938.

—— *The Natalians: further annals of Natal*. Pietermaritzburg: Shuter and Shooter, 1940.

Henning, M. W., *Animal diseases in South Africa*; 2nd revised edition. Pretoria: Central News Agency, 1949.

Herd, N., *The bent pine: the trial of Chief Langalibalele*. Johannesburg: Ravan Press, 1976.

Hertslet, L. E., *The Native problem: some of its points and phases*. Ntabamhlope: Hertslet, 1911.

Hobsbawm, E. J., 'Review of *Peasants, politics and revolution* . . . by J. S. Migdol', *Journal of Peasant Studies*, 5, 2, January 1978, pp. 254–6.

Hobsbawm, E. J. and Ranger, T., eds, *The invention of tradition*. Cambridge: Cambridge University Press, 1983.

Holden, W. C., *The past and future of the kaffir races*. Facsimile reprint. Cape Town: Struik, 1963.

Holleman, J. F., *Cash, cattle or women? A conflict of concepts in a dual economy*. Durban: University of Natal, 1962.

Horwitz, R., *The political economy of South Africa*. London: Weidenfeld and Nicolson, 1967.

Houghton, D. H., *Some economic problems of the Bantu in South Africa*. Johannesburg: SAIRR, 1938.

—— *The South African economy*. Cape Town: Oxford University Press, 1976.

Hunter, M., *Reaction to conquest: effects of contact with Europeans on the Pondo of South Africa*, 2nd edition. London: Oxford University Press, 1961.

Hurwitz, N., *Agriculture in Natal, 1860–1950*, Natal Regional Survey, vol. 12. Cape Town: Oxford University Press, 1957.

Hutchinson, B., 'Some social consequences of nineteenth century missionary activity among the South African Bantu', *Africa*, 27, 2, 1957, pp. 160–77.

Iliffe, J., *A modern history of Tanganyika*. Cambridge: Cambridge University Press, 1979.

—— *The emergence of African capitalism*. London: Macmillan, 1983.

—— *The African poor: a history*. Cambridge: Cambridge University Press, 1987.

Isaacman, A., 'Peasants and rural social protest in Africa', *African Studies Review*, 33, 2, September 1990, pp. 1–120.

Isaacman, A. and Isaacman, B., 'Resistance and collaboration in southern and central Africa, *c*. 1850–1920', *International Journal of African Historical Studies*, 10, 1, 1977, pp. 31–62.

Jenkinson, T. B., *Amazulu: the Zulus, their past history, manners, customs and language*. London: W. M. Allen, 1882.

Keegan, T., *Rural transformations in industrializing South Africa: the southern highveld to 1914*. Johannesburg: Ravan Press, 1986.

Kinsman, G. W., *Commentaries on native customs*. Pietermaritzburg, n.d.

Kjekshus, H., *Ecology control and economic development in East African history: the case of Tanganyika, 1850–1950*. Berkeley: University of California Press, 1977.

Klein, M. A., ed., *Peasants in Africa: historical and contemporary perspectives*. London: Sage, 1980.

Konczacki, Z. A., *Public finance and economic development of Natal, 1893–1910*. Durham: N.C., Duke University Press, 1967.

Krige, E.J., *The social system of the Zulus*, 3rd edition. Pietermaritzburg: Shuter and Shooter, 1957.

Kuper, H., *An African aristocracy: rank among the Swazi*. London: Oxford University Press for the International African Institute, 1947.

La Hausse, P., '"The cows of Nongoloza": youth, crime and amalaita gangs in Durban, 1900–1936', *Journal of Southern African Studies*, 16, 1, March 1990, pp. 79–111.

Lacey, M., *Working for Boroko: the origins of a coercive labour system in South Africa*. Johannesburg: Ravan Press, 1981.

Ladurie, E. Le Roy, *Montaillou: Cathars and Catholics in a French village, 1294–1324*, translated by B. Bray. Harmondsworth: Penguin, 1980.

Leverton, B.J.T., 'Government finance and political development in Natal, 1843 to 1893', *Archives Year Book for South African History*, part 1, 1970.

Luthuli, A., *Let my people go: an autobiography*. Johannesburg: Collins, 1962.

Mair, L., *African marriage and social change*. London: Frank Cass, 1969.

Mann, R.J., *The colony of Natal*. London: Jarrold, 1859.

Marks, S., *Reluctant rebellion: the 1906–1908 disturbances in Natal*. Oxford: Clarendon Press, 1970.

—— *The ambiguities of dependence in South Africa: class, nationalism and the state in twentieth-century Natal*. Johannesburg: Ravan Press, 1986.

Marks, S. and Atmore, A., eds, *Economy and society in pre-industrial South Africa*. London: Longmans, 1980.

Marks, S. and Rathbone, R., eds, *Industrialisation and social change in South Africa: African class formation, culture and consciousness, 1870–1930*. London: Longman, 1982.

Mason, F., *Native policy in Natal: past and future*. N.p., 1906.

Mayer, P., ed., *Black villagers in an industrial society: anthropological perspectives on labour migration in South Africa*. Cape Town: Oxford University Press, 1980.

Methley, J.E., *The new colony of Port Natal with information for emigrants, accompanied by an explanatory map*, 3rd edition. London: Houlston and Stoneman, 1850.

'"Mfecane" colloquium', *South African Historical Journal*, 25, November 1991, pp. 154–76.

Moller, V. and Schlemmer, L., *The situation of African migrant workers in Durban: brief report on a preliminary survey analysis*. Durban: University of Natal, Centre for Applied Social Sciences, 1977.

Murphy, F., 'Legitimation and paternalism: the colonial state in Kenya', *African Studies Review*, 29, 2, June 1986, pp. 55–65.

Nasson, B., *Abraham Esau's war: a black South African war in the Cape, 1899–1902*. Cambridge: Cambridge University Press, 1991.

Natal Land and Colonisation Company, *Report of immigration, settlement, occupation and cultivation*. London: The Company, 1905.

Natal, Department of Agriculture, *Notes on agriculture in Natal*. Pietermaritzburg, 1905.

—— *Agricultural industries and land settlement of Natal*. N.p., 1907.

Natal University, Department of Economics, *Experiment at Edendale: a study of a non-European settlement with special reference to food expenditure and nutrition*, Natal Regional Survey, Additional Report no. 1. Pietermaritzburg: University of Natal Press, 1951.

Odendaal, A., *Vukani Bantu! The beginnings of black protest politics in South Africa to 1912*. Cape Town: David Philip, 1984.

Osborn, R.F., *Valiant harvest: the founding of the South African sugar industry, 1848–1926*. Durban: South African Sugar Association, 1964.

Palmer, R. and Parsons, N., eds, *The roots of rural poverty in central and southern Africa*. London: James Currey, 1977.

Pearse, R.O., *Joseph Baynes, pioneer*. Pietermaritzburg: Shuter and Shooter, 1983.

Peate, I.C., ed., *Studies in regional consciousness and environment*. Freeport N.Y.: Books for Libraries Press, 1968.

Peires, J.B., ed., *Before and after Shaka: papers in Nguni history*. Grahamstown: Rhodes University, Institute of Social and Economic Research, 1983.

Phillips, J., *The agricultural and related development of the Tugela basin and its influent surrounds: a study in subtropical Africa*, Natal Town and Regional Planning Report, 19. Pietermaritzburg: Natal Town and Regional Planning Commission, 1973.

Phimister, I., *An economic and social history of Zimbabwe, 1890–1948: capital accumulation and class struggle*. London: Longman, 1988.

Phipson, T., *Letters and other writings of a Natal sheriff*, selected by R.N. Currey. Cape Town: Oxford University Press, 1968.

Plant, R., *The Zulu in three tenses: being a forecast of the Zulu's future in the light of his past and his present*. Pietermaritzburg: P. Davis and Sons, 1905.

Ranger, T.O., *Revolt in Southern Rhodesia 1896–7: a study in African resistance*. London: Heinemann, 1967.

—— 'Growing from the roots: reflections on peasant research in central and southern Africa', *Journal of Southern African Studies*, 5, 1, October 1978, pp. 99–133.

Reader, D.H., *Zulu tribe in transition: the Makhanya of southern Natal*. Manchester: Manchester University Press, 1966.

Roberts, R. and Mann, K., eds, *Law in colonial Africa*. London: James Currey, 1991.

Robinson, J., *A life time in South Africa: being the recollections of the first Premier of Natal*. London: Smith, Elder and Co., 1900.

—— ed., *Notes on Natal: an old colonist's book for new settlers*. Durban: Robinson and Vause, 1872.

Russell, G., *The history of old Durban and reminiscences of an emigrant of 1850*. Durban: P. Davis and Sons, 1899.

Russell, R., *Natal, the land and its story*. Pietermaritzburg: P. Davis and Sons, 1904.

Samuelson, L.H., *Zululand: its traditions, legends, customs and folklore*, new edition. Durban, 1974.

Samuelson, R.C.A., *Long, long ago*. Durban: Knox, 1929.

Schapera, I., *Government and politics in tribal societies*. London: Watts, 1956.

Schimlek, F., *Mariannhill: a study in Bantu life and missionary effort*. Mariannhill: Mariannhill Mission Press, 1953.

Shanin, T., *Defining peasants: essays concerning rural societies, expolary economies, and learning from them in the contemporary world*. Oxford: Blackwell, 1990.

—— ed., *Peasants and peasant societies*. Harmondsworth: Penguin, 1971.

Shepstone, S.W.B., *A history of Richmond, Natal from 1839 to 1937*. Durban: Singleton and Williams, 1937.

Shooter, J., *The Kafirs of Natal and the Zulu country*. London: E. Stanford, 1857.

Simons, H.J., *African women: their legal status in South Africa*. London: Hunt, 1968.

Slater, H., 'Land, labour and capital in Natal: the Natal Land and Colonisation Company, 1860–1948', *Journal of African History*, 16, 2, 1975, pp. 257–83.

Smith, R.H., *Labour resources of Natal*, Natal Regional Survey, additional report no. 6. Cape Town: Oxford University Press, 1950.

South African Native Races Committee, *The Natives of South Africa: their economic and social condition*. London: John Murray, 1901.

—— *The South African Natives: their progress and present condition*. London: John Murray, 1908.

Stichter, S., *Migrant labour in Kenya: capitalism and African response 1895–1975*. London: Longman, 1982.

Strong, W.E., *The story of the American Board.* New York: Arno Press, 1969.

Struthers, R.B., *Hunting journal, 1852–1856, in the Zulu kingdom and the Tsonga regions,* edited by P.L. Merrett and R. Butcher. Durban and Pietermaritzburg: University of Natal Press, 1991.

Stuart, J., *A history of the Zulu rebellion, 1906 and of Dinuzulu's arrest, trial and expatriation.* London: Macmillan, 1913.

Sundkler, B.G.M., *Bantu prophets in South Africa.* London: Butterworth Press, 1948.

Swanson, M.W., '"The Durban system": roots of urban apartheid in colonial Natal', *African Studies*, 35, 3–4, 1976, pp.159–76.

—— 'The urban factor in Natal native policy, 1843–1873', *Journal of Natal and Zulu History*, 3, 1980, pp.1–14.

Thompson, L.M., ed., *African societies in southern Africa.* London: Heinemann, 1969.

—— *The unification of South Africa, 1902–1910.* Oxford: Clarendon Press, 1960.

Trapido, S., 'Landlord and tenant in a colonial economy: the Transvaal, 1880–1910', *Journal of Southern African Studies*, 5, 1, October, 1978, pp.26–58.

Turner, S., *Portrait of a pioneer: the letters of Sidney Turner from South Africa, 1864–1901,* edited by D. Child. Johannesburg: Macmillan, 1980.

Turrell, R., *Capital and labour on the Kimberley diamond fields, 1871–1890.* Cambridge: Cambridge University Press, 1987.

Twentieth century impressions of Natal: its people, commerce, industries, and resources. N.p., 1906.

Tyler, J., *Forty years among the Zulus.* Boston: Congregational Sunday School and Publishing Society, 1891.

Van der Horst, S.T., *Native labour in South Africa.* Oxford: Oxford University Press, 1942.

Van Onselen, C., 'Reactions to rinderpest in southern Africa, 1896–97', *Journal of African History*, 13, 3, 1972, pp.473–88.

—— *Chibaro: African mine labour in Southern Rhodesia, 1900–1933.* London: Pluto, 1976.

—— *Studies in the social and economic history of the Witwatersrand, 1886–1914,* 2 vols. Johannesburg: Ravan Press, 1982.

Vilakazi, A., *Zulu transformations: a study of the dynamics of social change.* Pietermaritzburg: University of Natal Press, 1962.

Walker, C., ed., *Women and gender in southern Africa to 1945.* Cape Town: David Philip, 1990.

Walshe, P., *The rise of African nationalism in South Africa: the African National Congress, 1912–1952.* London: C. Hurst, 1970.

Warwick, P., *Black people and the South African War, 1899–1902.* Johannesburg: Ravan Press, 1983.

Webb, C. de B. and Wright, J.B., eds, *The James Stuart archive of recorded oral evidence relating to the history of the Zulu and neighbouring peoples,* 4 vols. Pietermaritzburg: University of Natal Press, 1976–1986.

Welsh, D., *The roots of segregation: Native policy in colonial Natal, 1845–1910.* Cape Town: Oxford University Press, 1971.

White, L., *Magomero: portrait of an African village.* Cambridge: Cambridge University Press, 1987.

Wilson, F., *Migrant labour.* Johannesburg: South African Council of Churches, 1972.

Wilson, F. et al., eds, *Farm labour in South Africa.* Cape Town: David Philip, 1977.

Woodley, V., *On the high flats of Natal: earliest pioneers of the Highflats/Ixopo area of southern Natal.* Highflats, 1984.

Wright, J.B. and Manson, A., *The Hlubi chiefdom in Zululand-Natal: a history.* Ladysmith: Ladysmith Historical Society, 1983.

Wylie, D., *A little god: the twilight of patriarchy in a southern African chiefdom*. Hanover, N.H.: Wesleyan University Press, 1990.
Yudelman, M., *Africans on the land: economic problems of African agricultural development in Southern, Central and East Africa, with special reference to Southern Rhodesia*. Cambridge, Mass.: Harvard University Press, 1964.

PAPERS, REPORTS AND THESES

Aborigines' Protection Society, *Annual report*, 1893–1908.
Atkins, K.E., 'The cultural origins of an African work ethic and practices, Natal, South Africa, 1843–1875', Ph.D., University of Wisconsin-Madison, 1986.
Ballard, C., 'The great rinderpest epidemic in Natal and Zululand: a case study of ecological break-down and economic collapse', African Studies seminar, University of the Witwatersrand, 1983.
Bitensky, M.F., 'The economic development of Natal, 1843–1885', MA, London School of Economics, 1955.
Bransby, D.I., 'The ecology of livestock production in Natal and Zululand', paper presented to the workshop on production and reproduction in the Zulu kingdom, University of Natal, Pietermaritzburg, 1977.
Christopher, A.J., 'Natal: a study in colonial land settlement', Ph.D., University of Natal, 1969.
Clegg, J., 'Ukubuyisa Isidumbu – bringing back the body', African Studies seminar paper, University of the Witwatersrand, 1979.
Colenso, H.E., 'The problem of the races in Africa', reprinted from *Asiatic Quarterly Review*, July 1897.
Dhupelia, U.S., 'Frederick Robert Moor and Native affairs in the colony of Natal, 1893 to 1903', MA, University of Durban-Westville, 1980.
Gillitt, C.A., 'Natal, 1893–1897: the alignment of parties and the fall of the Escombe ministry', BA (Hons.), University of Natal, 1965.
Hall, M., 'Ethnography, environment and the history of the Nguni in the eighteenth and nineteenth centuries', Collected seminar papers on the societies of southern Africa in the 19th and 20th centuries, 8, University of London, Institute of Commonwealth Studies, 1976–7.
Hamilton, C., 'Ideology, oral traditions and the struggle for power in the early Zulu kingdom', MA, University of the Witwatersrand, 1985.
Harris, V.S., 'Land, labour and ideology: government land policy and the relations between Africans and whites on the land in northern Natal, 1910–1936', MA, University of Natal, 1984.
Hedges, D.W., 'Trade and politics in southern Mozambique and Zululand in the eighteenth and early nineteenth century', Ph.D., London University, School of Oriental and African Studies, 1978.
Heydenrych, L.J., 'Die geskiedenis van Port Natal-hawe, 1845–1897', D.Litt. et Phil., Unisa, 1990.
Kannemeyer, H.D., 'The new Bantu society in Natal – its civilisation and culture, 1810–1942', Ph.D., University of the Witwatersrand, 1945.
Keegan, T., 'Primitive accumulation and class formation in the making of agrarian capitalism in South Africa', Collected seminar papers on the societies of southern Africa in the 19th and 20th centuries, 16, University of London, Institute of Commonwealth Studies, 1990, pp. 198–211.
Kotze, J.P., 'Die rinderpes in die Transvaal en die onmiddelike gevolge daarvan, 1896–1899', MA, RAU, 1974.

Krikler, J., 'The agrarian class structure of the Transvaal colony', Collected seminar papers on the societies of southern Africa in the 19th and 20th centuries, 16, University of London, Institute of Commonwealth Studies, 1990, pp. 166–97.

La Hausse, P., 'The struggle for the city: alcohol, the Ematsheni and popular culture in Durban, 1902–1936', MA, University of Cape Town, 1984.

Lambert, J., 'Sir John Robinson and responsible government, 1863–1897: the making of the first prime minister of Natal', MA, University of Natal, 1975.

—— 'Africans in Natal, 1880–1899: continuity, change and crisis in a rural society', D.Litt. et Phil., Unisa, 1986.

Machin, I., 'The isibhalo labour system in colonial Natal', paper presented to the History workshop on Natal in the colonial period, 24–25 October 1990.

Manson, A. H., 'The Hlubi and Ngwe in a colonial society, 1848–1877', MA, University of Natal, 1979.

Marable, W. M., 'African nationalist: the life of John Langalibalele Dube', Ph.D., University of Maryland, 1976.

Meintjes, S. M., 'The ambiguities of ideological change: the impact of settler hegemony on the *amaKholwa* in the 1880s and 1890s', paper presented to the conference on the history of Natal and Zululand, University of Natal, Durban, 1985.

—— 'Edendale, 1850–1906: a case study of rural transformation and class formation in an African mission in Natal', Ph.D. thesis, University of London, 1988.

Morrell, R., 'Differential access to the state: white farmers in the Natal midlands, 1900–1930', History Workshop conference, University of the Witwatersrand, Johannesburg, 1990.

Morrell, R., Padayachee, V. and Vawda, S., 'Banking, credit and capital in colonial Natal, 1850–1910', paper presented to the South African Historical Society biennial conference, University of Natal, Pietermaritzburg, 1989.

Padayachee, V. and Morrell, R., 'Indian traders in the Natal economy, c. 1875–1914', paper presented to the History workshop on Natal in the colonial period, University of Natal, Pietermaritzburg, 24–25 October 1990.

Rich, P., 'Black peasants and Ethiopianism in South Africa, 1896–1915', Development Studies Group paper presented to the conference on the history of opposition in southern Africa, University of the Witwatersrand, Johannesburg, January 1978, pp. 119–40.

Sanderson, J., *Polygamous marriages among the kafirs of Natal and countries around*, reprinted from the *Journal of the Anthropological Institute*, February 1879.

Switzer, L. E., 'The problems of an African mission in a white dominated, multi-racial society: the American Zulu Mission in South Africa, 1885–1910', Ph.D., University of Natal, 1971.

Unterhalter, E., 'Migrant labour and the Nquthu district of Zululand, 1879–1910', paper presented to the conference on the history of opposition in southern Africa, University of the Witwatersrand, January 1978, pp. 74–90.

—— '"The Natives appear contented and quiet": the Nqutu district of Zululand under British rule, 1883–1897', Collected seminar papers on the societies of southern Africa in the 19th and 20th centuries, 8, University of London, Institute of Commonwealth Studies, 1976–77.

Williams, G., 'Capitalism and agriculture: the South African case', Collected seminar papers on the societies of southern Africa in the 19th and 20th centuries, 16, University of London, Institute of Commonwealth Studies, 1990, pp. 141–8.

Wright, J.B., 'The dynamics of power and conflict in the Thukela Mzimkhulu region in the late 18th and early 19th centuries: a critical reconstruction', Ph.D., University of the Witwatersrand, 1989.

Index

Zulu words are entered under the stem and not under the prefix. Thus amaButho is entered under B. Proper names of places with a Zulu origin are, however, given as used in the colonial period. Thus Umgeni is entered under U. *Kholwa* names are entered under the surname; other African personal names under the first or given name.

Hlubi chiefdom   18, 25, 27, 29, 31–2, 43, 47,
  56, 71, 72
Homestead heads *see abaNumzana*
Homestead society
  adaptation to colonial presence   42–5
    passim
  alienation of   3, 112, 132, 135, 150–1, 161,
    166, 168, 170, 178–89 *passim*
  dependence on traders   95, 116
  deterioration within   3, 107, 127, 138, 177–
    80
  differentiation within   45
  generational conflict within   127, 135–6, 179
  growing crisis in   82, 99, 109, 113, 161
  impact of migrant labour on   123, 127, 135,
    136, 172, 178–80 *passim*
  impact of rinderpest on   148, 151–5
  impoverishment of   3, 41, 79, 152, 162,
    163, 169, 172, 173
  indebtedness of   116, 170–3 *passim*
  malnutrition in   163
  polygamy   17, 43, 45–7 *passim*, 51, 136, 177
  position of children   127, 146, 152, 163
  position of women   39–41 *passim*, 46, 52,
    62, 127, 135–7, 180
  position of young men   39, 40, 46, 52, 62,
    123, 127, 131, 135, 136, 179, 180
  in pre-colonial times   39, 42
  proletarianization   3, 173, 178
  relations with police   185–6
  relations with settler neighbours   79, 110
  resilience of   138, 145, 146, 161
  See also Agriculture, homestead; *ukuLobola*;
    Marriage; *imiZi*
Homesteads *see imiZi*
Hulett, James Liege   96, 150, 154, 169
Hunt, *Sub-Inspector* Sidney   1, 186
Hunting regulations   112

Ifumi mission reserve   17
Ilanga lase Natal   183
Immigration, settler   8, 71, 80, 82
Impafana reserve   11, 27, 43, 108, 112, 128
Impendhle division   112, 187
Impendhle reserve   12
Imprisonment   92, 170
Inanda division   45, 73, 81, 129, 180
Inanda mission reserve   35, 49, 51, 165
Inanda reserve   11, 47, 48, 106, 107, 111
Inanda Seminary   51, 136
Indaleni mission reserve   49
Indians   72, 78, 81, 89, 90, 93, 95, 113, 114, 163
Indwedwe division   145
Inkanyiso Yase Natal   125, 183
Interest rates *see* Usury
Invasion Losses Enquiry Commission   161
Ipepa lo Hlange   183

Ipolela division   12, 82, 89, 145, 149
Ipolela reserve   12
Irrigation   107–8, 163, 166
Isigebengu society   179
Ixopo division   47, 73, 75, 81, 82, 93, 112,
  129, 144, 146, 149, 152, 181

Johannesburg   80, 95, 99, 146, 172
Joyce, *Chief* T.   132
Justices of the Peace   59, 60, 101, 132

Kaduphi (Mbo chief)   28, 129
Kambule, Job   126
Kanyele, Philip   116
Kelly, Thomas   61
amaKholwa   50, 51
  agriculture   16, 17, 49–50, 114–18 *passim*,
    164–5
  and Bhambatha rebellion   184
  chiefs and *izinduna*   126, 164, 182
  drawing of rentals by   89
  and education   51, 167, 183
  exemptions   50, 58, 117–18, 167
  and the franchise   167, 183
  hostility to administration   125, 182–4
  impoverishment of   116–17, 164–5
  and individual tenure   49, 183
  land mortgages by   17, 117
  and missionaries   125, 136, 183–4
  as petty bourgeoisie   117, 125, 164, 167,
    183
  relations with homestead Africans   35,
    50–1, 125, 126, 135
  settler attitudes to   125, 183, 215
  and the South African War   183
  suppliers of produce   49–50, 117
  transport riders   49, 50, 115–16, 146
  See also Edendale; Driefontein; Mission
    reserves and stations
umKhosi ceremony *see under* Chiefs
Kinship   24, 25, 33, 34, 39, 51, 106, 111, 155,
  179, 181
Klip River county   26, 73, 78, 96, 124, 145,
  161, 164
Klip River division   75, 110, 153
Klip River reserve   10, 128
Knutsford, *Lord*   65
Krantzkop division   2, 145, 146
Kula (Qamu chief)   188
Kumalo, Johannes   17, 50, 126, 164
Kumalo, Luke   125
Kumalo, Solomon   125
Kunene, C.   117
Khuse chiefdom   188

Labour agents   95, 99, 100, 123, 167, 172
  see also Traders